Passion *for* Roses

Passion *for* Roses

PETER BEALES' COMPREHENSIVE GUIDE
TO LANDSCAPING WITH ROSES

Special photography
by Marianne Majerus

RIZZOLI
NEW YORK

For Joan

First published in the United states of America in 2005 by
Rizzoli International Publications, Inc.
300 Park Avenue South
New York, NY 10010
www.rizzoliusa.com

First published in Great Britain as *A Passion for Roses* in 2004 by
Mitchell Beazley, an imprint of Octopus Publishing Group Ltd.,
2–4 Heron Quays, London E14 4JP.

© Octopus Publishing Group Limited 2004

ISBN 0-8478-2693-7
Library of Congress Catalog Control Number 2004115562

2005 2006 2007 2008 / 10 9 8 7 6 5 4 3 2 1

While all reasonable care has been taken during the preparation
of this edition, neither the publisher, editors, nor the authors can
accept responsibility for any consequences arising from the use
thereof or from the information contained therein.

Commissioning Editor: Michèle Byam
Executive Art Editor: Sarah Rock
Design: Miranda Harvey
Editor: Lesley Riley
Special Photography: Marianne Majerus
Production: Sarah Rogers
Index: Sue Farr

Printed and bound in China by
Toppan Printing Company Limited

Jacket pictures
Front *Rosa* 'Mme Alfred
Carrière'

Spine *Rosa* 'Ferdinand
Pichard'

Back *Rosa* Double
Delight

Preliminary pictures
Half title *Rosa* 'Félicité
Parmentier'

Title page left *Rosa* 'Tour
de Malakoff'; right *Rosa*
'Mme Plantier'

Contents page left *Rosa*
'Raubritter' with white
foxgloves (*Digitalis*); right
Rosa 'Amy Robsart'

CONTENTS

6   Introduction

24   SPECIES ROSES
26   Introduction to Species Roses
29   Species Roses for the Garden
37   Rambling and Scrambling Species for
     the Garden

42   OLD GARDEN ROSES
44   The Albas
48   The Damasks
52   The Centifolias
56   The Gallicas
62   The Pimpinellifolias
66   The Moss Roses
72   The Chinas
78   The Portland Damasks
84   The Bourbons
90   The Hybrid Perpetuals
96   The Sweet Briars
100 The Rugosas
106 The Hybrid Musks
112 The Teas
116 The Older Hybrid Teas

118 MODERN ROSES
120 The Hybrid Teas
126 The Floribundas
132 The Modern Shrub Roses
144 The New English Roses

150 CLIMBING ROSES
152 The Noisette Roses and Climbing Teas
158 The Modern Climbing and Pillar Roses
166 The Climbing Hybrid Teas and Floribundas

170 RAMBLERS AND SCRAMBLERS
172 Introduction to Ramblers and Scramblers
174 The Wichurana Ramblers and Scramblers
184 The Multiflora Ramblers and Scramblers
192 Miscellaneous Ramblers and Scramblers

     PROCUMBENT AND
202 COMPACT ROSES
204 The Procumbent Roses
210 The Compact Floribundas and
     Miniature Roses

214 PLANT DIRECTORY
251 Hardiness Zones
252 Index
256 Acknowledgments

INTRODUCTION

A Passion Born

'William Lobb' and 'Tour de Malakoff' (*previous pages*) Arching down from above, the Centifolia 'Tour de Malakoff' mingles with the Moss rose 'William Lobb'. Also joining in the party in the foreground are the oriental poppy *Papaver orientale* 'Patty's Plum' and *Tradescantia*. This photo illustrates just how well roses of similar colouring can combine with widely differing plants to create a pleasing garden landscape.

'Tuscany Superb' (*below*) The major player in this tasteful scene is the Gallica rose 'Tuscany Superb', relaxed, as is its wont, among a variety of perennials including campanula and foxglove (*Digitalis*). Just visible, along the front, is a lavender hedge.

Looking back to my very first day working with roses, I remember the air was filled with an overwhelming scent of sweet briar and the hot sun shone incessantly. It was 1951 and I was just 15 and beginning my apprenticeship at the famous LeGrice nurseries in Norfolk. I had been set the task of weeding a thorny patch of sweet briar by Edward LeGrice himself. To this day, I wonder if I had been given this to do as a test, for I discovered later that "Father", as he was called by his staff behind his back, was a strict disciplinarian. If test it was, then I came close to failure for, with my scratched arms and aching back, I remember thinking at the end of the day: "If this is rose growing then I never want to see another rose." Somehow, however, I must have passed because from then on my work became more interesting and, under the excellent tuition and guidance of a great rose man, my lifelong love affair with roses began. Through his profound knowledge and deep affection for roses, and his desire to share this with others, a very satisfying working relationship evolved between tutor and pupil.

My apprenticeship was all embracing, covering seasonal tasks such as pruning, planting, pest and disease control, and all other aspects of good rose husbandry.

However, as time went by, my leanings were much more towards what I found to be the exciting side of rose growing, hybridizing and propagation. I became fascinated by watching LeGrice crossing different varieties and observing the diversity of the resulting offspring. Although, at first, my participation in this procedure was limited simply to writing labels and keeping records, I eventually graduated to making crosses of my own. None of these early crosses was ever good enough to be introduced, or given a name, but I still remember the thrill of seeing my very own creations come into flower for the first time. I recall one in particular, a beautiful dark velvety red bred from 'Tuscany Superb',

a rose LeGrice then used extensively in his breeding programme. My rose showed great promise early on but, in the following year, on the very first hot, sunny day as a maiden plant, its blooms shrivelled up and died.

Because of my apprenticeship my compulsory national service had been deferred and I was 20 when I became a soldier. That two year spell in the army broadened my outlook and boosted my confidence, but I was eager to resume my career.

During that time my abiding passion for Old roses was nurtured by reading the works of Graham Stuart Thomas. So strongly was I influenced by his writings that, just before I was due to finish my national service, I had the temerity to write to him to ask if he had a position for me at the nursery of Thomas Hilling of Chobham, Surrey, of which, at that time, he was a director. To my delight he took me on. I worked under him for about a year before he moved on, and I suddenly found myself custodian of that wonderful and famous collection, one that had taken Graham Thom as a long time to build up. This meant that I was able to spend a lot of my time getting to know the attributes and foibles of these roses, as well as learning to identify many of them by type and name.

As I learned more about the delights of Old roses and discovered more about their complexity, my love for them deepened, so much so that in some of my spare time I took to rifling through the shelves of second-hand bookshops looking for rose books. Gradually, I built up a large collection, to which I am still adding. At various times while rummaging, I came across the works of such eminent people as Nancy Steen, James Russell, and Vita Sackville-West, authors who fortified my passion and enhanced my appreciation of the written word as it applies to roses.

A Passion Realized

In the mid 1960s I started my own modest rose nursery and I soon found myself hybridizing again, at first on a small scale but, as time went on, rather more ambitiously. The first new variety I introduced was a fragrant, strawberry-coloured Floribunda called 'Penelope Plummer'. I cringe now when I recall that this rose was named after "Miss World" 1968. How politically incorrect that would be considered today! In fact, this Floribunda is first class, if a little flamboyant. I still have a soft spot for it and it appears in my catalogue to this day.

Another variety bred by me and introduced in 1973 is a shapely, fragrant, creamy white Hybrid Tea rose called 'Pinta'. The name was borrowed from the then Milk Marketing Board, which at that time was using the advertising slogan "drinka pinta milka day". Times were difficult then and I had little choice but to seek sponsors to help to keep my business going. Sponsorship was not always compatible with good taste and there were occasions when I was forced to swallow my pride. This was especially true in the case of 'Pinta'. During the year of its introduction, at the Royal National Rose Society's Summer Show, our stand had won a Challenge Cup. Much to our embarrassment, the Milk Marketing Board's publicity department brought along an actor who, to the utter amazement of my wife, myself, and other exhibitors, dressed up as a large black and white cat and was photographed licking cream from the cup! While this was going on my wife and I hid behind the stand. Other sponsored roses, all of which have proved successful for us, are 'Norwich Union', 'Everest Double Fragrance', and 'Norwich Castle'.

Since my early days as a rose nurseryman, the flower show has always been important, both as a vehicle for the promotion of new varieties, and as a means of marketing roses. Following a period of a few years on probation at less celebrated shows, I was eventually invited to exhibit at Chelsea, the world's most famous flower show. The first award I won there was of the lowest possible denomination, a Banksian Medal. It was received with great pride, encouraging me to do better next time. Prizes at Chelsea are not easily won and we slowly worked our way through the lower ranking awards, but it was to be 25 years before we eventually won the coveted Gold Medal, for a display of old-fashioned Shrub roses, Climbers, and Ramblers.

I mentioned earlier the works of Nancy Steen. Her book *The Charm of Old Roses*, published in the mid 1950s, inspired not only me but countless other rose lovers around the world, in particular, Nancy's fellow countrymen, New Zealanders. The devotees of Old roses in that country were among the first, if not the first, to form a specialized society to promote the cultivation and conservation of what they termed Heritage Roses.

This brings to mind my good friend Keith Money, himself a native of New Zealand. I well remember my first meeting with Keith. It was a hot day in midsummer at my nursery, then at Swardeston, near Norwich. He lived at Caston, a village not far

'Sanders' White Rambler' (*right*) The only pure white Rambler of the Wichurana group, 'Sanders' White' has wiry, relaxed growth, making it an ideal subject for arches and trellis. Beneath the arch here, a couple of bushes of the Gallica 'Rosa Mundi' provide a stylish contrast in colour. I recall seeing several superb examples of this lovely white Rambler in the white garden created by Nancy Steen.

away. Having heard that I was building up a collection of Old roses, he had come to see what I was up to. I soon realized that here was a kindred spirit, someone who loved roses, and my initial irritation at his intrusion into my time was quickly dispelled. Of about my own age, he was very well known internationally as an artist, author, and photographer. In fact, as the latter Keith collaborated with me in photographing roses to illustrate four little booklets I was writing on their history, published in the 1970s. These have now become collectors' items.

Before I met Keith he had already assembled a considerable collection of rare and historically important roses. Among these was 'Dame Edith Helen', which had previously been thought extinct worldwide. Even more importantly, his painstaking research had led him to rediscover 'Lady Mary Fitzwilliam', an old Hybrid Tea bred by the Victorian rose breeder Arthur Bennett and an important stud rose of its day. Keith had discovered this rose in a nearby garden and it was confirmed as authentic by an elderly Australian who, when shown Keith's photograph of the rose by his son Dean Ross, a professional rose grower, recalled seeing it in the early 1900s when he was starting the Ross family's nursery. At the time of its rediscovery this rose, too, had been thought commercially extinct.

From time to time, armed with secateurs, Keith and I made forays into the East Anglian countryside in search of old, obscure roses. When we saw one of interest over a fence or climbing on a wall or trellis, we would stop and knock on the door of the house and ask the surprised owner if we could have a look at his or her rose. In truth, few significant varieties were ever discovered in these escapades, but we always enjoyed the thrill of the chase.

At the time I first met Keith he was writing a biography of the ballet dancer Anna Pavlova, and one day he came to search through my rows of seedlings for a suitable rose to bear the great ballerina's name. His taste turned out to be impeccable for he selected a seedling rose that proved to be outstanding, a very fragrant, soft pink, Hybrid Tea type Shrub rose, which soon became one of the nursery's most popular varieties and, indeed, remains so to this day. Keith has now returned to New Zealand where he still grows roses with enthusiasm. When I stayed with him recently, the first rose to greet me on my arrival in the inimitable organized chaos of his garden was 'Anna Pavlova'.

'Anna Pavlova' plays a part in another fond memory I have concerning the late Queen Elizabeth the Queen Mother. Sandringham Flower Show, in my native Norfolk, has always been an important show for the nursery, and the Queen Mother visited the show regularly over a period of 36 years. On one occasion, while I was showing her around our stand, she remarked to one of her companions, the ballet choreographer Sir Frederick Ashton, "How nice it would be if a rose could be named especially for you Fred." I took this to be a royal command. Providentially, a few days after my return to the nursery from the show, I found a pure white sport on a bush of 'Anna Pavlova'. From this single plant I built up enough stock to enable me, two years later, to fulfil the royal wish by presenting Sir Frederick with his very own rose, named of course 'Sir Frederick Ashton'. Both the Queen Mother and Sir Frederick were highly amused to learn that his rose had been spawned from true ballet stock, keeping it in the family so to speak.

A Passion Abroad

I did not start my worldwide travels in search of roses and rose gardens until I was in my mid forties. Before then I had always thought, naively perhaps, that roses grew better in England than anywhere else. After all, the rose is the emblem of England and has played an important symbolical part in the history of the nation. However, on my travels I discovered that roses thrive in almost all parts of the world, and I have often felt envious when I have seen how well they perform abroad.

Roses love the climate of the southern states of Australia. My first visit to that country, in the mid 1980s, is deeply rooted in my memory. I was one of the guest speakers at an International Heritage Rose Convention in Adelaide. Soon after my arrival I was introduced to David Ruston, whom I now consider one of the world's great rosarians, thus beginning a friendship that continues to this day. David drove me to his gardens, which are situated about 300km (185 miles) north of Adelaide at a town called Renmark. We drove through the evening and into the night and I recall one of the most beautiful sunsets I have ever seen as we crossed the Murray River by ferry at Swan Reach. The next day was a serious rose day for me, spent exploring David's massive garden and finding roses that I had not seen since my apprenticeship days. Among these I found 'McCredy's Sunset' and 'McCredy's Yellow', to name but two Hybrid Teas, and 'Dainty Maid' and 'Dusky Maiden', two of his many Floribundas, which brought back memories of my early days with roses. With over 4,000 varieties, David has the largest collection of roses in the southern hemisphere. The day I spent in

Renmark must have been one of the hottest of that summer. The humidity level was also high because the entire garden was being irrigated by water pumped from the Murray River. By mid morning I was wearing a pair of David's two sizes too large wellies and a pair of his shorts, three sizes too large! It was the only time I have ever had to paddle through a rose garden. I remember seeing for the first time such roses as 'Bloomfield Dainty' and 'Bloomfield Courage', both of which are Climbers. The garden is surrounded by a

'Dainty Maid'
The Floribunda 'Dainty Maid' brings back memories of happy days at the beginning of my long love affair with roses. It was already established as one of the most popular Hybrid Polyanthas (now called Floribundas) when I started my apprenticeship with Edward LeGrice in 1951. He had raised and introduced 'Dainty Maid' in 1940, before being ordered by the government to put aside roses and grow vegetables for the war effort instead.

kangaroo-proof fence 2.5m (8ft) high, on which David was growing a multitude of Climbers and Ramblers, the most notable in my memory being a giant plant of 'Mermaid'. It must have been the biggest in the world then and it is probably even bigger now. I came across Climbing Tea roses growing arm in arm with orange and lemon trees, an interesting combination that, coming from colder climes, I had never seen before. Early the next morning I caught a bus that, 24 hours later deposited me, rather travel weary, in Sydney. I will always remember that hot day in David's garden. My stay in Australia was all too short.

On that same trip, from Sydney I flew on to New Zealand. This country, too, is full of good rose gardens and good rosarians, many of whom I count as my friends. I remember being shown the late Nancy Steen's white garden by her widower, David. It was thrilling to see a garden that had so inspired me from the pages of a book at an earlier stage in my life. Another superb rose garden is the Parnell Garden in central Auckland, and I spent several happy hours there browsing through the extensive rose beds. There are roses everywhere you go in New Zealand, from Auckland in the north to Dunedin and all stations south. In fact, it wouldn't surprise me to learn that there are more roses in New Zealand than there are sheep.

In Europe, there are many excellent rose gardens to be seen, both private and municipal, scattered all over the continent, from chilly Oslo to sunny Naples – an indication of just what a climate-tolerant plant the rose can be.

Secret gardens have always captured my imagination and although the owner of the garden behind the terrace house in the middle of Pithiviers, France, is known throughout the world, finding his garden was very difficult. I had always wanted to meet the man who lived there, the famous French rosarian André Ève. When I did so, although neither of us could speak the other's language, we were able to communicate without difficulty through the medium of roses. (One of the many things I have learned from my travels is that the rose knows no boundaries and, because of this, there are no language barriers between rosarians that cannot be overcome.) I spent a wonderful day with him in his enchanting garden where I saw, among many others, 'Souvenir de Mme Léonie Viennot' flowering away, high on a wall, and a huge specimen of 'Cerise Bouquet' reaching to the top of a very tall tree.

Pithiviers is not very far from Paris where there are two major rose gardens. First is the Roseraie de l'Haÿ-les-Roses, where a large collection of historical roses has been gathered together over many years, including some that cannot be seen anywhere else in the world. The other famous garden in this beautiful city is the Roseraie du Parc de Bagatelle. A special feature here are the many climbing and rambling roses trained on rope swags and obelisks, a superb sight from late June to mid July. Other French cities with major rose gardens are Lyon and Orléans.

Château Hex in Belgium was also a very rewarding experience for me, partly because of the many roses growing in the gardens surrounding the chateau, but also because of the owner Count d'Ursel's own love of roses, which he inherited from his

mother Countess Nanda d'Ursel. Roses of special note in my memory here are 'Sanders' White' and 'Debutante', both Ramblers, which were performing a graceful double act on tall obelisks.

Sizeable rose gardens abound in Germany, in cities such as Baden-Baden, Dortmund, Kassel, Karlsruhe, Uetersen, and Erfurt, to name only a few, all superbly designed and situated in parks and open spaces. Sangerhausen, which found itself behind the iron curtain during the Cold War, boasts the largest collection of roses in the world, with 7,000 varieties. More recently, the little city of Oelde in Westfalen has successfully redeveloped itself into a "garden city", with acre upon acre of gardens to explore. It was a pleasure to be involved in the planting of a rose garden here and, on its official opening in 2002, I named one of our new seedlings 'City of Oelde' especially to mark the occasion.

'Petite d'Hollande' and Pink Bells
A centrepiece sundial is the only indication that time even exists in this lovely secluded garden of roses totally integrated with a variety of other flowers and foliage. Among them are the ancient Centifolia 'Petite d'Hollande' and the modern Procumbent Pink Bells, proving that roses of all ages can grow together in harmony.

Italians, too, love their roses: there are superb municipal rose gardens in Rome, and Genoa and a large, eclectic private collection at Cavriglia has been lovingly compiled over many years by Professor Fineschi. There are also a good number of private gardens all over Italy. I was once commissioned to plant up a rose garden incorporating existing mature cacti on the Isle of Capri. It needed plenty of imagination! Without doubt, my favourite garden in the whole world is that of Ninfa, near Latina. It has been created over the past 80 years or so from a derelict city with a history that goes back to Roman times and became totally deserted in the late 14th century. It has now been transformed into a superb, highly atmospheric, woodland garden. Some seven ruined medieval churches rise randomly among the trees, and rose varieties from the past two centuries are scattered everywhere.

In the USA, although roses have to be protected from the severe frosts of winter in the north-eastern states, they really do flourish everywhere. In California, roses of all types thrive although, generally speaking, those of European provenance — in other words, the non-remontant varieties — do less well. This is because the summers are too hot and the winters too short and warm for them. The Old Teas and the China varieties flower almost through the entire year, as do many David Austin roses, which are widely grown in this state. (I do not like calling them "English" roses because, after all, the roses bred by any English breeder are English.) Likewise, Hybrid Teas, Floribundas, and Modern Shrub roses excel here, especially in maritime areas and in the vast fertile valleys, the latter providing the perfect environment for commercial nurseries to produce millions of roses, both budded onto rootstock and from cuttings. In California, the rose garden I know best is in the Huntington Botanic Garden, under the expert management of the Rose Curator, Clair Martin III. It accommodates a superb collection, beautifully laid out in various themed gardens, one of which is in Shakespearean style.

The state of Oregon has an even better climate than California for rose growing. Indeed, the city of Portland maintains a rose garden par excellence, attracting many thousands of visitors each year. Also in the state of Oregon, the Heirloom Roses nursery, owned by Louise and John Clements, offers a very comprehensive collection of all types of roses grown from cuttings. Roses propagated by this means, "own root roses" as they have become known, are beginning to dominate the commercial rose scene in the USA. Two other well-

known producers of "own root roses" are the Antique Rose Emporium of Brenham, Texas, owned by Mike and Jean Shoup, and Ashdown Roses in Landrum, South Carolina, run by Paul Zimmerman.

Canada has a harsh climate in the east but this does not stop roses being grown there in surprisingly large numbers, especially in and around Toronto and Montreal. As in the north-eastern regions of the USA, however, roses need covering to be sure they will survive through the coldest months of winter. West of the Rocky Mountains it is more clement and Vancouver and Victoria offer weather not dissimilar to that in Britain, the sort of climate that roses seem thoroughly to enjoy. I have spent many a happy hour browsing through a variety of rose gardens with rosarian friends in both the USA and Canada.

In 1990 I visited India to lecture at an Indian Rose Convention at Lucknow. I found many keen and enthusiastic rose growers there and it was a pleasure to see so many well-grown varieties in such good hands. Historically the first China roses were brought to the Indian subcontinent by way of the old silk route, eventually to find their way to the Middle East. While it is true that the British plant hunters brought roses back to Europe directly from China in the late 18th and 19th centuries, it should be remembered that roses of that type had been flourishing in India and the Arabian countries before then.

In recent years the Japanese have become very interested in roses. They have a strong, well-supported national rose society and they grow roses in most areas of their country with great success. I have been visiting Japan regularly since 1997 and it is always such a great pleasure to talk to so many dedicated gardeners devoted to roses. When the Japanese grow them they grow them well. Large rose gardens have been designed and planted both in and around Tokyo and further afield. A very good garden has been developed at Gifu, where there is a major collection of Species and Old roses as well as almost every Modern rose imaginable.

Another important garden, whose owners are proud of its rose collection, is that at Tateshina near Chino in the foothills of the Japanese Alps. This is called Barakura and it specializes in English-style gardening. It belongs to the Yamada family and, recently, my company introduced a new Bourbon rose discovered there – a dark plum-red sport of the striped 'Variegata di Bologna' – and named it 'Mrs Yamada' after the family matriarch. Miss Kay Yamada is a very famous gardener in her country and was awarded a Silver-Gilt Medal at Chelsea Flower Show in 2002.

In the UK, of course, most gardens have at least one rose, and even those who have no garden of their own can enjoy seeing them in a garden close by. For some reason (Belfast, Glasgow, Aberdeen, and the Queen Mary Rose Garden, London excepted), large municipal rose gardens are not common in Britain, but this is amply made up for by a wealth of superb gardens, open to the public, belonging to organizations such as the National Trust and the Royal Horticultural Society. In Scotland, good, comprehensive collections of roses can be found at both Edinburgh

and Glasgow Botanic Gardens. Another good garden of roses further north is at Drum Castle, near Aberdeen. However, it is the garden at St Albans, Hertfordshire, owned by the Royal National Rose Society that is the focus for roses in the UK.

A few privately owned gardens deserve special attention here for their excellence, both in the size and mix of their collections and for the way they are designed. Mottisfont Abbey Gardens, near Romsey in Hampshire, are run by the National Trust and, held within the confines of a spacious walled garden, have a treasured collection of Old garden roses in beds and borders and on structures. The gardens were designed and the varieties selected by the late Graham Stuart Thomas. They are now in the charge of David Stone.

Two privately owned gardens, both in Norfolk, are among the best in England. They are at Mannington Hall and Elsing Hall. The former is owned by Lord and Lady Walpole, the latter by David and Shirley Cargill. The Mannington Collection covers the evolution of roses from medieval times to this day. Elsing Hall has, over the past 20 years or so, assembled a fine ensemble of the Old types. The Royal Horticultural Society has collected a wide range of different varieties of roses at Wisley Gardens in Surrey, and has also planted a complete garden of roses, both old and new, at Rosemoor in north Devon.

This brings me to the end of a very quick tour around the rose gardens of the world. I have only touched upon their multiplicity and diversity. Such is the popularity and attraction of the rose that it could take ten volumes, twice the size of this one, and a pen writing at double the speed of mine to cover them all.

'Seagull' and 'Charles de Mills'
Almost smothering one of the doorways of the walled garden at Elsing Hall, Norfolk, in the UK, is the Multiflora Rambler 'Seagull'. Just below it is the Gallica 'Charles de Mills'. Had I not known where this picture was taken, I would have guessed, for the overall scene is so typical of the work of Shirley Cargill who, with her husband David, owns the hall. Foxgloves (*Digitalis*), poppies (*Papaver*), feverfew (*Tanacetum parthenium*), and geraniums are just a few of the plants making up the harmonious informality with the roses here.

Roses in the Garden Landscape

The genus *Rosa* is the only genus of plants from which it is possible to find a suitable subject to fulfil any role within the garden. It is therefore surprising to consider that, up until about the middle of the 20th century, roses were mostly isolated in order to form a distinct rose bed or separate rose garden. Until the early 1950s landscapers, garden designers, and private gardeners seldom if ever used roses for wider distribution within the overall garden scene.

Thankfully, nowadays, as well as being a major player, the rose has many other roles to perform, no matter how large or small the garden or how few roses are used. Such wider usage has become possible from the ever-growing popularity of Old Shrub roses over recent years and the wider availability of Modern Shrub roses from both specialist nurseries and good garden centres. Furthermore, the increasing use of both functional and decorative structures has provided a whole new range of settings for climbing and rambling roses within the garden.

We frequently read in modern lifestyle and gardening magazines about companion plants for roses, and most books on the subject these days usually include a chapter specific to this. Actually, roses associate comfortably with almost all other garden plants — so why not treat roses themselves as companion plants? A companion plant, to me, is one that by its very nature will not subjugate or quell the effect of its neighbours, blending in but at the same time adding one or more extra dimensions to a scene. This may be colour of flower, foliage, fragrance, or differing contours of height and shape.

Another feature that roses can bring to mixed planting schemes is that of seasonal enhancement. A herbaceous border, for example, one that is at its best in spring, can be enlivened in midsummer with a few old-fashioned roses. Few flowering shrubs outside the rose family ever bloom for longer than two to three weeks, so strategically placed roses planted in mixed shrubberies can work wonders if flowering seasons are correctly co-ordinated. Hips too, especially those of Species roses, can enhance a wild or woodland garden. They also provide a welcome source of tasty sustenance deep into winter for the birds.

Yet another element common in larger gardens is water, sometimes moving in streams, but more often as lakes and ponds. I love to see roses growing close enough to water for their reflections to be seen in it, and I love to

'Reine des Violettes' (*right*) One of the loveliest of all Old roses, the Hybrid Perpetual 'Queen of the Violets' is aptly named. In some of its moods it is violet and grey; in others, it takes on more pinkish shades, as here in the picture taken in my garden following a heavy shower of rain. In soft focus behind are some colourful foxgloves (*Digitalis*), which in some garden landscapes can be very useful plants for adding structure to relatively relaxed roses.

'Vanity' (*below*) The shocking pink Hybrid Musk 'Vanity' is seen here making a bold statement as it emerges from a clump of *Geranium* 'Johnson's Blue'. Colour combinations such as this can be eye-catching, but I feel they are perhaps best used sparingly, especially in a small garden.

R. wichurana
The rambling species
R. wichurana is seen
serving a useful purpose
here, clothing the banks of
the moat at Mannington
Hall, Norfolk, in the UK,
and cascading down to the
water. Like all roses, it
enjoys having its roots
constantly moist. This
species is the progenitor of
all the roses known as
Wichurana Ramblers.

see petals floating on its surface.
In smaller gardens, too, Compact
Floribundas and non-invasive
Procumbents can look extremely
effective if planted adjacent to ponds.

Hedges of roses have been part of
the garden scene for a long time but,
to my mind, they deserve to be more
popular. The more formal hedge can be
created from the once-flowering types,
which can be clipped into shape every
year after flowering. The Sweet Briars
are especially good for such a purpose.
Less formality in hedges can be
achieved with the use of almost any
type of rose, Rugosas undoubtedly
being one of the best.

The vogue for hard landscaping has
brought the patio to many gardens in recent years. Coinciding with the proliferation of
these paved areas, there has been a large increase in the use of shorter roses. These are
now generally called Patio roses, a name I patently dislike. I much prefer to call them
Compact Floribundas. Whatever their name, such roses are suitable for a wide variety
of uses. They are usually very colourful and easy to maintain, and being by nature small
and bushy, never outgrow their welcome in the small spaces in which they are
generally planted.

Patios or terraces lend themselves ideally as standing areas for pots and tubs, and
roses are very compatible with containers of all sizes. The Compact Floribundas are
particularly suitable for growing in 30cm (12in) containers, but I would love to see
many more roses grown in this way. Providing the container is large enough and the
compost nutritious enough, then any rose will grow in one, including Climbers and
Ramblers. In fact, all roses grown in this way usually respond superbly to the extra
tender loving care that is given to them. Daily irrigation is, of course, essential in
spring, summer, and autumn.

I have never been a great lover of standard roses — "tree roses" in the USA —
especially when grown in the open garden. One exception I make is when they are an
essential part of a formal planting scheme. However, standards are ideal pot plants,
half barrels proving excellent containers for them. On patios or terraces, however, I
prefer half standards, since their height seems to be in better proportion to the plants
around them, especially when close to a house.

Some roses, when mature, are broader than tall. These are commonly termed
Ground Coverers although I prefer the term Procumbent. Roses of this type need

space to develop and some actually make ideal short ramblers. Because they are seen as being very cost effective, more and more Procumbents are now appearing in rose catalogues and in garden centres. Many are very good subjects for mass bedding in lawns and are increasingly used in this way in parks and other municipal open spaces (although not always successfully, it has to be said). An attractive feature of this type of rose is that most are fully remontant. However, not all of them will cover the ground densely enough to suppress weeds, and it is best to see them growing as mature plants before choosing a particular variety.

Finally, I must mention roses for scrambling up into the branches of trees. I am glad to say that growing roses in this way is becoming more and more popular, and there are dozens of vigorous scramblers available today. Remember to provide a couple of strands of wire to help them to begin climbing; and plant them, if possible, on the cooler, darker side of established trees, so that they will seek the light from the sunnier side as they clamber up into the branches.

In the subsequent pages I have described a selection of roses that I am happy to recommend – roses you will enjoy living with and, if you care for them, I know will enjoy living with you.

'Dr W. Van Fleet'
Old apple trees make ideal natural supports for vigorous Scramblers such as the Wichurana 'Dr W. Van Fleet'. Here, it has clearly been established for several years. This rose is sometimes mistaken for 'New Dawn', whose flowers are identical. Unlike remontant 'New Dawn' however, 'Dr W. Van Fleet' blooms only once each summer; as a result, since nature does not provide for roses to grow and flower at the same time, it is far more vigorous.

SPECIES ROSES

T he things I like most about Species roses are the purity and simplicity of their flowers; in the main these are single, most having five petals, and show off their stamens beautifully. They are nature's roses, the wild roses of the world, distributed widely throughout all regions of the northern hemisphere. Although all types of roses now thrive in most temperate zones in the southern hemisphere, having been introduced there over the centuries, there is no evidence that any wild rose has ever evolved naturally south of the Equator. Species roses are to be found growing wild in four main regions: Europe, Asia Minor, Asia, and North America.

The European species

European species are fewer in number than those from other parts of the world, the most common by far being *R. canina*, the dog rose. Also widely distributed in Europe is *R. rubiginosa*, known as the sweet briar rose. This rose is apple scented, and until recently its botanical name was *R. eglanteria*. It is closely related to the dog rose. The Scotch rose, *R. pimpinellifolia*, once known as *R. spinosissima*, is frequently found wild in coastal areas since it does not mind impoverished sandy soils. These three species, along with the less common *R. arvensis*, the field rose, are happier in northern and eastern Europe than further south, but two that clearly find warmer climates to their liking are the so-called French rose, *R. gallica*, and *R. moschata*, the musk rose, both of which can occasionally be found in wilderness areas of the Mediterranean region. The genes of each of these species have had an influence – to a greater or lesser degree – on the highly bred roses grown in gardens today.

R. banksiae 'Lutea' (*previous pages*) This superb picture captures the refined exuberance of *R. banksiae* 'Lutea'. It also shows by the company the rose is keeping – tulips – just how early in the year it comes into flower. (A close-up view appears on p.38.)

R. canina (*below*) The dog rose is by far the most common of the European wild roses. Its favourite habitats are hedgerows and the margins of woodland. For many years, until the 1950s, plants of this species were used as understocks in the commercial production of garden roses.

The species of Asia Minor

Although they are seldom seen, two very important species grow wild in Asia Minor: *R. × damascena* and *R. × centifolia*. Both in their turn have contributed massively to the evolution of modern hybrid roses, but it may be that they are now extinct to nature. I am sure that the *R. × centifolia* available from catalogues nowadays is far too double in form to be even close to a true species.

Also indigenous to the Middle East is the lovely white single *R. pheonicia*; it, too, is significant as an early ancestor of modern hybrids. *R. foetida*, also from this region, gave rise in the distant past to *R. foetida* 'Persiana', which at the turn of the 20th century became the main progenitor of most of today's hybrid yellow varieties. *R. foetida* produced a bright orange sport called 'Bicolor', which has also been cultivated for a very long time, certainly since the 16th century, and possibly before.

R. canina hips
In winter the orange-red hips of the dog rose are a common sight in the countryside of most of northern Europe, providing tasty sustenance for both birds and small mammals. In the 1940s, when citrus fruit was scarce in Britain, rose hips, in the form of both syrup and jelly, were a valuable source of vitamin C. I collected them for this purpose when I was a schoolboy and was rewarded with a spoonful of the resultant syrup every day, before school.

The Asian species

The majority of Species roses native to Asia are found in its southern and central areas, several in the foothills of the Himalayas in the west, others in various parts of China in the east. A few come from Japan further south.

The most important species to come from Asia is undoubtedly *R. chinensis spontanea*, also known as *R. indica*. This rose is the parent of several of the Chinese hybrids brought to Europe in the late 18th and early 19th centuries, four becoming known as the "stud Chinas" (see p.72). When these were crossed with European and Middle Eastern species, the resulting offspring were found to be remontant, flowering twice or more in a season, which was almost a new phenomenon in Europe at that time. Except in isolated regions, *R. chinensis spontanea* is rarely seen in the wild today. In the early 1980s, however, it was found by plantsman Roy Lancaster who collected seeds for the Chelsea Physic Garden in London and Castle Howard in Yorkshire. This rose is quite different from the rose I know as *R.* 'Odorata', a name, wrongly in my opinion, frequently applied to *R. chinensis*.

Of all the garden-worthy wild roses, those from Asia have the showiest hips. These vary widely in form, from the drooping flagon shapes of *R. moyesii*, to the plump, rounded ones of *R. rugosa*, with many other shapes in between. The flowers of the Asian species are also wide ranging in colour, from bright reds to yellows and whites.

R. moyesii
This superb Species rose from western China makes a very good garden plant, either as a specimen on its own, or among other plants in mixed shrubberies. These beautiful single flowers are followed in autumn by pendulous, orange-red hips, which are plumply flagon shaped and slightly whiskery.

The North American species

The one feature that sets the North American species apart from the wild roses of other regions is that, with a few exceptions, they have very colourful autumn foliage. They are also generally more manageable as garden plants. The leaves of the pink-flowered *R. virginiana* are especially colourful: as summer subsides they turn to a stunning, rich tawny-gold. These are intermixed with lots of small, orange-red hips. Another species with pink flowers and richly coloured autumn foliage is *R. nitida*, which is somewhat shorter than *R. virginiana*. *R. blanda* is similar in many respects to the European *R. canina*, but is less shrubby in habit and has slightly larger flowers. *R. woodsii* grows in abundance in the hedgerows of Oregon and I collected my stock of this species from there. I also found *R. gymnocarpa* in the same area. Two of my favourite species from North America, however, are the lovely, large, single, lilac-pink *R. nutkana* and the similarly coloured, slightly smaller-flowered *R. californica*.

Wild native species are not so common in the southern parts of the USA but two species introduced from China escaped from gardens to become naturalized in the countryside, aided and abetted by birds dropping seeds all over the place. These are *R. laevigata* and *R. gigantea*. Both have single, creamy white flowers, are continuous flowering, very thorny, and bear sizeable, spiky, round, yellowish hips in autumn and winter. *R. stellata* can sometimes be found in the semi-desert regions of the south-west, tolerating dry conditions better than most other species. It has beautiful little mauve-pink flowers and is very thorny.

SPECIES ROSES FOR THE GARDEN

I have chosen 30 or so shrub rose species or near species to describe in these pages, grouping them by height: short – shrubs that normally grow to no more than 1.5m (5ft); medium sized – those that are usually 1.5–2.5m (5–8ft) high; and tall – those that are 2.5m (8ft) and above. These are followed by a selection of about a dozen of the best rambling and scrambling species – those that I consider most suitable for garden use. Most Species roses flower only once each year, relatively early in summer, but a few do bloom repeatedly, some carrying on into the autumn. Species roses are perhaps best left largely unpruned, as nature intended; if pruning must be done then the ideal time, I suggest, is early spring, after their hips have been consumed by birds.

R. pimpinellifolia
Commonly known as the Scotch rose, *R. pimpinellifolia* is frequently found in sparsely inhabited, coastal areas of northern Europe, especially where the soil is light and perhaps rather impoverished. A special feature is its black, spherical hips. It is superb in wild and woodland settings or as a dense, prickly, low-growing hedge anywhere in the garden.

The shorter species

There are quite a number of nature's pure roses that can be grown in smaller gardens without ever getting seriously out of hand, all usually staying below 1.5m (5ft) or so. One of the shortest, seldom taller than 90cm (3ft), is the mid-pink *R. nitida*, a species that looks especially effective in groups, serving as colourful ground cover. *R. gallica* is a similar size and also does well when planted in groups; its flowers are larger than those of *R. nitida* and a deep pink bordering on red. It is a pity that this attractive species is rarely seen in gardens today, even if only for old times' sake, because it is very significant as the main progenitor of all the hybrid Gallicas ever introduced.

No garden should be without at least one plant of *R. pimpinellifolia*, a rose that is naturally dense in habit, with abundant fern-like foliage. It bears

R. fedtschenkoana
This dense-growing species is one of very few continuous-flowering wild roses. Recent genetic research into the ancestry of roses suggests that, in addition to 'Quatre Saisons' (*R. x damascena bifera*), this species has played a part in bringing forth continuity of flower in modern roses.

soft creamy white, single flowers in great numbers in late spring, followed by round, mahogany to black hips. This species is an excellent mixer and always seems to fit in comfortably among shrubs and perennials. It will tolerate a little shade and is not too fussy about the soil in which it is asked to grow. Occasionally, it produces one or two flowers late in summer. 'Grandiflora' (also known as 'Altaica') is a taller form of *R. pimpinellifolia*, which I like very much. It has larger flowers although, I find, not such good hips.

Another species with delicate fern-like foliage and numerous thorns is the spring-flowering, soft primrose-yellow *R. primula*. The most endearing feature of this rose is the scent of incense exuded from its foliage and flowers, which becomes even more pronounced when the younger leaves are rubbed between finger and thumb. Although *R. primula* will tolerate some shade, its fragrance seems to be stronger when grown in sunny positions. I like to plant this species close to a path where its scent can be fully experienced when it is brushed against in passing.

The fern-like foliage of *R. elegantula* is soft to touch, as is the mass of moss-like, soft prickles, the colour of milk chocolate, on its elegantly arching branches. Its flowers are small, star-like, and lilac-pink in colour. This rose looks superb on clear, frosty winter mornings, when the hoar frost on its branches glistens and sparkles in the pale sunshine. The best form of this species is *R. elegantula* 'Persetosa'.

Two other roses, although not pure species as they are both hybrids between *R. rugosa* and *R. roxburghii*, also look good when covered with frost in winter. These are the soft pink, single-flowered *R. x micrugosa* and the pure white single *R. x micrugosa* 'Alba'. Both bear flowers throughout the summer. Their fruit is globular, spiky, and orange-red when fully ripe, and their foliage is very colourful, especially when seen in bright autumn evening sunlight.

R. fedtschenkoana, too, repeats its flowers, obliging us with heavy crops of single, pure white blooms from early summer through to autumn. Its foliage is soft in texture and greyish green in colour. It tolerates starved conditions well, but in very good soil may get taller than its usual 1.5m (5ft).

R. virginiana is, in my view, not only a superior species but one of the best garden shrubs. The slightly fragrant, single, pink flowers show off beautiful golden stamens when fully open, and are followed by an abundance of round, orange-red hips. Its bright autumn leaves are an absolute delight when seen in early winter sun. This species seldom outgrows its welcome in any garden. It will put up with impoverished soil and, although better in sun, will not mind a little shade. It is certainly one of the best wild roses I know for hedging. Tidy in habit, it usually grows to about 1.2m (4ft).

Like *R. virginiana*, *R. woodsii* originally came from North America; the form *fendleri* is now more commonly grown. In midsummer, it bears masses of single, lilac-pink flowers, larger than those of the true species, but perhaps its most attractive feature is its hips, which are large, red, and plump. This rose, too, tolerates some shade and does not need a particularly fertile soil in which to flourish.

Coming back now to another short rose with fern-like foliage, *R. ecae* bears masses of small, single, waxy, golden yellow flowers quite early each summer; in sheltered, warm gardens it will flower in spring. Upright in habit, with very thorny shoots, it mixes well with other plants but definitely enjoys special attention and fertile soil.

R. hemisphaerica, originally from western Asia, also likes to be mollycoddled. Its very double flowers are of deep sulphur-yellow but they rarely open properly if the atmosphere is damp. Notwithstanding this, patience and perseverance will be rewarded with an occasional perfect bloom. It needs a sheltered position, preferably in sun. It does well when grown in a sizeable container.

R. virginiana
Of all the wild roses, this North American species is one of the most rewarding as a garden plant. Its flowers first appear in midsummer and are followed in autumn by a profusion of small, red hips, which come along at a time when the foliage is beginning to change from yellow to rich tawny gold. *R. virginiana* is one of the best Species roses for hedging purposes.

R. x richardii
Not a true species but very ancient, R. x richardii is closely related to R. x damascena. Its origins are in and around Ethiopia, where it has been seen growing in the vicinity of tombs and churches, which accounts for its colloquial name, the holy rose. It makes a good garden plant, when it will become considerably wider than tall.

A seldom-grown species is *R. x kochiana*. Its single, mauve-pink flowers are borne among bright green leaves, these turning an impressive burnished gold in autumn. This rose is another good mixer and, in my opinion, looks especially good among grey-foliaged herbaceous plants and shrubs. It rarely grows to more than 90cm (3ft).

R. x macrantha, related to *R. gallica*, is a trailing shrub with medium-sized, single, fragrant flowers of soft blush-pink to white. Usually about 1.2m (4ft) tall, it needs space to expand, and given this will spread to at least 2.2m (7ft). Because it will tolerate a little dappled shade, it can be used to great effect beneath taller shrubs and trees, especially those that are not too dense.

Also wider than tall is the lovely *R. x richardii*, also known by three other names: *R. sancta*, St John's rose, and the holy rose. Related to *R. x damascena*, this is a very old species, or close species, although it was not introduced to Europe until 1902. Its fragrant, soft pink, single flowers are freely produced and sizeable. If I wanted to plant just one prostrate Species rose I would choose this one.

Finally, I come to *R. stellata*, at 90cm (3ft) one of the shortest species of all, best in the form *mirifica*. It looks more like a gooseberry bush but is even pricklier. Superb among herbaceous plants, its little single flowers are mauve-pink. It is a shrub that will happily endure the longest of droughts and also do well as a pot plant.

Species roses of medium height

Several of nature's roses can be said to be medium sized, that is 1.5–2.5m (5–8ft) high, and almost all are suitable for gardens. Some make good specimens on their own and others fit readily into woodland and wild settings. Most will tolerate at least dappled shade and a fair proportion are not too bothered by infertile soil.

One, in particular, that puts up with such soil is *R. × dupontii*, sometimes known simply as 'Dupontii'. This is an outstanding rose, with a close affinity to *R. moschata*. I have one about 2.5m (8ft) tall and almost as wide. Year upon year it gives me thousands of single, soft blush-pink to creamy white flowers, each with a boss of golden stamens. Its hips are bright red but, sadly, rather small and ordinary.

The strong-growing *R. canina* 'Andersonii' was a direct result of a cross between *R. canina* and *R. gallica*. This rose has an arching nature and is ideal for woodland planting. Its flowers are large, single, fragrant, and clear pink. These precede lots of oval, orange-red fruit each autumn.

R. villosa also has single, mid-pink flowers, followed by apple-shaped, whiskery, crimson hips. Its greyish green foliage has a slight downy texture. Previously known as *R. pomifera* or the apple rose, this European species has been grown in gardens since the 1770s. There is a double form called *R. villosa* 'Duplex', or Wolley-Dod's rose.

The burr rose, *R. roxburghii*, is an ancient Chinese rose that has caused some confusion over the years. The first form to arrive in Europe had fully double flowers, and was in fact a cultivated form but introduced as a species; known today as *R. roxburghii roxburghii* or *R. roxburghii* 'Plena', its colour is deep lilac-pink. The species itself (*R. roxburghii normalis* today), with large, single flowers of a more delicate colour, was introduced later on. Both forms bear succulent hips, resembling small, unopened chestnut husks. These ripen to rich yellow in autumn, changing to red in winter.

R. roxburghii
The fruit of *R. roxburghii* develop on short stalks among the leaves, which are themselves borne close to the stems. The fruit usually form in pairs, as the picture shows, a feature that is not quite so obvious with the flowers.

R. glauca
This picture shows
R. glauca's flowers at
about double their actual
size, thus accentuating
their charm when set
against the glaucous, bluish
purple foliage and similarly
coloured stems of this
Species rose.

R. webbiana is a rose with lots of character. Its habit of growth is semi-pendulous, its foliage glaucous grey-green, and its numerous little, single flowers soft rosy pink. Its best feature, however, is its colourful red fruit, which hang like small, oval bottles on long, arching branches from mid-autumn well into winter each year.

Another semi-pendulous species is *R. willmottiae*. This has greyish green foliage and small but numerous, single, lilac-pink flowers. Its hips are small and oval. Both this species and *R. webbiana* are excellent when used on their own, as specimen plants, in lawns and open spaces. Neither will be too unhappy if planted in dappled shade.

Semi-shade presents no real challenge to *R. macrophylla*. This species, however, is better in the form 'Doncasterii', which is very upright in stature. Its almost thornless wood is plum coloured and well endowed with purple-tinted foliage. Its hips are large, oval to bottle shaped, and bright orange-red in colour.

R. xanthina hugonis, Father Hugo's rose, is closely related to the bright yellow *R. xanthina* 'Canary Bird', better known simply as 'Canary Bird', and the two have much in common. Father Hugo's rose, though, is a little more graceful in growth, with flowers that are a slightly softer yellow. Like 'Canary Bird', this species blooms in about the middle of spring each year.

The last in my selection of the medium-sized species is *R. glauca*, known until recently as *R. rubrifolia*, in my opinion the most useful Species rose of all. This superb shrub has glaucous, plum- to purple-coloured wood, its young growth being thornless.

Its flowers, if a little insignificant among the foliage, are quite beautiful in form, single, and soft blush-pink, blending superbly with the purple foliage. In the autumn, its hips hang in large bunches, reddish purple in colour and each about the size of a small grape. The growth habit of this species is dense and upright and it will thrive almost anywhere. In fact, there are few uses within the garden to which *R. glauca* cannot be put. It will even grow on walls as a small climber.

R. glauca hips
Combining superbly with the bluish purple foliage, the fruit of *R. glauca* ripen first to the bright red colour seen here; they then slowly change to deep crimson, and end up plum-purple. Eventually they provide tasty meals for the birds.

The taller species

While all the tall species will reach large proportions, growing at least 2.5m (8ft) high and sometimes more, it must be borne in mind that even the medium-sized ones will also make quite big plants if grown in really good soil. The tall, wide types, of course, are not really suitable for small gardens. They fit best into wild gardens and into shrubberies; they are also ideal for forming impenetrable hedges and barriers.

For hedging, the first of the taller species to come to mind is *R. rugosa*, which makes one of the best hedges of any of the wild roses. The wild form is not as well known as its many excellent hybrids. A native of Japan, it is one of very few species that bear their flowers continuously; these are single, fragrant, and mid- to deep pink, and are followed by sizeable, round, bright orange-red hips. *R. rugosa* has plenty of thorns, and its foliage is dense and dark green. Irritatingly, it produces suckers far too readily and these often emerge some distance away from the parent plant.

A species of which I am very fond is *R. forrestiana*, a statuesque plant with stiff, mahogany-coloured branches. These are thorny and clothed with blue-green leaves. The flowers are single, deep pink, and fragrant, and are followed by generous quantities of small, oval, orange to red hips.

Large, red, flagon-shaped hips follow the soft pink, single flowers of *R. davidii*. These are borne profusely all along stiff, thorny branches in early summer. Its foliage is leathery, dark green with a touch of gloss. This is a lovely versatile species, well worth space in any garden of substance.

R. setipoda is similar in stature and structure to *R. davidii*, but its flowers are a much deeper pink, and its flagon-shaped hips are a little narrower, but equally large and colourful.

R. soulieana is a grey-leaved species with a graceful but dense, arching habit. It will, however, get very tall, especially in situations where it can assert itself. In fact, it could easily be classed as a Rambler. It has a good crop of small, white, single, fragrant flowers each summer, followed by bunches of small but numerous, orange-red hips, a spectacular sight especially from a distance.

The most unusual of all the Species roses is *R. omeiensis pteracantha*, sometimes called *R. sericea pteracantha*. The pure white flowers of this very vigorous rose are made up of only four petals, a flower form unique to this species. They are borne in late spring and followed by small, drooping, bright orange-red hips. The thorns are by far its most outstanding feature: large, wedge-shaped, translucent, and cherry-red when young, they are especially beautiful when seen in bright morning or evening sunlight.

'Master Hugh' is another, taller form of the relatively thornless *R. macrophylla* mentioned earlier, but this rose bears massive, drooping hips, which have to be seen to be believed. They are plumply urn-shaped and turn bright red in mid-autumn, lasting well into winter. These are preceded by large, soft cerise-pink, single flowers, which sometimes partially conceal themselves among the purplish foliage.

RAMBLING AND SCRAMBLING SPECIES FOR THE GARDEN

Those of nature's roses that ramble and scramble are quite diverse in type, coming as they do from a wide range of different classes within the genus. Some are very flexible in their climbing habit, and others have rigid tendencies. Many contain themselves to fairly modest dimensions, while a few are almost unstoppable and climb to great heights. It is for these more vigorous plants that I like to use the term scramblers, but this is not an official classification – unlike Ramblers which is the accepted term for all roses capable of rambling.

Some Ramblers are practically evergreen, even in harsh climates, and a few have greyish foliage. Several, before shedding their leaves, give a good display of colour as winter approaches. Nature is clever, of course, and the majority of the flowers of Ramblers are white or creamy white in colour, because, in their natural habitat, they need to be clearly visible among the foliage if they are to be fertilized by bees and other insects. Quite a number are fragrant. By the end of summer they can be overflowing with red or orange hips: a gastronomic pleasure for the birds, and a joy to those, like me, who consider berries one of the most rewarding features of roses.

Species roses in their scrambling forms are very useful. In most cases, however, except on walls and up into trees, they do not fit easily into smaller gardens. They come into their own in wooded, wilder spaces, where they blend naturally into the landscape; some form themselves into clumps of ground cover, especially where sunshine is able to filter through the leafy canopies of any trees around. Grown as tree scramblers, they add an extra dimension to the wild garden scene; they can also look at home on structures such as fences and trellis.

There are 20–25 Species roses that can climb but some, while interesting, are quite obscure and seldom seen other than in botanic gardens and dedicated rose collections. I have selected about a dozen to discuss here.

R. omeiensis pteracantha
This unusual Chinese species is easily recognized by its very sharp, wedge-shaped, translucent, red thorns. Only a very few of its close relatives have such attractive, pernicious armoury. Another unique feature is its flowers, each of which is composed of only four petals; all other single roses have five.

The field rose, *R. arvensis*, is Britain's only true native Rambler, and it is a very lovely rose. Its single, pure white flowers are roughly the same size as those of the dog rose, *R. canina*, and have beautiful golden yellow stamens. The fruit that follows the flowers, though, is rather a dull red. The plant produces many flexible shoots, which thread their way up into trees as well as scramble through undergrowth and hedges. They are only slightly thorny, and bear plenty of darkish green leaves. If allowed to develop, *R. arvensis* will reach an ultimate size of 3–5m (10–15ft). In all honesty, however, I prefer coming across this rose in the wild to seeing it in my garden. Incidentally, *R. arvensis*, in its time, was the progenitor of several double forms of garden roses, including 'Dundee Rambler', 'Bennett's Seedling', and 'Venusta Pendula'.

The four forms of *R. banksiae*, natives of China, are considered a little tender in northern Europe but should be comfortable enough as long as they are grown on a warm, sheltered wall rather than on a structure in the open. *R. banksiae banksiae*, also known as *R. banksiae* 'Alba Plena', bears masses of small, semi- to fully double, white flowers in cascading clusters; the other white form, *R. banksiae normalis*, has clusters of single flowers. *R. banksiae* 'Lutea', or Lady Banks' rose, is a marvellous rose by any standard, with bright yellow, double flowers in many clusters. The fourth is a very beautiful, single yellow named *R. banksiae* 'Lutescens'. All the Banksian roses flower in late spring in northern Europe, three or four weeks earlier in warmer climates. They are thornless and have plenty of light green foliage. In friendly habitats they will all grow to considerable sizes. An added bonus is their perfume, which is quite alluring.

One of the most vigorous of all roses, *R. brunonii* has sometimes been distributed erroneously as *R. moschata*. However, it blooms much earlier than the latter species and its white, fragrant flowers are borne in larger corymbs. The foliage is greyish green and its fruit, when fully ripe in mid-autumn, is bright red in colour but rather inconspicuous. There is a superior form called 'La Mortola' with larger, more luscious foliage and more numerous, grander flowers.

R. helenae is my favourite of all the scrambling species. It is a very vigorous plant, with grey-green foliage, and bears small, distinctively perfumed, single, creamy white flowers, each cuddled up tightly to the other in large, cascading corymbs. Its best feature, though, is its copious crop of hips,

R. banksiae normalis
(*right*) Thought to be the species form of the Banksian roses, *R. banksiae normalis* is here showing off in the company of *Wisteria sinensis*. It is by far the most vigorous of the group, needing lots of space to flourish.

R. banksiae 'Lutea'
(*below*) Flowering in mid-to late spring, this beautiful rose is always one of the first to come into bloom each year. Its season may be short, but this minor misdemeanour is amply made up for by the sheer number of flowers, and by the way they are flaunted against a background of copious, light green foliage. (See also the photograph on p.24.)

R. gentiliana
This species from China has many medium-sized clusters of white flowers, borne among plenty of almost evergreen, glossy leaves. They are followed by small, plumply oval, orange-red hips. In the foreground here are evening primroses (*Oenothera biennis*).

which hang in large bunches like redcurrants from when they first ripen in mid-autumn right through until midwinter.

I come now to *R. moschata*, mentioned in passing earlier. It has fragrant, single, white flowers, which are produced in large, loose clusters from midsummer onwards. This is a relatively short-growing rose, sometimes behaving more like a large shrub than a rambling species. Dense in habit, it has soft, greyish foliage. It is a very old rose, dating back to before the 16th century. It was lost to commerce for many years, before being rediscovered at Myddleton House, Essex, in the UK, by Graham Stuart Thomas in the 1970s. It makes an excellent garden plant and deserves wider attention.

The small white flowers of *R. multiflora* are perhaps most attractive when seen from afar in the branches of trees. The plant roots easily from cuttings and is used as understock in some parts of the world; it can be found growing wild in all sorts of places, its seed having been scattered far and wide by birds. In the USA it is considered a weed. The best use to which it can be put in the garden is as hedging when, if pruned regularly, it will serve well as a living boundary or dividing barrier.

Another slightly contentious scrambler is *R. mulliganii*, which for many years was distributed wrongly, as *R. longicuspis*. The small, white flowers of *R. longicuspis* have a strong fragrance, while *R. mulliganii* is only slightly scented. This species is vigorous and makes a superb tree scrambler. Its orange hips are quite small, but profuse in number.

If large, glossy foliage is reason enough for growing a rose then *R. sinowilsonii* is the one to plant. It is said by some to be a little tender in cooler climates, but I have never found it so. Its leaves, by rose standards, are huge, polished, and bright green, changing to colourful tawny-yellow in the autumn. Although not over generous with its single, white flowers, these are fragrant and are carried in showy, well-spaced trusses. Some consider this rose to be synonymous with *R. longicuspis*, but it is quite different from the *R. longicuspis* I once knew. More generous with its flowers is *R. gentiliana*, a scrambler not dissimilar to *R. sinowilsonii*, with large, glossy leaves.

I first came upon the beautiful *R. bracteata* growing in the open at La Landriana, a lovely garden near Rome. In England, I had seen it only in conservatories, as it is not thought hardy enough to grow out of doors. I have now seen it in other Mediterranean and Californian gardens and over the last three or four years have grown it in a large pot here in Norfolk; so far, it has survived. It has large, soft primrose-yellow flowers amid a multitude of foliage and many thorns. Here, it takes a rest in late summer, flowering again in late autumn; in warmer climates it flowers throughout the year.

The most vigorous scrambling species of all is, without doubt, *R. filipes* from China. However big the tree or structure on which it is grown, it will take it over with a vengeance. These days it is more commonly seen in the form 'Kiftsgate', which, if anything, is even more vigorous than the species and has larger flowers; these are fragrant, single, and produced in large panicles. The reddish hips are small but most attractive en masse. It is well endowed with healthy, mid-green foliage and is very thorny. It is, in fact, an ideal rose to use as a burglar deterrent.

R. wichurana has much to commend it as a species. It bears masses of fragrant, single, off-white flowers in corymbs, a little later than most others of its type. It puts out slender, flexible shoots, which lend themselves to scrambling into trees. Almost evergreen, it can also make a good ground-cover plant. In the late 19th and early 20th centuries it was used extensively as breeding stock, and quite a few of its offspring — including 'Albertine' and 'New Dawn' — remain popular today. In my earlier books, written only a few years ago, I followed the lead of all other authors in using the name *R. wichuraiana*, which is now considered incorrect by the powers that be in plant nomenclature. I believe in accuracy in all things, but surely, even if wrong, a precedent was set at the time the rose was first named in 1860. Now, with the name changed to *R. wichurana*, every book published until recently is rendered inaccurate — irritatingly, including mine. So be it!

R. filipes 'Kiftsgate'
A superior form of *R. filipes*, which was introduced from western China in 1908, this rose was found at Kiftsgate Court, Gloucestershire, in the UK, in 1954 and has since been distributed widely around the world under this name. The original plant at Kiftsgate is one of the biggest roses in Britain, covering several large trees.

OLD GARDEN ROSES

The Albas

Having been in love with them from an early age I now realize that the Alba roses have for ever been disadvantaged. Disadvantaged because, in the eyes of so many, they suffer from the drawback of flowering only fleetingly, for just a few weeks each summer. Other Old garden roses, including the Damasks, the Gallicas, and the Centifolias, also have a short flowering season, but the Albas are such beautiful roses that it seems to me especially unjust that they should be shunned for this one slight frailty. Moreover, plants such as daffodils bloom only once each year (albeit gratifyingly well in advance of roses), as do lilac, cherries, and almost all other flowering shrubs. These are never cold-shouldered simply because of their transient performance in their respective seasons.

The anonymous author of one of my favourite little books, *The Flower Garden* (1839), refers to the Albas as having been cultivated in the gardens of Europe from time immemorial. Certainly we are safe to assume that some of the older forms go back at least to Roman times. The author lists no fewer than 42 different varieties of Alba roses, but today most specialists offer no more than a dozen or so. Although their origin is somewhat obscure, there can be little doubt that the original Alba owes much of its genealogy to the dog rose, *R. canina*, as evidenced by the healthy, grey-green foliage and shrubby habit of growth of its garden-worthy descendants. *R. x damascena* is usually deemed to be the other likely parent of the Albas, clearly a potent mix of genes in the bringing forth of fragrance. To me no other roses have the same refinement and pervasiveness of perfume as has this group. However fleeting their flowers, the few Albas that have come down to us from centuries past are surely well worth space in any modern garden, on the strength of their fragrance alone.

ALBAS FOR THE GARDEN

The name Alba, meaning white of course, is a little misleading for, although there are several pure white Alba roses, including 'Maxima' and 'Semi Plena', most are actually varying shades of pink. Irrespective of their colour, given fair weather in which to bloom, they almost all border on the divine for sheer good looks. They are also among the easiest of roses to grow. Their paramount virtue, however, is the way they cohabit so generously with most other garden plants.

I have always taken a special interest in the Albas, probably because I love fragrant roses of white and soft colours. My favourite, without a doubt, is 'Maiden's Blush'. This is a rose I remember from my childhood and, for me, few pleasures can surpass

'Hermosa' (*previous pages*) This China rose dates right back to 1840 yet it flowers continuously throughout summer, contradicting the generalization that all Old roses have a very short flowering season. The blooms of 'Hermosa' are fragrant, and its stems rather thorny.

that first viewing each year of one of its perfect blooms, its blush-pink petals opening to a full, exquisitely perfumed cushion. There are two forms of this rose, 'Great' and 'Small'. 'Great Maiden's Blush' reaches heights of 5m (15ft) on walls or trellis or up into trees and 1.8m (6ft) or so as a free-standing shrub, while 'Small Maiden's Blush' seldom gets to more than 1.2m (4ft). In my travels around the world I have also come across considerable variation in colour among roses labelled as 'Maiden's Blush', some heavily blushed pink, others hardly blushing at all. 'Cuisse de Nymphe' is the French name by which this lovely rose is also known. Were I allowed to take just one rose with me to solitary confinement on some far-off desert island, this would most certainly be my choice.

'Maxima' is believed by many to be the white rose of York, the emblem of the Yorkist faction involved in the Wars of the Roses in 15th-century England. It has also had many other names in its time, including the Jacobite rose, Bonnie Prince Charlie's rose, the Cheshire rose, and 'Great Double White'; the latter is very descriptive for, when open, the flowers are full of pure white petals, occasionally showing the faintest hint of blush in dull weather. Its fragrance is not unlike that of 'Maiden's Blush'. As a

'Maiden's Blush'
I consider 'Maiden's Blush' to be one of the most beautiful of all roses. Its fragrance is refined and evocative. It was first introduced to me when I was at a very young age, and although it is perhaps too far fetched to believe that its discovery influenced my choice of career, it certainly stimulated an early interest in garden plants.

'Königin von Dänemark'
Sharing space with
Clematis 'Prince Charles',
'Königin von Dänemark',
one of the deepest pink
of the Albas, has formed
itself characteristically into
an upright but densely
bushy plant. This picture
also shows the abundant,
healthy, grey-green foliage
so typical of all the Albas.

plant, 'Maxima' is thorny and well endowed with grey-green leaves. It makes a good, tidy shrub, and it can also be easily trained for use as a small wall climber.

A few very good Albas were introduced into Europe in the early 19th century, presumably the result of deliberate hybridization or selections from randomly sown seed, and I have chosen three to describe here. The first is 'Jeanne d'Arc', introduced from Vibert, France, in 1818. This rose has lots of creamy coloured, fragrant flowers, but its many petals quickly bleach to white in hot sun. It is useful as a tidy, medium-sized shrub for mixed shrubberies and herbaceous borders. 'Königin von Dänemark' or 'Queen of Denmark', 1826, has slightly smaller flowers than most Albas. These emerge from flat-topped buds to become very double, their colour a deeper pink than most of their kind. Sometimes the weight of a cluster of flowers causes its rather thorny stems to arch downwards from a fairly rugged, but not over tall plant. This superbly fragrant rose is best in groups of three, especially if each is given a little support. The third of the trio is a stocky but charming cultivar called 'Félicité Parmentier', introduced in about 1828. An upright shrub with the usual healthy, greyish green Alba foliage, it has many fully double flowers with reflexing petals forming delicate blush-pink pompons.

'Chloris', also known as 'Rosée du Matin', is a very ancient Alba of unknown provenance. It is another medium-growing cultivar. Adding to the charm of its satiny pink flowers are the small green carpels that emerge from the centres of its tightly packed petals. In all respects 'Chloris' is a typical Alba.

The Alba that I consider to have the loveliest foliage is 'Celestial' or 'Celeste'. Its leaves are lush, leaden grey-green and plentiful, providing a superb foil for loose, silky pink, deliciously scented flowers. 'Celestial' is the sort of rose that mixes well with all types of shrubs and herbaceous plants. Even if neglected, it never seems to get out of hand. I like to plant a few of these in different parts of the garden, to come upon by chance from time to time, so to speak.

'Semi-Plena', as the name suggests, has fairly informal flowers, with most clones — and there seem to be several — having enough pure white petals to form a nicely shaped bud. Fully open, they show off attractive golden stamens. Also known as *R. alba* 'Nivea' and *R. alba* 'Suaveolens', this rose dates back to well before the 15th century, and some consider that it — and not 'Maxima' — is the historical white rose of York. In truth, no one knows for sure. My own view on this is that it could, perhaps, have been *R. alba*, a lovely, pure white, single rose flowering in early summer. I have seen it growing wild in the hedgerows of Norfolk, and it would have been found all over Europe in the 15th century. It has a good scent and, in autumn, its oval hips are of similar colour to those of the dog rose, *R. canina*, but smaller. Indeed, it is not unlike *R. canina*, but with greyer foliage, and it may well be a white form of that species.

Finally, 'Mme Plantier' and 'Mme Legras de St Germain' — two fully double, pure white, fragrant Albas that are difficult to tell apart. Neither is totally typical of this group. Their foliage is soft to touch — a fact that rather suggests distant Damask ancestry. Both are fairly free of thorns and make good tall shrubs or small climbers.

'Celestial'
This is one of several Albas of unknown provenance, all of which very likely go back to well before the 15th century. *Penstemon* 'Port Wine' provides the ideal companion for this delightful soft pink, very fragrant, trouble-free rose.

The Damasks

An exquisite fragrance is the most alluring feature of the Damask roses. One or two of the oldest Damasks have long been highly valued by perfumeries in the Middle East for making attar of roses, and Damask roses are among the best for use in pot-pourri. In terms of colour, the flowers are all some shade of pink or white, and grace the garden with their presence for about three weeks each summer (much longer in the case of one or two varieties).

It is said that the first Damasks came to Europe at the time of the crusaders. In fact, some say that they were brought back from the Middle East by the crusading knights themselves. There is no reason not to believe this; certainly among the ranks of the Damasks are some of our oldest roses. As regards their genealogy, I believe the ancient Damasks have more *R. gallica* in their make-up than hitherto thought.

DAMASKS FOR THE GARDEN

The main recognition features of Damask roses are their downy, soft to touch foliage and rather short flower stalks; also, they almost all have very thorny stems. Usually relaxed in growth and unobtrusive in behaviour, Damasks lend themselves ideally as companions to many other shrubs and perennials. In all, there are about 20 varieties. I will discuss about half of these, in alphabetical order.

'Blush Damask' blooms very freely early each summer. It is a tidy shrub, growing to about 1.2m (4ft) tall, and being dense and thorny makes an almost impenetrable hedge, a purpose for which I would use it above all others; it can also excel itself as a specimen shrub. Its full, flat flowers are mid-pink, fading to soft pink around the edges, and are very fragrant.

'Celsiana' dates back to before 1750 and has been well loved by gardeners ever since. It can reach up to 1.5m (5ft) in height, but it is not as

'Kazanlik' (*right*)
An ancient, semi-double Damask, 'Kazanlik' is grown in large quantities in Bulgaria for the aromatic qualities of its flowers. Its petals have been collected and distilled into attar of roses for centuries.

'Ispahan' (*below*)
Although all the Damasks except 'Quatre Saisons' bloom only once each summer, in full flush they give a concentrated display, as can be seen here. Not only is every flower of 'Ispahan' very seductive in appearance, but each one has a most beguiling fragrance.

'Leda'
Also known as the painted Damask, this captivating rose is of unknown origin but shows some Gallica influence in its foliage. Were it continuous flowering, it would almost certainly be classified as a Portland Damask. It never gets tall or out of hand. I have always loved the name 'Leda', that of the mythical queen seduced by Zeus while he had taken the form of a swan.

dense in habit as 'Blush Damask'. Its flowers are not quite fully double and are a lovely shade of clear pink, fading a little to blush in hot sun; they are extremely fragrant and the rose is worth growing for this alone.

A rather unDamask-like rose is 'Hebe's Lip', which some say could be a cross between *R. × damascena* and *R. rubiginosa*. Its flowers are rather more than single, and whitish in colour with red edges to the petals. It is strongly scented, and flowers very freely in early summer. Its foliage is somewhat coarse and growth a little ungainly; nevertheless I am fond of this rather unusual shrub rose, which is never obtrusive in any position in the garden. It also has two other names 'Reíne Blanche' and 'Rubrotincta'.

No one really knows the provenance of 'Ispahan', which dates back to before 1832, except that, as its name suggests, it was found in a garden in Ispahan, western Persia (Iran), by an anonymous rose fancier. It is also known as 'Rose d'Isfahan'. It is a superb example of a Damask, but with fewer thorns than most. Rich pink in colour, its blooms are very fragrant, and shapely in form. This is one of my favourite Damasks, making an ideal pot or border plant; it is fairly upright in growth and, although non-remontant, flowers very freely in early to midsummer each year.

'Kazanlik' or 'Trigintipetala' is a very ancient rose, grown for centuries in Bulgaria specifically for the perfume industry there. I cannot lay my hand on my heart and say that this rose would have survived as a garden plant until now had it not been for the superb fragrance of its warm pink flowers. It sprawls a bit and is very thorny; it is also very healthy and good in a wild garden, but, in truth, it will grow anywhere.

Another Damask with its origin shrouded in mystery is 'Leda', probably an early 19th-century rose. Its flowers are fragrant, medium-sized, and very double, with a button of incurving petals in the centre; they are soft blush in colour, brushed red at the margins. I have found it very healthy, and although not a repeat flowerer it is beautiful with just its one flush. Shorter than most of its kind, at only 90cm (3ft), I find it fits well among a variety of different plants.

One of my favourites of all roses is the pure white Damask 'Mme Hardy', a sumptuous and refined rose that should be in every garden. It is deliciously fragrant and very generous with its one and only flush of flowers in early summer. Upright and tidy in habit, its one fault is its dislike of rain, but this is forgivable in such a virtuous rose. Plant it anywhere in the garden, and keep it well fed and watered, and it will give a wealth of pleasure in return for these favours.

Undoubtedly of great antiquity, 'Omar Khayyám' was first propagated in England from a rose planted on the grave, in Suffolk, of Edward Fitzgerald, celebrated for his 1859 translation of Omar Khayyám's *Rubáiyát*. It had grown there from the seeds of a rose found on the 12th-century Persian poet's tomb in Nishapur. It is its provenance that makes this rose so important, certainly not its garden-worthiness, but perhaps this is unkind, for it really is quite a nice rose. It does, however, need lots of tender loving care. Its flowers are silvery pinkish in colour and muddled in shape. Never reaching more than 90cm (3ft) in height, it is best on a patio or terrace in a sizeable pot.

'Quatre Saisons', or autumn Damask, is an extremely ancient rose. It is thought to be the result of a cross between *R. gallica* and *R. moschata;* it is also named *R.* x *damascena bifera* or *R.* x *damascena semperflorens*. It was an early form of this Damask, crossed in turn with two of the first hybrid Chinas, that led to the Portland and Bourbon roses. Quite apart from all this history, as a rose it has much to commend it. Its flowers are fragrant, soft pink in colour, and beautifully formed, and they are arranged in tightly packed clusters. As a shrub it is not too untidy and about 1.2m (4ft) high.

The last of the Damasks I have selected to discuss is very much a collectors' rose. This said, it will grow in almost any type of soil and is quite indifferent to position. Its name is 'York and Lancaster', more properly *R.* x *damascena veriscolor*, the name being a clue to its colouring, which is a mixture of deep pink and white. The coloration is erratic: sometimes only one flower in a cluster is white, sometimes only half a flower, and so on. It is clearly a sport of 'Kazanlik', and has certainly been around since before its recorded date of 1550. It is more than possible that when the Tudor rose, the emblem of the British royal family, was first designed in 1485, this unusual rose was its inspiration.

'Mme Hardy'
Seen here against a backdrop of wattle, this superb, pure white rose has been one of the most popular Damasks since its introduction in 1832. Like most white roses, it suffers a little in wet weather; but given a spell of successive fine days in midsummer, it is absolutely charming.

The Centifolias

I am familiar with about 25 varieties of Centifolia roses, or Provence roses as they are also called, this being almost the entire collection. No one really knows their true origin, nor is anyone altogether sure about their evolution through the centuries. It is clear, however, that their genealogy is very mixed and includes among other species *R. gallica* and *R. × damascena*. In the past there appear to have been many more Centifolia roses: hundreds of different varieties were thought to have been developed in Holland in the 16th and 17th centuries and, since the Dutch have always been such good horticulturists, there is no reason to doubt this. Even accepting that so many roses of various kinds have become extinct over the years, I am still rather mystified as to why so few Centifolias have survived to this day.

Although rose literature over the ages does not record this, I believe that the Dutch rose breeders had stock of ancient Centifolia-type roses with which to work, perhaps roses pre-dating Roman times. This theory is borne from the fact that most Centifolias that have survived until now have flowers that are far too double for easy hybridization. Furthermore, the climate in Europe is said to have been colder three or four centuries ago than it is now, and breeding roses would have been difficult without much artificial heat. I believe those Centifolias that have become lost to us today were the single and semi-double forms, which would have been much easier to hybridize, with only the fully double offspring being selected for cultivation and wider distribution — as cut flowers perhaps, the main purpose for which the Dutch would have grown them. Such full-petalled roses are seen in many of the paintings by the Dutch and Flemish old masters and other artists of the day, often shown being worn as decoration by equally well-proportioned women, or in posies, vases, and elaborate arrangements of other flowers and fruit.

CENTIFOLIAS FOR THE GARDEN

It is not surprising that Centifolias have been depicted time and again by artists down the ages, for without question they are very beautiful roses. The majority have flowers composed of many petals — the name *centifolia* means one hundred leaves — all packed together to create flat, very double cushions when fully open. Although one or two members of this group are white and a few others are reddish shades, pink is by far the predominant colour of Centifolias as a whole. Almost all flower only once in a season. Another consistent attribute of the group is fragrance, which is distinctive and almost intoxicating in strength.

'Fantin-Latour'
Sumptuous is a word I use sparingly in describing a rose, but I have no hesitation in using it for 'Fantin-Latour'. Were I much younger I might even call it scrumptious. When this rose is in flower, for just a few short weeks each summer, one glance and one sniff remind me of why I have always been in love with roses.

As plants, the Centifolias are a very mixed bunch: some have very thorny stems, others are quite smooth, and they range from the small and tidy to the tall and untidy. This diversity of habit makes it possible to utilize them in almost any position within the garden; and if they are planted among other types of shrubs, their once-flowering nature need not be too much of a drawback.

The following ten Centifolias are those I consider the best for any garden, beginning with *R. × centifolia* itself. This complex rose has been around since before 1600; in olden days, it was known colloquially as the cabbage rose. Its colour is intense bright pink, and its flowers have more petals than those of any of its relatives. It is also one of the most thorny members of the group. In normal soil it will naturally make a very lax plant, growing to a height of 1.8–2.2m (6–7ft), but I have seen plants as climbers growing on the walls of old houses and into the branches of trees; and I once came across one scrambling up into a hedgerow, presumably planted there long ago by a public-spirited countryman. There is an ancient form called 'Bullata', distinguished from *R. × centifolia* by its foliage, which is much larger and more luscious, and

'De Meaux'
This Centifolia from the late 18th century is one of the shortest members of the group, and an ideal candidate for growing in small groups or in pots. Like most of its kind it has a lovely fragrance. It is seen here showing off its ability to flower in great profusion, in early to midsummer every year.

crinkled-like lettuce leaves. There is a third form, which is slightly more refined in having a lovely button of petals in the centre of each flower; it is also brighter pink in colour. It is known by three names: *R. x centifolia* 'Major', 'Centfeuille des Peintres' and 'Rose des Peintres'.

One of the white forms of the Centifolias is 'Unique Blanche', which dates back to 1775; it is also known as white Provence and 'Vierge de Cléry'. In early summer it produces lots of fragrant flowers, which are composed of many silky textured petals. The plant is relaxed in habit and is a useful mixer, especially because it happily tolerates partial shade. 'Juno', the other white Centifolia, is a more refined hybrid dating back to 1832. Its flowers blush soft pink. The plant's proportions are very much like those of 'Unique Blanche', perhaps a little less relaxed, with considerably fewer thorns and more numerous dark green leaves.

Among the smallest of the Centifolias is the little charmer 'De Meaux', which has been around in gardens since before 1790. Seldom growing to more than 60cm (2ft) tall, it was once extensively used as a pot plant and sold as such in the flower markets of Paris. Today it also looks good in a container, perhaps on a patio or terrace, or it could be used as a portable rose, to be moved around in the garden on a whim. If planted direct into the ground it is better in groups of three or five. Its numerous flowers, appearing in early and midsummer, are small and soft pink with frilly petals.

Another short-growing variety dating back even further than 'De Meaux' is 'Pompon de Bourgogne', also known as *R. burgundica*, the Burgundian rose, and 'Parvifolia'. In early summer this delightful little rose adorns itself with lots of small, pompon-like flowers, varying in colour from rosy pink to claret. This rose will be an asset to any mixed border, especially if, like 'De Meaux', it is planted in small groups or in pots and moved into position as required.

The rich rose-pink 'Spong' also makes an excellent container plant and, although a little taller than the previous two varieties, reaching about 90cm (3ft) maximum, it too will be happy in small groups among herbaceous plants and low-growing shrubs.

'Robert le Diable' has flowers of a colour that is very difficult to describe: crimson, lilac, and grey all merged together is the nearest I can get. On cloudy days, though, the overall effect of such a mixed colouring is purple. Each flower is very double.

A much taller variety in this group, with similar colouring to 'Robert le Diable', is 'Tour de Malakoff' (also known as 'Black Jack'), a rose that

'Tour de Malakoff'
Also known as 'Black Jack', 'Tour de Malakoff' is seen here peeping through, and coordinating with, *Clematis* 'Mme Julia Correvon'. Although clematis can be rather intimidating to some roses, I expect 'Tour de Malakoff' simply to take such presumptuous competition in its stride.

needs the support of a stake or obelisk. This lovely rose is also highly scented and generous with its flowers in early and midsummer.

R. × *centifolia* 'Variegata', better known as 'Village Maid', is a tallish shrub rose with very strong, thorny shoots. Its flowers are soft off-white, randomly striped purplish pink; these are very fragrant and produced freely in early summer.

Finally, I come to one of the best-loved and most popular of all the Centifolias — 'Fantin-Latour'. This is a rose that is certainly one of my favourites, and will always be in my top ten of all roses. Mysteriously for such a beautiful rose, there are no records of its origin or parentage, but from its appearance I believe it will have several Gallica genes in its constitution. Its foliage is smooth, greyish green, and softer to touch than that of others in its group; it also has fewer thorns and is more upright in growth. Superbly fragrant, its shapely, fully double flowers are a delicate soft shade of pink. This rose will fit comfortably among other plants, and I have seen it growing as a climber, to twice its normal height of 1.5m (5ft).

R. × *centifolia*
This classically old-fashioned style flower has opened up from a cup-shaped bud to a superb arrangement of petals, with just a hint of golden anthers showing through to tempt the bees – if they have not already been enticed by the refined and all-pervading perfume from this delightful bloom.

The Gallicas

R. gallica officinalis
One of the oldest of our present-day garden roses, *R. gallica officinalis* is also known by two other names, the apothecary's rose and the red rose of Lancaster. Here it is photographed adjacent to the Moss rose 'Gloire des Mousseux' and numerous other plants, including delphiniums. It will never get much taller than seen here, about 90cm (3ft).

The Gallicas form one of the oldest groups of roses, and their genealogical influence has carried forward right through to almost all Modern roses. In earlier times there were many more Gallicas than there are now, and they were the most popular garden roses up to the end of the 18th century. In fact, the Empress Josephine is said to have grown over 150 different varieties in her collection at Malmaison; and many more were bred after that time, mostly in France. In Victorian times and before, Gallicas were called French roses or roses of Provins.

One of the oldest is *R. gallica officinalis*, also known as the apothecary's rose and, after its adoption as the emblem of England's House of Lancaster in the mid 13th century, the red rose of Lancaster. Another very famous Gallica is the red and white striped 'Rosa Mundi', which is a sport of *R. gallica officinalis*. An apocryphal legend has it that this rose was named for Rosamond Clifford, a mistress of Henry II of England, after it was discovered growing close to her grave.

GALLICAS FOR THE GARDEN

As garden plants the Gallicas are
extremely useful for, with a few
exceptions, they all contain themselves
to a manageable size. One or two are a
little floppy, but most form reasonably
compact, bushy plants. Their posture
and dimensions make them ideal for
integrating among a wide variety of other
shrubs. A few would not be incongruous
in modern garden settings. All are
suitable for use as pot plants.

Few, if any, Gallicas are really thorny,
and although their foliage is a little
coarse to touch, it is usually of a good
dark to mid-green colour and prolific.
If grown on their own roots these roses
sucker very freely. Generously produced
in midsummer, their flowers range from
single to very double in form. They
provide an amplitude of colour from soft
pink to deep crimson and purple, but
there are no whites. Some, although by
no means all, have a pleasing perfume.
Incidentally, since their hips are of little
or no ornamental value, it is a good
policy to deadhead all Gallicas after flowering, to help keep them in shape.

'Rosa Mundi'
At some time during the
early days of its existence,
R. gallica officinalis
mutated to bring forth the
lovely striped rose 'Rosa
Mundi', which is now one
of the best known of all
the Old roses. As well as
being a good mixer, it also
makes an excellent low-
growing hedge, especially
if clipped into shape after
flowering each summer.

About 50 worthwhile varieties of Gallicas have come down to us from their
heyday, from which I have selected 15 to discuss in more detail here. While not
necessarily well known, those included are roses I can vouch for and some I just
happen to like.

Placing them in no particular order, I start with 'Agatha', a fully double rose of a
deep raspberry colour with paler edges, which dates back to before 1818. 'Empress
Josephine' is rather similar, but of softer colouring and with fewer petals. Both are
fragrant and grow to about 1.5m (5ft). These two belong to a small group of hybrid
Gallicas known as Frankfurt roses, their main differences from true Gallicas being
slightly coarser leaves and taller stature.

A fine Gallica, shorter in stature than the previous two, at 1.2m (4ft), is a lovely
rose called 'Belle de Crécy'. It has very double, magenta-coloured flowers heavily
overlaid with greyish purple, with a fragrance as alluring as their colour and form.
These are freely produced, and are borne on strong but thinnish shoots, which

'Empress Josephine'
Here overlooked by the giant feather grass (*Stipa gigantea*) and stag's horn sumach (*Rhus typhina*), 'Empress Josephine' never seems to mind sharing with other kinds of plant. It is fragrant and very floriferous for about three weeks each summer. This hybrid Gallica dates back to before 1815.

sometimes sag from the weight of the blooms they carry. This rose enjoys the good life and anything less than a fertile soil will cause it to sulk.

There are one or two striped Gallicas, the most famous of which is, of course, 'Rosa Mundi', already mentioned. This rose is easier to grow than 'Belle de Crécy' and, while it responds well to special treatment, will suffer hardship without complaining. Because it is a sport from *R. gallica officinalis*, its red and white striped flowers occasionally revert to its parent's colour of deep reddish pink. Like its parent, it makes a superb low-growing hedge and I know several very good gardens where both roses excel themselves as such. Simply clipping with shears every year after flowering will keep the hedges of these two roses in trim. Both are fragrant. In dry seasons, both are prone to mildew but this is not usually a problem, since the disease does not take hold until after the flowers are spent. Another lovely striped Gallica is the magenta, pink, and soft purple variety 'Camaieux', dating back to 1830. Its flowers are sizeable and almost fully double, with their petals arranged in loosely formed rosettes, and they have a pleasing scent. Tidy if rather arching in habit, this shrub has healthy, greyish green foliage.

'Alain Blanchard' is a delightful semi-double Gallica: its sizeable, slightly scented flowers are coloured crimson smudged with purple, and have an array of golden stamens. Perhaps a little taller than average, at about 1.2m (4ft), this rose makes a relaxed but nevertheless tidy plant, which is blessed with lots of dark green foliage.

Dating back a very long time, much earlier than 1848, the date recorded for its introduction, is one of the most beautiful of all Gallicas, 'Tuscany Superb'. Its flowers are fragrant and composed of about three layers of velvety textured, deep crimson petals, which surround a lovely arrangement of golden stamens. The effect of gold and crimson together is quite stunning.

Two other Gallicas that fall into the very deep crimson-purple colour range are 'Cardinal de Richelieu' and 'Charles de Mills'. The flowers of the former, when fully open, are packed with petals, which curve in at the centre of the bloom. 'Charles de Mills' is considerably darker and more double but, on opening, its petals lie flat like a cushion, making a composition of perfect symmetry. Sadly, 'Cardinal de Richelieu' has only a faint fragrance and 'Charles de Mills' none at all — at least I cannot detect any — but in both cases, their sheer full-face beauty more than compensates for this.

'Alain Blanchard'
Thought to be a cross between *R. x centifolia* and *R. gallica*, this rose at first glance seems to be just an ordinary dark red cultivar with a large central boss of golden yellow stamens. Closer inspection, however, is very rewarding, for its ten or so petals are like swatches of luxurious, maroon velvet, each one lightly dappled red and smudged purple, forming a unique, very beautiful flower when fully open. As should any rose of this colour, it has a lovely fragrance.

Another Gallica of unusual colours, a mixture of lilac, purple, pink, and grey, is 'De la Maître d'École'. Its fully double, perfumed blooms are very large, opening to give a quartered effect, with a green eye in the centre. It has good, dark grey-green foliage and strong stems which, like those of 'Belle de Crécy' and some other Gallicas, arch down with the weight of the flowers.

The deep violet-magenta Gallica called 'Hippolyte' seems deliberately to arch its stems downwards, causing one to stand on one's head to observe its many flowers (the effort of doing so is well worthwhile). Its flowers are double and small for a Gallica and produced in very large numbers. By virtue of its relaxed nature, the plant needs space to expand, but will seldom grow taller than 90cm (3ft).

'Président de Sèze', also known as 'Mme Hébert', is another Gallica with flowers made up of a mixture of lilac and magenta colours, this time more muted, with pale grey edges to its many petals, and very fragrant. A tidy bush, it grows to about 1.2m (4ft) tall and spreads almost as wide. If not kept in hand by pruning, it can become quite scrawny.

A lovely, very ancient Gallica is the semi-double 'La Belle Sultane', also known as 'Violacea', a name that succinctly describes the mottled violet-purple colour of its flowers. This rose, too, has prominent golden stamens.

One of the palest Gallicas is the blush-pink 'Duchesse de Montebello'. Its incurving, fully double flowers are deliciously scented. I love this rose especially when its soft-coloured flowers are seen arm in arm with some of the purple- and crimson-coloured Gallicas. As a shrub, it will reach around 1.2m (4ft), with a naturally tidy, upright disposition.

To finish this chapter, I include a rose that is something of a contradiction among Gallicas, but one that, to my mind, should be in every garden. Its name is 'Complicata'. It is one of the few roses in this group to produce single flowers: these are bright pink in colour, with conspicuous yellow stamens, and they are fragrant. Unlike most others of its kind, which are rather tidy by nature, 'Complicata' tends to have a sprawling, scrambling habit. If regularly pruned, it can be used as a medium-sized shrub; allowed freedom of expression, however, it will happily climb up into the branches of trees or through hedgerows.

'Complicata' (right)
Enlarged to over twice its natural size, 'Complicata' is seen here as being pure and chaste – quite the opposite of what its name suggests. It will tolerate poor soil, act either as a shrub or as a tree climber, form a hedge, and happily cohabit with different kinds of shrubs. As if all this were not enough, 'Complicata' is also fragrant and has generous amounts of healthy foliage.

'Président de Sèze'
(below) Blue is a colour that blends superbly with many deep pink Old roses, especially those with discreet bluish pigments of their own showing through. In this picture *Campanula latifolia* has been captured in soft focus, providing a perfect background colour for the beautiful Gallica 'Président de Sèze'.

The Pimpinellifolias

The Scotch rose, *R. pimpinellifolia,* is a native of Britain, but it especially enjoys the climate of Scotland, hence its common name. The botanical name comes from the similarity of the leaves to those of burnet, or *Pimpinella*; and the species and its offspring are also known as Burnet roses. Until fairly recently, however, the Pimpinellifolias were known as Spinosissimas, a reference to the many thorns and spines that clothe their stems.

This group of roses first came about as garden plants around 1800, when seedlings cultivated from a wild Pimpinellifolia plant found in Scotland yielded double, variously coloured flowers. Clearly, this wild rose, helped by the bees, had indulged in a liaison with a cultivated garden rose to spawn such colourful, double offspring. Such was the appeal of these lovely little shrubs that many double and semi-double forms, as well as the most colourful single forms, were launched onto the rose market during their heyday. In *The Flower Garden*, published in 1839, at least 50 named varieties are listed, their colours varying from pure white through the spectrum to purple and yellow. One of the reasons for the abundance of varieties is the plants' willingness to root from cuttings; they were also widely distributed by enthusiastic growers simply pulling up rooted suckers and passing them on to friends.

Pimpinellifolias flower early in the season, indeed they give us some of the first roses of summer, but they produce only an occasional bloom later on. Following the introduction of remontant roses to the wider scene, it was just a matter of time before the popularity of these little shrubs started to decline. There are still quite a lot growing in old country gardens, easily recognizable by their spiky spines and soft fern-like foliage. In the past very few records were kept of their nomenclature, and nowadays few people can name them; I certainly have problems of recognition myself.

'Double Pink Burnet'
(*right*) A superb conglomeration of plants shows this little Pimpinellifolia in a sandwich of iris and lupins. Once upon a time this delightful rose would have had a more seductive name, but with the arrival of remontant roses such as Portlands and Bourbons, it and many others of its kind vanished almost into oblivion, and most of their names were lost.

PIMPINELLIFOLIAS FOR THE GARDEN

In recent years this happy group of roses has started to enjoy a new lease of life; the few still left are very adaptable and will fit comfortably into most gardens, making their presence felt with charm and personality. They are excellent as low-growing hedges, so dense that they will keep out even the most headstrong of the neighbours' cats. Such hedges seldom need much attention, just tidying up with shears after the hips have finished each winter — hips, incidentally, that are mostly mahogany or purple in colour. Scotch roses also cohabit well with each other and groups of two or three different varieties grown close together can look good, especially in more informal

'Old Yellow Scotch'
Older yellow roses are scarce, but the rose I know simply as 'Old Yellow Scotch' is a very lovable cultivar from past times. It is a compact form of 'Harison's Yellow' and seems to be deeper in colour than 'Williams' Double Yellow'; perhaps it is a different clone of one of these?

settings. These roses tolerate shade better than most, and may confidently be used to provide undergrowth for woodland. They look effective scattered here and there in herbaceous borders and in the front of shrubberies. They are all very attractive when their foliage turns to burnished gold and bronze-purple in late autumn. It almost goes without saying that roses of such modest sizes make excellent container plants. If grown in pots it is good policy to put them into a balanced compost, but in open ground they adjust readily to any type of soil, making themselves especially at home in lighter soils.

Having already dealt with the wild forms under Species roses (see p.29), I begin my selection with four varieties that, through lack of proper names, are distributed by description. The first, 'Double White Burnet', is a lovely fragrant rose with cupped flowers borne in great profusion among fern-like, dark green foliage. It is very thorny, compact in growth, and about 90cm (3ft) high. The next is 'Double Pink Burnet', which differs from the white form only in the colour of its blooms. Likewise 'Marbled Pink Burnet', which has flowers, as the name implies, marbled or mottled pink and white. The fourth is 'Irish Marbled Burnet', again identical to the others except in colour, which is marbled and mottled purple, pink, and white.

'Old Yellow Scotch' has semi-double flowers of deep, unfading yellow. A little taller than the others of its type, at 1.2m (4ft) or more, it probably dates back to the late 18th century. Other yellows in this group are the fully double 'Harison's Yellow', which is also known as the yellow rose of Texas, and 'Williams' Double Yellow', with slightly fewer petals, dating back to 1828. All these make good hedging plants.

A rose of unknown date, but clearly old, is a lovely semi-double called 'Falkland', with cupped flowers of lilac-pink, paling to soft pink with age. Growing in tidy, compact fashion, it has typical fern-like foliage, and its hips, when ripe, are deep maroon in colour and oval to round in shape.

'Mary Queen of Scots' is always a special pleasure to me when it comes into bloom in late spring. Its slightly fragrant, single flowers are creamy white in the centre, deepening to lilac in the middle of the petals, as if painted by a brush, and then paling at the edges to soft pink. Produced in great abundance, they are followed by a good crop of small, dangling, oval-shaped hips in polished mahogany to purple.

'Mrs Colville' is one of the Pimpinellifolias that could be wrongly named because old books describe several different roses as being single and deep red to magenta in colour with a white centre. This particular rose is marginally less thorny than the others and its foliage fractionally less fern-like, but it is still, clearly, a true Pimpinellifolia. Its hips are maroon and conical and sit among bright autumn foliage.

'Single Cherry' is a real delight: its cherry-red flowers, a little larger than those of some of its sister roses, are borne on a bushy plant that mostly stays below 90cm (3ft); its round hips are deep maroon in colour. As with 'Mrs Colville' and 'Mary Queen of Scots', its date of introduction is unknown.

Another rose I have never been able to date precisely is 'William III'. Of tidy, upright disposition, it has semi-double, rich maroon flowers, paling to magenta, and bears chocolate brown hips among dense, fern-like foliage. I am aware of at least two other roses of this name, one of them producing single flowers.

'Glory of Edzell' is taller than the average Pimpinellifolia, growing 1.2m (4ft) tall in the best soils. It has single, clear pink blooms with paler centres and comes into flower fairly early each season. Its foliage is fern-like but a little less so than others of its type.

'Stanwell Perpetual' is quite different from others of its group, probably a cross between 'Quatre Saisons' and *R. pimpinellifolia*. Produced throughout summer, the very fragrant, soft pink flowers are large and fully double, with incurving petals in the centre. They appear amid lots of greyish green, fern-like leaves, which are, regrettably, sometimes blemished, the older leaves becoming mottled purple. The plant will grow as tall as 1.5m (5ft) and equally wide. Unlike most other Pimpinellifolias it will sulk in anything but the best soil, but neither this nor its tarnished foliage should put anyone off growing this lovely rose.

'Mrs Colville'
Although it is only once-flowering, 'Mrs Colville' produces an abundance of blooms, covering the plant in early summer. That it is scented is a bonus. None of the Pimpinellifolias ever gets big or awkward, making them ideal for cultivation in pots. Later in summer and autumn, most members of this group produce black, purple, or mahogany hips.

The Moss Roses

Moss roses are different from all other roses by virtue of the mossy beards that form around their calyces, flower stalks and, sometimes, their leaf stalks and stems. Usually the moss is green, but it may be brown or mahogany coloured. It is soft to touch, except in a few varieties when it is crispy, and it is usually heavily aromatic, especially when rubbed between finger and thumb.

No one is absolutely sure how and when the first "roses with whiskers" came about but 'Common Moss', one of the most beautiful of all, is clearly closely related to *R.* x *centifolia*. It can be traced back to before 1700 but is probably much older. In fact, almost all Moss roses are of Centifolia origin, most raised in France throughout the 19th century. In terms of colour they are a mixed bunch, from almost pure white to very dark crimson-red. In their sizes, too, they range from little more than 90cm (3ft) to around 3m (10ft). Most are in bloom from early to midsummer, but there are a few that flower again later in the season.

Mosses clearly fascinated the Victorians and nursery catalogues of the time listed a huge number of different varieties, about 50 of which have come down to the 21st century. I believe that those that are now with us have survived more from the novelty of their moss than from any virtue as garden plants, or quality of flowers. Perfume, though, is another matter, for they all have plenty of that.

MOSS ROSES FOR THE GARDEN

Such is the diversity in the ranks of the Mosses that it is not difficult to find one to fulfil any purpose in the garden. Generally, however, they make good shrubby shrubs, since their pastel shades make them relatively unobtrusive. Although they can tolerate some dappled shade, by and large their preference is for sunny, airy positions. Some of the shorter varieties will happily grow in containers. Several of the taller ones, which are naturally rather sprawling, make good pillar roses.

I love Mosses to be grown close to the edges of borders, alongside paths, or next to lawns, for from here the mossy buds can be touched or brushed against in passing, releasing their aromatic fragrance. In fact, every time I come in contact with their aroma, my mind goes back to the balsamic remedies for colds that were rubbed on my chest as a child.

From the 50 or so different Mosses available today, I have had to harden my heart and choose only 16 to discuss. The first is one of only two or three with lots of Damask genes in its constitution, 'Alfred de Dalmas', also known as 'Mousseline',

which dates back to 1855. This is an interesting, attractive rose of a soft creamy pink colour. Its flowers are semi-double with a good scent, and it has lots of khaki-coloured moss on both its buds and its stems. Its flowering season is much longer than that of other Mosses; in fact it is in bloom throughout the summer. If it were not for its moss it would probably be classified as a Portland Damask. This lovely rose seldom gets taller than 60cm (2ft). It has many uses in the garden: it is good as a pot plant, but is also useful in borders, on its own or in groups.

'Blanche Moreau', introduced in 1880, is a lovely white rose with maroon-coloured moss and fully double, fragrant flowers. The plant is of upright growth, and its slender shoots are well mossed; its foliage, rather surprisingly for a white rose, is darkish green. Sometimes, it will produce an intermittent bloom or two in the autumn, a trait probably inherited from a distant relative, perhaps the Damask rose 'Quatre Saisons'.

A Moss rose that curbs itself to no more than 1.2m (4ft) in height is the very dark reddish purple 'Capitaine John Ingram'. The flowers of this variety are not over large but they are shapely and fully double, and they are quite strongly scented. Its dense, purplish brown moss spreads all over the calyces, receptacles, and stems, and is

'Chapeau de Napoléon'
The deep pink colouring of this Moss rose can just be seen in this picture as petals emerge from a bud. The buds are unique, the shoulder of moss on the sepals forming into the shape of a cocked hat, hence the name 'Chapeau de Napoléon'. It is also known as crested Moss.

fragrant with the aroma of pine. This classy rose was introduced in 1855. It is very useful for mixing into shrubberies.

'Chapeau de Napoléon' is very unusual. Its fully double, highly scented, deep pink flowers are embellished by raised tufts of moss on the calyces which, on close inspection, are shaped like cocked hats, giving the rose its name. As a plant it is rather sprawling and open, with shoots well dressed with grey-green foliage. Given its head, it can grow to 1.5m (5ft) high. I have seen it used effectively as a short climber on a wall. Raised in 1826, this rose is also known by two other names, *R.* x *centifolia* 'Cristata' and crested Moss.

I have already mentioned 'Common Moss', a rose that crops up all over the place. It is also sometimes called old pink Moss. If a pink Moss rose occurs in an old garden, it will almost certainly be this one. Bright deep pink in colour, this ancient rose is very double and superbly fragrant. Its moss, which spreads from buds to stems, is very dense, mid-green in colour, and has an aroma redolent of freshly sawn pine. As a shrub it grows to 1.2m (4ft), but will get even taller if planted by a wall.

'Comtesse de Murinais' is a medium to tall rose of a beautiful, soft pink to cream colour, with delicious, fully double, highly scented flowers, which bely its ordinariness in other ways. Its moss is bristly to touch, and exudes the strong, lingering smell of balsam. Growing to a height of about 1.5m (5ft), this rose has somewhat lanky stems, and benefits from the support of a wall, pillar, or trellis.

'Deuil de Paul Fontaine', raised in 1873, is one of the darkest of all the red Mosses, but it is certainly not the best behaved, qualifying for mention only on the strength of its occasional habit of repeating its flowers in late summer. Seldom growing taller than 90cm (3ft), it has large, fully double flowers that open flat. Its reddish green foliage changes to mid-green later, and the moss is similarly coloured. This rose could well have some Portland in its ancestry.

I have loved the delightful, soft pink Moss rose 'Général Kleber' since I first saw it in flower in the 1960s. I recall feeling then that such a beautiful rose should not be named after a man, let alone a general. Of a colour I call "icing-sugar pink", it is fully double and overflowing with perfume. The dense moss on its buds exudes the fragrance of fresh pine needles. It seldom outgrows its welcome in any situation, and will reach about 1.2m (4ft) in height.

Although in no way vulgar, 'Gloire des Mousseux' has probably the largest flowers of all the Mosses; these are soft blush-pink in colour. Its foliage, which is inclined to mildew late in the season, is dark green, and its moss even darker. The plant is rather scrawny but can be kept under control by annual pruning.

Also known as red Moss, the very lovely 'Henri Martin' is one of the most free-flowering of all the Mosses, with fragrant, bright red flowers borne in large clusters. Its moss is reddish tan in colour, and the foliage bright green and always healthy. Given a little support this rose makes a superb shrub to a height of about 1.5m (5ft).

Pinkish green moss generously adorns the flower buds and receptacles of the soft pink 'Mme Louis Lévêque'. Both flowers and moss are fragrant. Sturdy and upright, it seldom gets much taller than 1.2m (4ft); I have seen it growing very happily in a large pot.

'Gloire des Mousseux'
This picture captures superbly the many petalled, globular form of the lovely Moss rose 'Gloire des Mousseux'. It also shows the delicate, silky texture of its petals. The perfume of this rose is almost intoxicating. Its moss is very dark green and packed tightly around the calyces, receptacles, and flower stalks.

'William Lobb' (*above and right*) This enduringly popular rose is also sometimes called old velvet Moss because of the texture of its petals. Two of its other features show clearly in the photograph above: first the density of the green moss, which takes on a pinkish hue with age; second, the huge number of buds that make up a cluster of its blooms.

In the photograph on the opposite page, 'William Lobb' harmonizes with campanulas and Armenian cranesbill (*Geranium psilostemon*). Again, the rose is showing off several of its many virtues: unpretentious colouring, durable, grey-green foliage, and a huge quantity of flowers.

The only British rose I have selected from among the Mosses is the very double, deep glowing pink 'Mrs William Paul', flowering very freely in early summer. Its moss is a coppery colour and covers the calyces and most of the rest of the young stems. Its foliage is dark green and crisp to touch. It was introduced in 1869 by William Paul, one of the leading English rose growers of the Victorian era.

'Old Black' is another name by which 'Nuits de Young' is sometimes known, and this sums up its colour almost perfectly. Its fully double flowers are small, with loosely arranged petals, and they are strongly fragrant, as is the dark-coloured moss that surrounding the buds, flower stalks, and receptacles. A relaxed shrub with plenty of dark green foliage, 'Nuits de Young' grows to about 1.2m (4ft), and has much to commend it.

'Robert Léopold' is the youngest of the Moss roses, having been raised in 1941 by Monsieur Buatois of France — rather bravely perhaps, since the Mosses had fallen from favour at the beginning of the century, superseded by the longer-flowering Hybrid Teas. As well as the most recently introduced, 'Robert Léopold' is also the only Moss worth growing that has any yellow in its flowers. These are semi-double and bright pink with yellow deep down in the centre, and they repeat spasmodically in autumn. This rose has ginger-coloured moss covering the calyces and extending well down the stems, and its foliage is darkish green.

A short-growing Moss rose, suitable for smaller gardens, is 'Salet,' usually growing no taller than 90cm (3ft). This said, in very good soil it can reach 1.2m (4ft). Not the most heavily mossed of its type, its flowers are very double, clear deep pink, and scented. Tidiness of habit lends it well to cultivation in pots. 'Salet' is a very amenable rose, introduced in 1854.

Finally, I come to 'William Lobb', introduced in 1855. This is a tall, arching rose probably best as a climber. Grown as such, it can reach up to 3m (10ft). It has fragrant, loosely formed, semi-double flowers in a cocktail of purple, lilac, grey, and silvery pink — the overall effect, from a distance, being magenta. The moss of this rose is not dense, but is soft to touch and pinkish green in colour; the foliage is also soft textured and greyish green. 'William Lobb' is one of the most popular Moss roses, and I will always find room for it on a structure or wall in my garden.

The Chinas

Judging by the flowers depicted in the ancient arts and crafts of China, roses have been revered for their beauty and cultivated there since the tenth century, if not before. The roses that are classified as Chinas today are in themselves an important group of garden plants, valued especially because they flower continuously and have a fairly high resistance to disease, but they are also significant genetically in the development of Modern roses. Most of these owe their ability to flower twice or more in a season to genes inherited long ago from China roses.

One of the first hybrid Chinas to arrive in Europe came in 1789 in the form of 'Old Blush', a soft pink variety. A few years later a red form was introduced, this one coming via India; it was, at first, called 'Bengal Rose' but later became known as 'Slater's Crimson' or *R. chinensis* 'Semperflorens'. Two more came from China during the next few decades: 'Odorata', also known as 'Hume's Blush', and 'Parks' Yellow' or *R. x odorata* 'Ochroleuca'. These four became known collectively as the "four stud Chinas". All were related by natural fertilization to *R. gigantea*, and this mix of genes would later lead on to the Portlands, the Bourbons, the Tea roses, and so on.

Over the years I have acquired stock of all four of the original Chinas and I am satisfied that they are authentic but, it must be said, their legitimacy has been challenged by others from time to time. I try to keep an open mind on matters of authenticity but the issue usually boils down to what else could they be, if they are not the real thing; I am never able to answer that question. Sometimes, I must admit, I find these challenges of authenticity, however well meant, get in the way of the more pleasurable side of rose appreciation.

Generally speaking, the Chinas are happiest in warmer parts of the world, so the ultimate size of plants is much smaller in northern Europe than in the Mediterranean region or California, for example. Also, in my travels, I have noticed that the colour of Chinas is usually stronger in hot climates. Another factor for consideration is their hardiness. Although most will survive the rigours of a colder climate, an abnormally harsh frost may well damage shoots and these will need pruning out in spring. There are several Chinas that actually thrive in Europe, one or two as far north as Scandinavia, and in the northern regions of North America, although they will all need protecting from the worst ravages of winter in these areas.

Although most Chinas are very happy in open sites, even in cooler climates, I am a great believer in growing roses in pots, tubs, urns, and other containers, and it is in these, if of sufficient size, that the majority thrive. Most Chinas have several

'Mutabilis' (*right*)
This delightful China rose clearly has a sense of humour. Not only does it keep one guessing about just how tall it might grow – anything from 90cm to 1.8m (3–6ft) – but it also adjusts its flower colour according to the prevailing weather; it normally starts straw-yellow and ages to deep red over two or three days, but sometimes makes this transformation in just one day. Seen here with 'Mutabilis' is the foxtail lily *Eremurus x isabellinus* 'Cleopatra'. Beginning to tumble over the roof of the building in the background is the Multiflora Rambler 'Veilchenblau'.

characteristics in common, one of the most obvious being that they have few thorns of consequence. Another common factor is their young foliage, which is usually orange-red. Thirdly, they all have relatively thin, angularly arranged shoots and stems, and none of them likes to be pruned too hard on a regular basis. Most bear their flowers in clusters and, unlike many other roses, whose colour fades with age, the flowers of Chinas tend to become deeper in colour as they get older.

CHINAS FOR THE GARDEN

By far and away the most popular China is the lovely 'Mutabilis', a rose whose behaviour is rather erratic. It may grow for several years at 90cm (3ft) – the average height of Chinas – then, for reasons best known to itself, it will suddenly grow taller. I have seen plants of this variety 3m (10ft) tall on walls. Its flowers are single and initially buff-yellow but, once fully open, they change colour through various shades of pink to red. They have very little scent but are produced in great numbers, like swarms of butterflies, throughout summer. 'Mutabilis' is also known by two other names, 'Tipo Ideale' and *R. turkestanica*. Despite its unpredictable behaviour it makes a superb pot plant; I have also seen it used very effectively as a hedge, and it can double as a small climber for walls.

Another popular China rose is 'Cécile Brünner', the Maltese rose, also known as the sweetheart rose. It is small, both in stature and in flower size, but makes up for lack of dimensions by blooming profusely throughout summer. Soft pink in colour, and mildly scented, its flowers mimic miniature Hybrid Teas and make lovely buttonholes. I sometimes think its foliage is too sparse but this weakness is balanced by its abundance of flowers. Like all Chinas, it is an excellent pot plant and is good in greenhouses and conservatories. Out of doors, it sits happily with a diversity of plants, especially shorter perennials. There is a climbing version with flowers that perfectly replicate those of the bush form, but in all other respects it is a contradiction, for it will become massive on a tree or wall and will overwhelm all but the strongest trellis. After its first flush in early summer, this form blooms only spasmodically.

The flowers of 'Bloomfield Abundance' are almost identical to those of 'Cécile Brünner', except that they have longer, more feathery sepals. 'Bloomfield Abundance' (known in the USA as 'Spray Cécile Brünner') is also

'Old Blush'
'Old Blush' or 'Parson's Pink', as it is also sometimes called, is one of the oldest of the Chinas, first coming to Europe in 1789. Along with other roses from China, it was quickly put to stud, giving many new generations of roses the ability to repeat their flowers.

much taller and more vigorous in growth. Much discussion has taken place in the rose world as to the true identity of these two Chinas but, although I have strong opinions on the matter, I have no wish to get involved in this controversy in this book.

'Old Blush', one of the first hybrid Chinas, has retained its popularity and enjoys considerable longevity, growing contentedly in old cottage and farmhouse gardens. It also fits well into the more modern garden, where it can be useful either as a bush or as a small climber. Its colour is deep blush-pink with soft lilac undertones. It is semi-double, continuous flowering, and fragrant.

'Perle d'Or' is one of the few Chinas with yellow in its make-up, although in this case the yellow is bronzy and fades to creamy white, especially on the outer edges of the petals. The shapely, fully double blooms are mildly scented and are held upright in sizeable clusters. Its foliage is a little sparse but this is atoned for by the sheer quantity of flowers it produces in successive flushes. Its growth is reasonably upright and its stems not over thorny. Left to its own devices, it will get to a height of around 1.2m (4ft) and spread to 90cm (3ft). This rose mingles well with plants of any colour, even those in the hot shades of red and orange. Like all Chinas, 'Perle d'Or' does not like being pruned too hard, preferring to be left to develop its own shape and form.

One of the best of the red Chinas is 'Cramoisi Supérieur', of which there is also a climbing form. The flowers, produced in clusters, are slightly more than semi-double, crimson, and have only a modest perfume. In cooler climates the bush form seldom gets taller than about 90cm (3ft); the Climber, which I believe should be much more widely grown, is far more ambitious and capable of growing to about 4m (12ft). As a

bush, 'Cramoisi Supérieur' is continuous flowering; as a Climber, after a prolific first flush, it flowers only spasmodically. I have seen this rose in warmer parts of the world growing to at least double the sizes I have quoted. The bush form is known in the USA and Bermuda as 'Agrippina'. Placing it in the garden is not difficult for, again, I feel that red will go with most other colours.

A China rose of which I have become very fond is 'Sophie's Perpetual', which is clearly an old rose, but one of unknown provenance. My stock was given to me by the late Humphrey Brooke, who put together a wonderful collection of Old roses in his garden in Suffolk. This is really a short climbing rose and is best grown as such in warm climates. However, I like to grow it as a shrub, when it will reach a height of about 1.8m (6ft). Its flowers are fragrant and loosely formed, in a colour that is best described as a mixture of cherry-red and silvery pink. They are arranged in smallish clusters that follow on from each other throughout summer and autumn. The colour is not so easy to use within the garden but it does look good on a red brick wall, and here it will reach at least 3m (10ft).

The darkest of the red Chinas is the almost black 'Louis XIV', which grows only to 60cm (2ft). It is semi-double, moderately fragrant, and flowers all summer. I find it a little lacking in foliage for my taste but, even so, well worth growing. Another red, this one much taller at about 1.8m (6ft), is the old variety 'Grüss an Teplitz', with very double, shapely flowers and a spicy perfume. Being very floriferous it makes a good garden plant, especially if given the support of a short tripod or stake. The flowers of 'Slater's Crimson', one of the varieties used in developing remontancy in roses, are bright red and double; growing to 90cm (3ft), this rose is best used in the garden as a pot plant. Another bright red of about the same size is 'Sanguinea', also known as 'Miss Lowe's Rose'; this is sometimes confused with 'Slater's Crimson' but they are quite different. I have them both and can confirm their separate identities.

Although the colour yellow is scarce among the Chinas, 'Arethusa', a rather lovely little rose raised in 1903, has sizeable, double flowers of soft yellow, with orange shades deep down among the petals. It is extremely healthy and I can recommend it as a companion to perennials. The variety 'Comtesse du Cayla' is a semi-double, bright orange-pink with yellow at the base. It grows to about 90cm (3ft) and is very generous with its fragrant flowers. As well as amalgamating well with brighter-coloured perennials and shrubs, it makes a well-proportioned pot plant.

'Hermosa', raised in 1840, is a silvery pink, very double rose, good for small gardens. It is fragrant, free flowering, and rather thorny. Again, I advise growing this rose in a container of some sort or by a wall. Another brightly coloured rose that lends itself well to pot culture is the semi-double, salmon-pink 'Mme Laurette Messimy'. If it grows taller than 60cm (2ft) it will be enjoying its habitat. 'Irène Watts' is a very lovely little China rose of blush-pink with a deeper-coloured centre. Seldom taller than 45cm (18in), it makes an attractive bedding plant. The flowers are fragrant, very double in form, and open flat with muddled petals. I always enjoy the company of this delightful rose. In recent years it has become confused with a pink form of the Floribunda 'Grüss an Aachen' (see p.128).

Now to return to 'Odorata' and 'Parks' Yellow', two of the original stud Chinas. These two roses are sometimes listed as Tea roses but I feel they are better placed here as Chinas. 'Odorata' has double, blush-white, fragrant flowers and is quite vigorous, to 1.8m (6ft). Growing to about the same height, 'Parks' Yellow' has numerous flowers in its first flush and a spasmodic crop later; the blooms are fragrant, semi-double, and pale sulphur-yellow with orange-tinted edges, the orange deepening as the flowers mature. Both this rose and 'Odorata' need to be grown in sheltered positions in cooler climates since they are susceptible to damage by severe frost.

Finally in this section on Chinas I must mention one of the most unusual of roses, 'Viridiflora', commonly known as the green rose, whose flowers consist of clusters of brown-tinted green petal-like sepals. It is hardly more than a talking point in the garden but well worth growing for that alone, and it is much sought after by flower arrangers. It will grow anywhere and does not seem too bothered by the quality of the soil into which it is planted.

'Viridiflora'
More a novelty than a garden rose, the flowers of 'Viridiflora' are made up of ragged bundles of green and purple-brown bracts. These oddities come in very large numbers, without a break, all through the summer and autumn. Everything else about the plant is quite normal. Perhaps not surprisingly, this rose is popular with flower arrangers.

The Portland Damasks

Until recently it was generally thought that the first Portland Damask rose came about from a chance cross between 'Quatre Saisons' (*R.* x *damascena bifera* or autumn Damask) and a China rose, probably 'Slater's Crimson'. From recent genetic fingerprinting, however, it would seem that other genes, in particular those of *R. gallica*, are also part of the ancestry of the Portland Damasks. The science of genetic fingerprinting is beginning to shed new light on the origin of all rose groups, not just the Portlands, causing long-accepted rose genealogy to be redefined.

Whatever its ancestry, the first Portland rose came on the scene in the late 18th century. It was called simply "the Portland rose", later becoming known as 'Duchess of Portland'. Both names are still in common use today. This rose produced a succession of flowers throughout the summer, a relatively new phenomenon that, as I have mentioned before, must have sent ripples of excitement through rose fraternities. As a consequence, the Portland rose was quickly put to stud, thus initiating the beginnings of this charming group of roses.

Most Portlands are fully remontant and all are fragrant to some degree. They are very accommodating, seldom reach heights of more than 90cm (3ft), and are relatively disease resistant; they also have plenty of good foliage. In all there are about 12 varieties available from specialist growers of older roses. I love them all. About half a dozen are widely available today, all of which will give pleasure to those who wish to grow an Old garden rose or two, but don't have acres of space in which to do so.

PORTLAND DAMASKS FOR THE GARDEN

One of the most endearing features of Portlands is their willingness to mix with companion plants. Without exception, any variety will fit in anywhere, and never intrude into the space of another. Portlands look good in pots, tubs, or urns, placed on patios, terraces, or any other hard-surfaced area. In older gardens especially, their old-world dispositions give them considerable advantages over more

modern roses. They also have a significant role as bedding plants, particularly in large beds or borders, where their softer colours and demure characteristics are perhaps more desirable than those of the more flamboyant types.

Again, I write about these roses in approximate order of popularity, starting with 'Comte de Chambord' – not only one of the best Portlands, but also one of the better Old garden roses. Raised in 1863, it is testimony to both its stamina and its good looks that it can now be found in almost any garden where Old roses are featured. It makes a bushy plant with lots of foliage and, such is its easy-going nature, will be in bloom almost continuously through the summer. Its flowers are very fragrant, very double, and initially high centred, becoming flat when fully open. They are rich warm pink in colour, reminding me of pink icing sugar. The plant's normal height is about 60cm (2ft). 'Comte de Chambord' is known as 'Mme Knorr' in the USA.

The lovely, soft pink 'Jacques Cartier' is another rose with a different name in the USA; there it is called 'Marchesa Boccella'. It is continuous flowering, very double, and fragrant, and I never cease to be amazed that such a beautiful rose can emerge from such an insignificant-looking bud. As a plant, it grows to about 90cm (3ft) if not regularly pruned. However, from time to time, it will send up taller rogue shoots; these serve little purpose and should be pruned off. Its foliage is slightly coarse in texture, deeply veined, and dark green.

I must come back, for a moment, to the different names used for these last two roses: who knows which are correct – the American or British? As a nurseryman, I am only too well aware of how names of roses can become muddled and, when this occurs, it sometimes takes a long time to realize that a mistake has happened. By then, though, it is rather difficult to put it right. I try to keep an open mind as to which names are the right ones; in the case of these two roses, I can only comment as follows: I once grew a rose called 'Mme Knorr', which was very similar to 'Comte de Chambord', so similar that I dropped it from my list; there seemed little point in growing both varieties. That 'Mme Knorr' had fewer leaves and was more prone to disease than my 'Comte de Chambord'. In my view these are unquestionably two distinct roses, and one should not be regarded as synonymous with the other. As for 'Jacques Cartier', I have known this Portland by this name all my life, ever since I started growing Old roses under Graham Stuart Thomas in the 1960s. It is almost certainly the same rose as that grown in the USA as 'Marchesa Boccella', but to me – and virtually every nursery in Britain – its correct name is 'Jacques Cartier'.

My next choice of Portlands is 'De Rescht', of unknown provenance. Its flowers, made up of many shortish petals, open to tightly packed cushions of rich fuchsia-red, changing to purplish red with age and, occasionally, to pinkish red in hot sun. They are very fragrant and sit among a mass of dark green foliage. This rose will grow anywhere in the garden and thrives on the extra care it receives if grown in pots. Over the years I have noticed how much it enjoys the freedom to grow as it likes; this permitted, it should be hard pruned every three or four years to prevent it becoming too leggy.

'Jacques Cartier'
(*left*) One of the most beautiful Portlands, 'Jacques Cartier' is seen here, full face and magnificent, at about three times its natural size. Who could possibly resist such a rose? As a plant, it has good foliage, and goes on mass-producing sumptuous blooms like this one all through the summer every year.

'De Rescht'

The maroon, powder-puff blooms of 'De Rescht' contrast here in both colour and form with the flowers around it: elder (*Sambucus*) at the back and, standing up in the foreground, *Epilobium angustifolium album*. The rose seems quite at ease with the competition, substantiating my point that roses make excellent companion plants.

A rose of similar colouring to 'De Rescht' is 'Arthur de Sansal', raised in 1855, which has survived until now despite a propensity to mildew and rust. Undoubtedly its survival has something to do with its very beautiful, crimson-purple flowers, coupled with its quality perfume. The flowers are large, of rosette form, and produced repeatedly. Regrettably, its foliage has little to commend it. 'Arthur de Sansal' is best grown in a pot, when it can be fed, watered, and sprayed regularly.

'Indigo' is even older than 'Arthur de Sansal', dating from about 1830. Its name aptly describes the deep purple of its flowers, some of which occasionally have a very thin white stripe. These flowers are very double and, when fully open, show off golden stamens. Fragrance is another of this Portland's virtues; it also produces blooms all summer long amid an abundance of rich green foliage on a bushy, upright plant.

'Pergolèse' is a very good Portland, again very old, having been raised in 1860. This is another rose of rich crimson-purple colouring but, in this case, sometimes paling to lilac. Its fully double flowers are produced in clusters and are well scented. They appear regularly throughout the summer. The influence of its Gallica genes can be seen in its dark green foliage.

'Marbrée' makes a good shrub, which is taller and a little more upright than others of its kind, reaching about 1.2m (4ft). Its flat, double flowers have slightly fewer petals than most other Portlands. Their colour is purple and pink, smudged together to give a mottled appearance; regrettably, they have little or no scent.

To end my selection of Portlands I go back to the original Portland rose, 'Duchess of Portland'. Historically, it deserves attention as the first of its race but it is also a very worthy garden plant. Borne in good numbers from late spring to autumn, its fragrant flowers are made up of about a dozen cerise-red petals and, when fully open, allow a display of rich golden stamens. A special feature is the way they nestle among healthy, dark green leaves. As a plant, it requires little attention to thrive. It will tolerate a little shade and looks very good when grown in sizeable groups.

'Arthur de Sansal'
This very beautiful rose from 1855 is one of the most free flowering of the Portlands. It also has a good fragrance and makes a tidy plant. Over the years, however, unlike others of its group, it has developed occasional afflictions such as a proneness to both rust and mildew. However, observing just one of its beautiful blooms close up helps me to forgive this rose its little foibles.

The Bourbons

The French island of Bourbon, now renamed Réunion, in the Indian Ocean, is considered to be the birthplace of the first Bourbon rose. I say considered because, although this is the most widely held belief, there is a minority of experts who believe its birthplace was Calcutta, India; but this book is not the forum for these discussions. There is no argument, however, about which rose was the first of the Bourbons: it was 'Rose Édouard', the progeny of a China rose, probably 'Old Blush', and the Damask rose, almost certainly an early form of 'Quatre Saisons'.

When 'Rose Édouard' arrived in France in about 1818, nurserymen were quick to recognize its potential: its rounded, fully double, deep pink blooms were borne repeatedly through the season, making it not only a highly marketable rose but also very good breeding stock. At that time, apart from the Chinas themselves and one or two Portlands, repeat-flowering roses were few and far between. These were good years for roses, their popularity ever increasing as they became more widely grown in the gardens of the wealthier people of the day. Much of this popularity had been engendered by the Empress Josephine's patronage of the European rose-growing

nurseries. Just before the first Bourbon came along, the Empress had planted a very large collection of roses at her home, the Château de la Malmaison, near Paris, and had the foresight to employ an artist to record it for posterity; his name was Pierre Joseph Redouté and he later became world famous for his botanical paintings of roses.

Following the introduction of 'Rose Édouard', it took only a short time for rose breeders and nurserymen to capitalize on such an exciting new strain. Soon a veritable orgy of cross-pollination of roses took place, especially in France. From then on, throughout the 19th century, Bourbon roses were introduced in their hundreds to an ever eager public. Few, however, were good enough to sustain their popularity for long, and by the early 20th century most had been dropped from commercial catalogues. Those that survived are still with us today and, such is their usefulness as flowering shrubs and small climbers, they are likely to remain with us in perpetuity.

BOURBONS FOR THE GARDEN

Most of the world's specialists in Old roses now list around 40 different Bourbons, and a few more, rather rarer ones are to be found in public and private rose collections. Those commercially available today are a mixed lot, some short and bushy, others tall and ungainly. They also vary in colour from pure white to deep red, with the majority being of various shades of pink; there are no yellows. A few flower only once in a season. I have selected 20 to discuss here. Some, it must be said, are martyrs to black spot but I, for one, can live with that. Spraying with suitable fungicides will obviously assist in the control of this disease, but I am inclined to use only sprays that are more natural. In any case, the best control of rose diseases is good husbandry, which means regular feeding and watering to keep plants free from stress.

Another way of minimizing diseases is to grow roses among different types of plants. If other plants are between them then diseases are less likely to spread from one rose to another. In fact Bourbons, being repeat flowerers and very good mixers, make superb companions for a variety of shrubs and perennials and will add colour and fragrance to any herbaceous border or mixed shrubbery. There are a few climbing Bourbons and some taller shrubs useful for both walls and trellis.

Year after year, the two most popular Bourbons are 'Mme Isaac Pereire' and 'Zéphirine Drouhin', both deep pink shades, the former purplish pink. Both can be grown either as shrubs or as climbers, and both flower throughout the summer and have the virtue of a strong scent. Here, however, the similarity between them ends. 'Mme Isaac', as she is usually called, has an abundance of thorns on stout, unyielding stems, while 'Zéphirine's branches are thinner, totally smooth, and thornless. Neither, however, is perfect, for if not kept well fed and regularly watered, both will easily be troubled by black spot.

These Bourbons came into the world in Victorian times and both have produced sports during their lifetime. A paler pink form of 'Mme Isaac' named 'Mme Ernst Calvat' came shortly after 'Mme Isaac's introduction, and 'Zéphirine's sport 'Kathleen

Harrop', which is also pale pink, came along 50 or so years later. Both sports behave very much like their parents, although I have noticed a tendency by 'Kathleen Harrop' to grow a little less vigorously than 'Zéphirine Drouhin'.

The next most popular Bourbon is 'Souvenir de la Malmaison'. This beautiful, fully double, soft blush-pink variety is not over vigorous but, if lightly pruned each year, its dense, bushy shape can be maintained. An endearing feature is its strong, sweet scent. In many ways this rose, which is unlikely to reach more than 90cm (3ft), is better grown in association with other types of plant, its soft colouring being especially good with blue and lavender shades. Raised in 1843, it is by no means the oldest Bourbon, but it is the perfect rose to commemorate Josephine's work at Malmaison. In 1893 a climbing sport of this lovely rose was discovered in England and has since made its mark as an excellent wall plant. Sadly, the flowers of both forms hate wet weather, responding to this by "balling up" and failing to open properly.

Although not as widely grown as 'Souvenir de la Malmaison', its semi-double, soft blush-pink sport 'Souvenir de St Anne's' is a real delight. Discovered by the late Graham Stuart Thomas in 1950, this rose has inherited all its parent's refinements but, if anything, is a little healthier; it is also far less sensitive to a damp atmosphere.

Close on the heels of 'Souvenir de la Malmaison' in terms of popularity comes the bright rose-pink 'Louise Odier'. Dating back to 1851, it has by now fully established its credentials as a continuous-flowering, fragrant rose, which never gets big or untidy. This is one of only a few Bourbons I would use for mass planting, and groups of three or four would never look misplaced among grey-foliaged perennials or shrubs.

A pair of very lovely, continuous-flowering varieties comes next: 'La Reine Victoria', which is a rich lilac-pink, and its mother-of-pearl pink sport 'Mme Pierre Oger'. Both are generous with their highly scented, silky petalled flowers each summer, and in good fertile soil will bloom well into autumn. I will always find room for these two roses in my garden, especially in pots because they really express themselves when grown in this way.

I now come to a group of three striped Bourbons, the best known of which is 'Honorine de Brabant', a tall, rather relaxed, relatively thorn-free shrub that is also good as a shorter-growing climber. Its mildly fragrant flowers, initially globular, later loosely formed, are off-white and heavily striped lilac and pinkish purple. These are produced all summer, but are partially hidden among the dense, greyish green foliage. 'Commandant Beaurepaire' is another densely leaved shrub, which grows to about 1.2m (4ft). It has lots of full, fragrant, crimson flowers, striped and mottled purple and white. It looks especially good in a mixed border. The third of the striped Bourbons is 'Variegata di Bologna', by far the most thorny and also the most floriferous. It seldom gets taller than 1.5m (5ft) and usually stays at about 90cm (3ft). Its flowers are very fragrant and cabbage-like in form. As I have written elsewhere, with their irregular purple stripes on a background of creamy white, they remind me of the stirred semolina pudding and blackcurrant jam served at schoolday lunches.

Although not a repeat bloomer, 'Blairii No. 2', a climbing Bourbon, is certainly worth growing on any structure where it can be allowed its head for, when in full flower, it is unforgettable. Opening flat, its very fragrant, fully double flowers are composed of many deep pink petals, which pale to blush around their edges as they age. After shedding its flowers in midsummer, it invariably sulks and gets mildew, but this, to me, is only a minor inconvenience.

A rose I have adored for a very long time is 'Adam Messerich', introduced in 1920 by Herr Lambert of Germany; this was a brave introduction at that time for the Hybrid Tea roses were then becoming rather fashionable. This is another remontant shrub rose that easily doubles as a climber, and I have seen it growing happily up into the branches of an old apple tree. It has few thorns and good foliage, and its freely produced flowers are fragrant, loosely double, and reddish pink in colour.

The red Bourbon 'Gipsy Boy' or 'Zigeunerknabe' was also bred by Herr Lambert in the early part of the 20th century. It, too, cannot decide whether it is a shrub or climber; I prefer it as the latter. Its foliage is coarse in texture, as are its very thorny stems, and it blooms only once, in midsummer. Its flowers are full of petals but open to display a good array of golden stamens. Its usual colour is dark red – almost purple – but in hot, sunny weather this turns to a rather muddy pink. All its faults fade into insignificance, however, with one noseful of its perfume.

'Louise Odier'
Introduced in 1851, this classic Bourbon is still popular today. What this picture cannot show is its captivating perfume, one sniff inviting another, another, and another. Here the rose is surrounded delightfully by horned violet (*Viola cornuta*).

I have a great sentimental attachment to 'Bourbon Queen', another rose that is unable to make up its mind what it should be, shrub or climber. In 1958 I found a stray plant of this rose growing among brambles halfway up the mound of Pembroke Castle in west Wales. At the time I was out walking with my wife to be and, later, her mother Freda, then in her late fifties, told us that she could remember seeing this rose growing in the exact same place when she was a child, proving that this Old rose has a far stronger constitution than most I know. Its foliage is extremely healthy, grey-green in colour, and produced on long, sturdy, thorny stems. Its fragrant flowers are globular until fully open, when their silky, rose-pink petals become muddled around a centre of soft yellow stamens. Unfortunately, it flowers only once each summer.

The variety 'Mme Lauriol de Barny' is much like 'Bourbon Queen' in colour, form, and fragrance. It is also healthy and vigorous and blooms intermittently through the summer. I love this rose and use it in a variety of situations, not least in semi-shaded spots where it can be relied upon to flower well, year upon year. In fact, this rose requires less attention than most of its kind and is not too fussy about the soil in which it is planted. It is also a useful pillar rose. Once established, I suggest underplanting it with sweet peas: the combined fragrances are very rewarding.

Another Bourbon of similar colouring, perhaps a little paler pink, is the cup-shaped 'Coupe d'Hébé', but this is even taller in stature and will need some support if it is not to sprawl over adjacent shrubs. I like to plant this rose where it can be appreciated on the strength of its perfume alone.

'Prince Charles' is a Bourbon of unknown origin, first recorded in 1918. It is a quite vigorous, fully double red and has a sound constitution. Regrettably, it blooms only once each summer, otherwise it would be far more widely grown. Even so, this one is well worth being given enough space to develop to its full height of 1.5m (5ft).

To round up my selection of Bourbon roses, I must include 'Boule de Neige', a white rose of mixed disposition, sometimes rather good, sometimes rather poor. It has few thorns, and is stiff and upright in growth, with mid-green leaves. Each bud is like a little ball, which opens up into a superbly scented, pure white globe. Find a spot for this rose where it can do its own thing. Do not allow it to be smothered by other plants and keep it well fed and watered; it will then give you great pleasure in return.

'Honorine de Brabant'
(*right*) Reminding me of raspberries and cream, the blooms of this pleasing Bourbon are sometimes hidden, as if bashful, among copious foliage. Tall, free flowering, and not too thorny, 'Honorine de Brabant' can be grown either as a shrub or as a small wall plant.

'Blairii No. 2' with
***R. filipes* 'Kiftsgate'**
(*below*) These two roses make an unlikely pair, although in terms of colour the combination works. What happens as regards ultimate sizes is quite another matter, for although 'Blairii No. 2' is robust and vigorous, it is unlikely ever to keep up with the irrepressible 'Kiftsgate'. Both are fragrant and, later on in the autumn, 'Kiftsgate's small, single, white flowers will be followed by a crop of bright red hips.

The Hybrid Perpetuals

The Hybrid Perpetuals, HPs as they are commonly known, started to emerge soon after the Portland Damasks and at about the same time as the Bourbons. The main differences, more apparent now perhaps, with hindsight, than then, are that most HPs have high-centred flowers, and the plants are not usually as tall as the Bourbons but are considerably shorter than Portlands. It must be said that the term Hybrid Perpetuals is something of an exaggeration; the usual flowering season is from early summer through to autumn, but few ever flower continuously throughout that time. To my mind the name "Hybrid Repeats" would be more accurate.

In the early days of their slow rise to prominence the HPs were not fully recognized as a separate group of roses but, by the Victorian era, as flower shows became increasingly fashionable, many Hybrid Perpetuals were bred, rather for the size of their flowers than for garden purposes. By then, too, the cut flower trade was taking off and some HPs were bred specifically to satisfy this demand. As with the Bourbons, hundreds of varieties started to appear in the catalogues of the day; by that time, Britain had begun to lead the world in rose breeding, and HPs were bred by such prominent English rosarians as Henry Bennett and William Paul. Again as with the Bourbons, many varieties failed to make the grade, and within a few years of their introduction had fallen by the wayside. Many that flourished in Victorian times and right through to the 1950s, thriving in the sulphur-laden atmosphere of the industrialized world, became miserable failures as the air gradually became cleaner and diseases such as black spot took hold. Today, hundreds of HP varieties are just names to conjure with in old catalogues and books, having become extinct in cultivation.

HYBRID PERPETUALS FOR THE GARDEN

A number of the taller Hybrid Perpetuals make excellent flowering shrubs, and are best grown as such, although regular pruning and feeding will be needed to reinvigorate the plants each year. Deadheading is also important to ensure, as much as is possible, a flush of flowers late in the season. The shorter varieties are best treated like Hybrid Teas and pruned fairly hard each spring. There is no doubt that, with perhaps one or two notable exceptions, HPs require a little bit of extra attention to keep them at their best, and adopting a regime of regular feeding, watering, and spraying is well worthwhile.

In the past the technique known as "pegging down" was popularly used to grow Hybrid Perpetuals. This involves taking the long shoots of the taller varieties and fixing

'Baronne Prévost'
One of the first Hybrid Perpetuals ever introduced, 'Baronne Prévost' has a lovely old-fashioned, multipetalled form and an alluring fragrance. Its first flush of flowers, in summer, is prolific; its second, in autumn, more sparing. A rather thorny and lax plant, it benefits from hard pruning annually to help to keep it tidy.

them down to the ground with pegs, spacing them as evenly as possible around the plant. These shoots will then produce lateral shoots and, after flowering, these are spurred back, as with fruit trees. In this way, each main shoot should flower happily for several years before it needs pruning out and replacing by another. "Pegging down" has rather gone out of fashion, being deemed too labour intensive these days; but it is still a valuable technique for gardeners, since one plant can be encouraged to cover quite a large area, producing masses of flowers into the bargain.

Today, about 70 Hybrid Perpetuals are available from the rose specialists of the world. Many more can be found in major collections such as those at Sangerhausen in Germany, L'Haÿ-les-Roses in France, Cavriglia, Italy, Ruston's Rose Garden, Australia, and Mottisfont Abbey, England. I have selected 17 that I consider the best for description in the following pages. They are in alphabetical order.

Introduced in 1868, 'Baroness Rothschild' (known as 'Baronne Adolphe de Rothschild' in its native France) is a sport of a now extinct variety. For a sport to have survived for so long is recommendation in itself. Soft clear rose-pink and silky in

texture, its flowers are fully double and are held on strong, erect stalks. A minor talking point about this rose is its perfume, or lack of it: I can detect a fragance, others cannot. In growth, this rose is stocky and upright, seldom attaining a height of more than 90cm (3ft). The greyish green leaves are firm, crisp to the touch, and densely packed on thorny branches.

'Baron Girod de l'Ain' is a most interesting rose, with very fragrant flowers made up of many petals of crimson-red, each with a distinct white margin and crinkled around the edges, reminding me of a carnation. Its mid-green foliage is a little inclined to mildew. If planted in good soil, it will grow to about 1.2m (4ft).

The flowers of 'Baronne Prévost', a rose that dates from 1842, are rather like those of a Centifolia, packed full of deep rose-pink petals. They have a delicious fragrance and are borne very freely initially, but a little spasmodically later on. Growth is coarse and the stems strong and thorny; the foliage is plentiful but rough to touch. All in all, it makes a useful shrub to mix with other bushy plants.

Another attractive HP is a bright cerise-red called 'Dupuy Jamain'. Its flowers are large and, in its heyday, they would undoubtedly have won prizes at shows. This rose is fragrant and free flowering, and has healthy, grey-green foliage, borne on stout, moderately thorny stems. Growing to a maximum height of about 1.2m (4ft), it is, again, a useful plant for mixed shrubberies or for borders.

Despite a sensitive temperament and slight proneness to disease, 'Éclair' is a favourite of mine. It has superbly fragrant flowers, which are very dark red, almost black in colour; they are beautifully cup shaped at first, becoming flat and quartered later on, when fully open. This beauty was rescued from the brink of oblivion, and sent to me by the late Mrs Margaret Wray of Langport in Somerset in the late 1980s — a most valuable rediscovery.

'Empereur du Maroc' is fragrant and of very similar colouring to 'Éclair' except that it has a little more crimson in its fully opened flowers. It is also rather more straggly in growth, with very dark green foliage that is prone to rust in dry, warm weather; the secret is to keep the plant's roots well watered. It is best grown with support, and it will also make a useful pillar rose.

The very beautifully formed flowers of 'Enfant de France' are a joy to me each summer when the plant first comes into bloom. They are quite sizeable, fragrant, and mid- to soft pink, and the petals have a texture like satin. This rose seldom grows to more than 90cm (3ft), its posture upright and non-intrusive, with good foliage.

Striped roses are, I suppose, an acquired taste but one that is always a favourite is 'Ferdinand Pichard'. Quite apart from its unique colouring of carmine-red, soft pink, and greyish white, it also has a lovely fragrance. The flowers are sizeable and double in form. These are carried proudly among good, healthy, greyish green foliage, and after a short rest in late summer are repeated in autumn. The plant's normal height is about 1.2m (4ft) and it will grow just as wide. This is one of the youngest of the Hybrid Perpetuals, having been introduced as late as 1921.

'Ferdinand Pichard' (*left*) Introduced in 1921, this was one of the last Hybrid Perpetuals ever to be raised. All its life it has had to compete with Hybrid Teas, and it is only through being such a delightful novelty, with pink and grey striped flowers, that it has survived until now. This said, it is still a first-class rose. Dominant in front is *Salvia sclarea turkestanica,* a form of biennial clary.

'Prince Camille de Rohan'
Any very dark red Hybrid
Perpetual would have
immediately become
popular in Victorian times,
as indeed did this rose.
Even though, later on, it
was superseded by the red
Hybrid Teas, it survives to
this day on the strength of
having a finer texture to its
petals and a stronger
fragrance than most of its
competitors.

'Frau Karl Druschki', which dates from 1901, is probably the purest white of all roses. Its large blooms are high centred in bud, opening blowsy and dishevelled; unfortunately they have no scent, and they also dislike wet weather. A tall-growing, rather rigid shrub, reaching 1.2m (4ft), it is a superb rose for "pegging down", as described earlier. It produces plenty of foliage, which is mid- to grey-green in colour with a leathery texture. There is also a very good climbing form with the same name, dating from 1906.

The clear, very bright red HP called 'Général Jacqueminot' was a sensation when it was introduced in 1853 since its colour was the brightest red ever seen in a rose, and the variety remains popular in Old rose circles even today. Pointed buds open fragrant, loose, and ruffled. The plant will grow up to 1.2m (4ft) in height, and can become untidy. Its mid-green foliage is coarse to touch and sometimes prone to mildew and rust; its stems are quite thorny.

One of the tallest HPs, perfect for the "pegging down" technique, is the very lovely, fragrant, rich dark red 'Hugh Dickson', raised in 1905. It reaches a height of 2.5m (8ft) when planted in open ground, but it can easily double as a climber, when it will grow as tall as 4m (12ft). It has healthy, maroon-tinted, dark green foliage.

If you require an Old rose for mass bedding then 'Mrs John Laing' is ideal. It can always be relied upon to stay at about 90cm (3ft) and, if regularly pruned, can be kept below that. Its fragrant flowers are full and shapely, of an unfading, soft to mid-pink colour, and borne among plentiful, mid greyish green foliage.

If size of flower is a consideration then 'Paul Neyron' should be grown. It is a rose that has some of the biggest flowers of all: when fully open they can easily reach 15cm (6in) in diameter. They are also very fragrant. Their colour is bright warm pink with deeper and paler highlights, and they are held on stout, relatively thornless stems, which are generously furnished with leathery, dark greyish green foliage. As a shrub it will stay at about 90cm (3ft).

The blush-pink, globular, fully double blooms of 'Paul's Early Blush' are heavily scented and produced among healthy, dark greyish green foliage. Its branches are stout and thorny and the bush grows to about 90cm (3ft).

'Prince Camille de Rohan' has lovely blooms, which are flat and cushion-like when fully open. But this rose is very perplexing: sometimes it is as near perfect as a rose can be; at others it is very disappointing, mainly because of its proneness to mildew. Leaving aside its foibles, it deserves attention for its colour alone, which is like that of blackcurrant jelly; the flowers are also very fragrant. As a plant it can grow to 1.2m (4ft), but is more likely to stay at about half that height.

Without a doubt 'Reine des Violettes' is a rose I will always have in my top ten of all roses. It will sometimes need extra attention to flourish, but it is lovely in all its moods, even when not at its best. Its large, flat flowers open from insignificant buds and are a mixture of violet, lilac, silver, and grey, with hints of pink here and there. In some lights it can look purple. It has plenty of foliage, which is greyish green and slightly downy to touch. It grows up to 1.5m (5ft) in fertile soil.

Finally in my choice of Hybrid Perpetuals, I must include another beautiful dark red, this time a climbing rose with lots of class. It is 'Souvenir du Docteur Jamain', with almost fully double, fragrant blooms, in a colour best described as like that of good claret. This rose grows to 4m (12ft) on a warm, sheltered wall and flowers freely each summer. It should never be planted in a hot, sunny site because its blooms will scorch. Its foliage is dark green and its shoots almost thornless. It dates back to 1865.

'Reine des Violettes'
This is one of a few very special roses that I will always have in my garden. Its many worthy attributes include fragrance, ample grey-green foliage, and tidy, upright, almost thornless growth, not to mention the charm it exudes when cut and placed in a vase. If it has a fault, it is that its blooms open too quickly and shatter in the wind.

The Sweet Briars

This group of vigorous shrubs is derived from the European native species *R. rubiginosa*, previously *R. eglanteria*, commonly known as the sweet briar rose. It is from this wild rose that today's hybrids have inherited their distinctive apple-scented foliage, although only once have I found this species growing wild in the countryside. The natural *R. rubiginosa* is a dense shrub with many sharp prickles. It has one prolific flush of flowers in early summer, followed in early autumn by an abundance of whiskery, oval, orange-red hips. I am slightly mystified as to why some enlightened young rose hybridizer has not worked on Sweet Briars, since they are healthy and appear to me to be just waiting to have their numbers increased. This thought is not new: Graham Stuart Thomas made the same point, more eloquently, in his classic work *The Old Shrub Roses*, first published in 1955.

The majority of Sweet Briars available today were bred by just one man, Lord Penzance, during the last decade of the 19th century. Recognizing the potential appeal of apple-scented foliage, he crossed the common sweet briar with several different hybrids to bring forth a fascinating group of roses, which are large in stature, healthy in disposition, and ornamental in both flowers and fruit. I have often wondered how Lord Penzance came to name his roses, but it has now been drawn to my attention that they all carry the names of characters in the works of Sir Walter Scott.

SWEET BRIARS FOR THE GARDEN

Sweet Briars make ideal shrubs to naturalize in wild gardens. As well as having aromatic foliage, they flower for about three weeks at the beginning of summer, and in most varieties the flowers are followed by a good crop of bright red hips. Once the plants are established to the required size, it is a good plan to prune them annually after the hips are all gone to encourage new young shoots to grow; it is the new growth that is the most heavily scented. Sweet Briars are naturally sturdy and will make good on pillars, tripods, and trellis. They almost all form excellent hedges in and around the garden, where they do not mind being kept in shape by regular clipping. Nowadays, the complete collection of Sweet Briars numbers about 17, of which I have selected eight to discuss as a fair representation of the group.

A spectacle when in full flower, 'Amy Robsart', introduced in 1894, is a vigorous rose that can get up to 3m (10ft) high, but is better pruned annually in winter and kept to about 1.5m (5ft). At this height it will stay dense and bushy. Its slightly apple-scented flowers are large, almost single, and deep pink in colour, enhanced by soft

yellow stamens. The flowers are succeeded by oval, slightly hairy, orange hips. Its foliage, which is very healthy, has a fragrance redolent of apples. The variety 'Anne of Geierstein', introduced in the same year, is similar to 'Amy Robsart' except that it has single, bright crimson flowers.

'Flora McIvor' was also introduced in 1894. Its flowers are single and white in colour with pink edges to their petals. Of all the Sweet Briars I am most fond of this one. In stature it is slightly shorter than the previous two and I can detect a slightly stronger apple scent from its foliage than from the others.

Introduced in 1892, but probably much older, is the shorter-growing 'Janet's Pride', also known as 'Clementine'. It is believed that it was the fragrant foliage of this variety that first prompted Lord Penzance to start rose breeding. Its creamy white flowers are bordered with pink and are smaller than those of any of the other Sweet Briars, although produced just as freely.

'Amy Robsart'
This delightful pastoral scene shows how some of the Old Shrub roses can harmonize with nature. Here, the almost single Sweet Briar 'Amy Robsart', the Multiflora Rambler 'Russelliana', and an unrecorded Gallica, probably 'Charles de Mills', all mingle beneath the oak, while one of the geese stands and looks on in curiosity.

'Lady Penzance' (*right*)
Almost all the Sweet
Briars were raised by Lord
Penzance, an English
judge, and were
introduced by him in the
early 1890s. Many are of
unknown parentage, but
'Lady Penzance' is a cross
between *R. rubiginosa*
and *R. foetida* 'Bicolor', as
the flowers clearly show.
All Sweet Briars have
apple-scented foliage,
although the aroma is
stronger in this cultivar
than in any other.

'Magnifica' (*far right*)
This superb Sweet Briar
was raised in Germany in
1916. It mixes superbly
with shrubs of most other
genera, and of its own
kind. It is seen here
growing beneath a
mountain ash (*Sorbus
aucuparia*), into which
the rumbustious Modern
Shrub rose 'Cerise
Bouquet' has scrambled
and is just visible in the
shadows. I spy a thistle,
too, and a sucker – but
then, this picture was
taken in my own garden!

A rose I have had growing in my garden for a very long time and one that seems to be quite rare is 'La Belle Distinguée'. Its foliage is very Centifolia-like and gives off a slight aroma of apples; its flowers are fully double and scarlet in colour. This interesting rose forms a useful, dense shrub, usually growing no taller than 90cm (3ft).

'Lord Penzance' and 'Lady Penzance' were first introduced in 1894 and, in most respects, are very similar, each having soft green leaves, lightly coloured green wood, and foliage and flowers with good scents. In fact, the only rose to match these two for degree of apple scent is the species *R. rubiginosa*. The flowers of 'Lady Penzance' are salmon-pink overlaid coppery yellow, and those of 'Lord Penzance' are buff-yellow with only a hint of pink. Both have single flowers and attractive stamens.

The lush, dark green foliage of 'Magnifica', which was raised in 1916, is less aromatic than that of any other Sweet Briar. This is a vigorous and bushy rose, growing to 1.2m (4ft), and it has semi-double flowers of deep pink with hints of purple.

'Manning's Blush' is quite different from any other Sweet Briar, having fully double flowers, blush-white in colour; well scented and nestling among dark green, aromatic foliage, they recur regularly throughout summer. This is a rose for the smaller garden since it is easy to keep within bounds at around 90cm (3ft), although in good soil it will get to 1.5m (5ft). Older than all the others, it was first recorded as early as 1800.

An extremely vigorous and, indeed, prickly Sweet Briar completes my selection: the bright red, near single 'Meg Merrilies', which has a discreet white eye in the centre of its fragrant flowers; its foliage, too, is fragrant. Like all Sweet Briars, it has lots of stamina and it will reach 2.5m (8ft), or even taller, when grown on a wall.

The Rugosas

A native of Japan and other parts of eastern Asia, *R. rugosa* could well have been used as an ornamental plant for much longer in that part of the world than elsewhere. In Europe, the earliest record of *R. rugosa typica* dates back to 1796, but it took some considerable time for it to become widely known. In fact, its wider distribution came more from its prowess as a rootstock, especially in the production of standard roses, than from any ornamental value. *R. rugosa* spent almost one hundred years in comparative obscurity, then it began to dawn on the rose breeders of the day that here was a remontant species with great potential as a parent. Several first-class Rugosa roses were introduced between 1890 and 1915, including 'Roseraie de L'Haÿ' from France in 1901, 'Hansa' from Holland in 1905, and 'Fru Dagmar Hastrup' from Denmark in 1914, but only a few came into being after that. (Those that did will be discussed under Modern Shrub roses later on.)

This lack of attention by breeders over the years is surprising since Rugosa hybrids have much to commend them as garden plants, making usually healthy, easy-going shrubs that flower throughout much of the summer and sometimes beyond. Hardiness is their most valuable asset although, it must be said, one of their frailties is a dislike of hot climates, especially when they cannot rest for a while over winter. Temperate maritime areas, however, present them with no problems; in fact, the hybrids closest to the true species seem to enjoy growing by the sea and will not mind light, sandy soils; they do sulk a little, though, if asked to grow in chalk or heavy clay.

R. rugosa 'Alba'
The hips produced by the lovely, single, white-flowered *R. rugosa 'Alba'*, seen here on their way to ripening to a much deeper red, are some of the biggest of any rose. Most Rugosas have fruit of this shape, which hangs on the bush until fully ripe, making tasty dinners for hungry birds, field mice, and even squirrels in the cold midwinter.

RUGOSAS FOR THE GARDEN

With so many virtues and so few foibles, it perhaps goes without saying that Rugosas can perform almost any task asked of them in the garden. The most common use to which they are put is for hedging, and no other type of rose can fulfil this role so effectively; the shorter, more compact types being best for formal dividing hedges, the taller for the less formal. Another use is as specimen plants in lawns and open spaces, for

which their long flowering season makes them ideal candidates, their hips and autumn colouring prolonging the season well into winter. Groups of Rugosas also look good in mixed shrubberies and they are increasingly planted en masse in public parks, as well as being used to great effect as screens and barriers. The following 15 Rugosas are, arguably, as good as they come.

One of the most useful is the white form of the species, *R. rugosa* 'Alba'. In fact, I can think of no role that this rose is not capable of playing within the garden. Its superbly scented, single flowers are silky in texture, with golden yellow stamens adding to their simplicity and purity. They appear regularly on thick, thorny stems throughout summer and into autumn, the later ones coinciding with large, round, red hips, borne among unblemished, dark green foliage. *R. rugosa* 'Alba' reaches heights of up to 1.8m (6ft); it makes a marvellous hedge and is a good companion for other plants in mixed shrubberies.

First coming on the scene in 1894, 'Belle Poitevine' is a Rugosa with considerable charisma. Growing quite tall, to 1.8m (6ft), it blooms prolifically and continuously throughout summer. The large, almost double flowers are bright pink blushed with soft magenta, and they open a little tousled to show off creamy yellow stamens. They are also highly scented. 'Belle Poitevine' carries a good crop of hips well into winter, and its foliage is very healthy, wrinkled, and lightish green in colour.

'Pink Grootendorst'
The individual flowers of this sweetly scented Rugosa hybrid have fringed petals, rather like those of carnations or pinks (*Dianthus*). As in all four of the Grootendorst cultivars, they are arranged in tightly packed clusters. The flowers of the other Grootendorsts are of red, crimson, and white.

'Blanc Double de Coubert', one of the most beautiful Rugosas, was introduced two years earlier than 'Belle Poitevine' but has become better known over the years. A cross between *R. rugosa* and the Tea rose 'Sombreuil', it has double, pure white flowers that are very fragrant and produced continuously all through the summer. Its foliage is abundant and mid-green in colour, taking on golden-amber shades in autumn. Only occasionally do its flowers set hips. Growing to 1.5m (5ft) or thereabouts, it is again good as a hedging plant, and mixes well with both its own kind and other shrubs.

A very vigorous Rugosa from Germany, 'Dr Eckener' has semi-double, fragrant, soft yellow flowers heavily overlaid bronze and pink; these are of considerable size and borne repeatedly throughout summer. This is a spreading plant with coarse, dark green foliage and many sharp thorns on its long stems. Left to its own devices 'Dr Eckener' will reach 3m (10ft) tall and grow equally wide; it is just the rose for a part of the garden that requires privacy.

'Fimbriata', introduced in 1891, is a rather unusual Rugosa, the parent of which is the Noisette rose 'Mme Alfred Carrière'. 'Fimbriata' is also known as 'Phoebe's Frilled Pink' and 'Dianthiflora', the latter name being a reference to the small, semi-double, dianthus-like flowers; these are blush-pink fading to white and are arranged in small clusters on upright, light green stems. Good as a flowering shrub in mixed shrubberies, this rose never gets too tall, remaining at about 90cm (3ft) even without pruning; however, some pruning is essential if the plant is to keep any sort of shape.

Like 'Fimbriata', the following four Rugosas have flowers reminiscent of those of dianthus but with more petals. They are all closely related, being sports from one another. The first, the deep red 'F.J. Grootendorst', was introduced in 1918. Making up the quartet are soft pink 'Pink Grootendorst', 'White Grootendorst', which is more ivory-coloured than white, and the crimson 'Grootendorst Supreme'. All are scented. From time to time, these roses revert back to one another, and it is not unusual to see flowers of all four colours in the same cluster. The growth of each is rather coarse and the stems rather thorny, and pruning is important to keep them constantly rejuvenated.

One of the most popular Rugosas with municipal landscapers these days is the lovely, silvery pink single 'Fru Dagmar Hastrup', which is especially useful as a ground coverer since it is dense in growth and as wide as it is

'F.J. Grootendorst' (*right*) This is the original red form from which all of the other Grootendorst roses originated as sports. Here it shows its prolific flowers and abundant foliage. What cannot be seen, though, are its vicious thorns. Behind the rose is the black elder *Sambucus nigra* Black Beauty.

'Mrs Anthony Waterer' (*below*) Just a little extra tender loving care is needed to get the best from this strongly fragrant Rugosa. It is very thorny and will make a dense hedge, so dense as to be the perfect deterrent to even the most persistent of domestic pets.

'Roseraie de l'Haÿ'
The lovely utility Rugosa 'Roseraie de l'Haÿ' grows so densely that it can easily be used as a hedge. The bud emerging from among the abundant foliage and the fully open blooms are clues to its continuity of flower. A particular feature of this Rugosa is its fragrance, redolent of cloves.

tall, at around 90cm (3ft). By the end of the summer this shrub will have produced hundreds of flowers, each one followed by a bright red, rounded hip. Its leaves are very dark green and numerous. Its uses are multifarious and, despite the fact that it is seen everywhere these days, I still love this special little Rugosa.

If I had to select just one Rugosa for my garden it would be 'Hansa', a shrub that is tidy and bushy and stays that way without too much attention. The fragrant flowers are fully double and reddish purple in colour, and they precede the largest hips of all the Rugosas. A special feature is its crisp, dark green foliage. 'Hansa' can perform many functions in the garden, from hedging to specimen plant. Most Rugosas are not happy with their roots contained, but this one does make a good pot plant.

'Max Graf', a spreading Rugosa 60cm (2ft) tall and four times as wide, is good for staying close to the ground and covering banks, mounds, and old tree stumps. Its foliage is plentiful and very dark green, and it produces numerous single flowers of a deep silvery pink, but these seldom set fruit.

'Mrs Anthony Waterer' has semi-double flowers, deep red to crimson in colour, which are highly scented. Not a tall rose, at 1.2m (4ft) maximum, it has very dark green foliage and stems with many thorns. This rose makes a tidy hedge but also looks good in a mixed shrubbery; it can be temperamental, being rather prone to mildew, and needs a little extra care to give of its best.

Often used by landscape gardeners and garden designers these days is 'Roseraie de l'Haÿ', and deservedly so for, apart from being quite lovely and heavily scented, it is also a utility rose. The almost double, crimson-purple flowers appear all through the summer. The plant has good dark green foliage, which is colourful in the autumn. Its only fault is that it seldom sets hips and, when it does, they are not over large.

Another utility Rugosa is 'Scabrosa', a foundling that is older than its declared date of 1950. Pronounced stamens accentuate the large, single, magenta-cerise flowers, which have plenty of fragrance and are followed by hips larger than those of most others of the group, like small tomatoes. With crisp, dense, mid-green foliage, this rose is perfect either as a divider within the garden or forming a boundary hedge.

Finally, I come to another white Rugosa, called 'Schneezwerg' or 'Snow Dwarf' and dating back to 1912. This lovely rose has much to commend it, with semi-double, white flowers which, when fully open, display a lovely cluster of yellow stamens to good effect. The maximum height of this thorny and rugged bush is about 1.2m (4ft). Its fruit are round and bright red, and often appear together with the flowers later in the season. As well as being good for hedging, this rose is a superb mixer among other shrubs and herbaceous plants.

'Scabrosa'
Clearly seen here are 'Scabrosa's heavily veined leaves, setting off its silky textured flowers with their delightful golden yellow stamens (shown a little larger than life size). Add in fragrance, and sizeable, tomato-shaped hips later in summer and this superb rose is complete. Like all Rugosas, it is especially good for hedging.

The Hybrid Musks

Such are the changing fashions in gardening that the Hybrid Musks were held in little regard when first introduced, but nowadays are a very important group of shrub roses. Although they have some musk rose genes in their make-up, they really owe more in pedigree to *R. multiflora* than to *R. moschata*. Almost all were raised between 1913 and the start of the Second World War, with the majority bred by an English clergyman, the Rev. Joseph Pemberton. Clearly, Pemberton was ahead of his time: the fashionable roses then were the rather formal Hybrid Teas and Hybrid Perpetuals, and at first no one knew quite how or where to grow these new, more relaxed shrubs. It is a tribute to Pemberton's work that these roses are now automatic choices where continuous-flowering shrub roses are required. Some of Pemberton's roses were introduced after his death by his gardener, W.A. Bentall, who also went on to introduce some very good varieties of his own.

In his work, Pemberton used only free-flowering roses, especially those with cluster flowers, crossing them with the more traditional roses of the day, and creating shrubs with larger, more fully double flowers than had been seen up to that time. As the foundation, Pemberton used 'Trier', a seedling from a rambling rose called 'Aglaia' which, in turn, had been bred from a cross between *R. multiflora* and a Noisette variety called 'Rêve d'Or'. One of his first seedlings was 'Danaë', raised in 1913. After this he introduced roses regularly, year on year, well into the 1920s.

Some believe that the relatively youthful Hybrid Musks belong among the Modern roses, rather than with the Old roses, which are normally defined as those that pre-date the arrival of the first Hybrid Tea, in 1867. In my view, however, the demarcation between Old and Modern needs to move forward from time to time, just as it does with cars, for example. This is the principle I have adopted, shifting the cut-off date between the two to 1940. With this delineation the Old roses now embrace important groups such as the Hybrid Musks as well as the classic early Hybrid Teas. Future generations of rose devotees can move the defining date on, as appropriate.

HYBRID MUSKS FOR THE GARDEN

All the Hybrid Musks have many features in common, the most important of which is continuity of flower. Secondly, they are all roughly the same height, making it possible to use them for multifarious purposes. Nearly all are fragrant to some degree, and they almost all carry their flowers in large clusters. Most have few thorns of consequence. With one or two exceptions, where mildew is a nuisance, they are all very healthy.

Over the years, some of the best characteristics of the Hybrid Musks have been carried forward into Modern Shrub roses and, consequently, the demarcation line between the two groups has become a little blurred. Apart from the Modern Shrubs, no other group of roses is as versatile in its potential as the Hybrid Musks. They are excellent for use in mixed shrubberies and some are superb as individual specimen plants. They are all very gregarious, easily making themselves comfortable among a wide variety of other types of plant. Furthermore, such is their adaptability that most will make extremely good hedges, especially of an informal type. As if this is not enough, they are also very useful for growing in pots, tubs, urns, or any other hollowed-out object that may be available. In terms of general husbandry, they are fairly easy going but, as with most roses, the more fertile the soil the better the results. There are no golden rules about pruning Hybrid Musks; it depends on where they are planted and the purpose to which they are put. Hedges of Hybrid Musks can be clipped with shears, specimen plants simply tidied up from time to time, and those associating with other plants pruned according to the size required.

There are about 25 different varieties of Hybrid Musks around today, of which ten or so are widely available. I am fond of all these roses and have found it very difficult to select just 15.

I start with 'Ballerina', which was first introduced in 1937 and is nowadays one of the most popular roses for general garden use. It is never without flowers throughout the summer, each one small, soft pink, and single and part of a large cluster on a stem

of sometimes more than 100 blooms. When first introduced it was considered rather mundane but, since about the 1960s, its utilitarian attributes have found it a wider public. 'Ballerina' benefits from regular pruning and deadheading and will grow about 90cm (3ft) high in good soil. I also love 'Belinda', introduced a year earlier. It is a much deeper pink and its flowers are more double than those of 'Ballerina', but in all other respects the two are very similar.

'Buff Beauty' must be included, for it is a lovely example of the Hybrid Musks. Its flowers are sometimes produced singly but are more often in large clusters. Double and a little muddled in shape, they are bright buff-yellow in colour, fading almost to cream in hot sunshine. They are not short of fragrance. The foliage is tinted bronze when young but changes to dark green on maturity. The plant will never get more than 1.2m (4ft) high, but could well exceed this measurement in width; sometimes the weight of the clusters of flowers, added to the natural arching habit of the rose, causes the shrub to become very wide if it is not pruned.

'Cornelia', introduced in 1925, adopts a similar arching posture to 'Buff Beauty'. It too is free flowering and carries its semi-double, shrimp-pink flowers in equally large clusters. It usually grows to 1.5m (5ft) in height, and its foliage is bronzy coloured, ageing to very dark green. This rose is particularly good in the autumn, when the flowers it produces are more colourful, giving the plant a much more definite presence than earlier in the year.

Also carrying its flowers in clusters, although not such large ones, 'Danaë' has semi-double flowers of mustard-yellow, paling to creamy yellow in hot weather. Tidy in habit, the plant has chocolate-coloured young foliage, which changes to mid-green with age. It can grow up to 1.2m (4ft) tall in good soil. As I mentioned before, this was the first of the Hybrid Musks bred by Pemberton.

'Daybreak', another Pemberton rose, introduced in 1918, opens to soft primrose from deeper yellow buds. The fragrant, semi-double flowers are well spaced in sizeable clusters. Its young branches and foliage are reddish brown and turn to darkish green with maturity. In normal soil 'Daybreak' will reach a height of about 90cm (3ft).

If I were forced to choose, I would say that the fragrant 'Felicia' is my favourite Hybrid Musk. Its flowers are larger than any of those previously discussed and are composed of many

'Buff Beauty' (*left*)
This superb picture shows 'Buff Beauty' in all its stages, from bud through to mature flower. It also highlights a slight imperfection – that of paling quite quickly in hot sun. Yet this rose has so many other good points that I, for one, can overlook such a fault. In any case, the autumn flowers will be deeper in colour and less likely to fade. Here, the rose is ably coping with the embrace of a sizeable group of white geraniums.

'Felicia' (*below*)
Of all the Hybrid Musks, if I had to choose just one, it would be 'Felicia'. This rose has good deportment and carries its fragrant flowers in sizeable clusters against bluish green foliage. A good all-rounder, it is especially fine as a hedging rose.

'Penelope' (*right*)
A relatively small group of 'Penelope's flowers is seen here in the company of *Euphorbia griffithii*. Usually this lovely Hybrid Musk has much larger clusters. As a plant it is fairly relaxed in growth and has abundant foliage. Unfortunately, by the end of each summer, it tends to become mildly afflicted by mildew.

'Francesca' (*below*)
This enchanting Hybrid Musk will grow up to 1.2m (4ft) tall and equally as wide. It makes an ideal informal hedge. Although paling slightly over time, the large sprays of flowers are composed of blooms of differing ages, so the overall effect from a distance is bright yellow – no doubt the attraction for this foraging honeybee.

more petals. They are borne in clusters, but these are not as densely packed as those of other Hybrid Musks mentioned so far. In growth 'Felicia' is upright and tidy, with coppery tinted foliage which, when mature, is of a bluish green shade. This rose grows to a manageable size of about 1.2m (4ft).

'Francesca' is an arching Hybrid Musk with slightly fragrant, semi-double flowers, which are yellowish apricot in colour, and arranged in very large clusters. Its stems are purplish green, well furnished with glossy dark leaves; it has hardly any thorns of consequence, and will reach a height of 1.2m (4ft).

'Moonlight' has fragrant, soft lemon to white flowers; each of these has a double layer of petals and, when fully open, shows off a centrepiece of golden stamens. The flowers are produced in clusters, which are well spaced on the plant. Its foliage is darkish green and, as a shrub, it can get as tall as 1.5m (5ft).

One of only a few red Hybrid Musks is 'Nur Mahal'. Its flowers are slightly more than single, quite large, and fragrant. Its growth is upright and its foliage mid- to dark green. Introduced in 1923, it is not, I feel, as well known as it should be.

'Pax' is the largest of the Hybrid Musks, both in size of bloom – up to 10cm (4in) – and size of plant – which can be up to 1.8m (6ft). Its loosely formed flowers are fragrant and creamy white in colour. Its stems are darkish green and relatively free of thorns.

Another very good white Hybrid Musk is 'Prosperity'. Its produces sizeable clusters of fully double flowers and, in some weather, a hint of pink can be seen in the central petals of each bloom. The foliage is dark and glossy and the stems carry only a smattering of biggish thorns. It dates back to 1919.

A delightful, semi-double, pinkish cream Hybrid Musk, 'Penelope' also produces its fragrant flowers in clusters. These are borne amid greenish purple foliage, on stems that are fairly free of thorns. Its one fault is an ability to develop mildew for the most flimsy of reasons.

'Robin Hood' is a rose that, over the years, I have grown to like very much. It is not over tall, normally getting to about 90cm (3ft) high, has lots of good foliage, and puts out large

trusses of small, semi-double, pinkish scarlet flowers, which are unobtrusively speckled white. I use this rose more and more at the front of borders to provide a splash of muted scarlet. It was introduced in 1927.

To complete my collection of Hybrid Musks I must include 'Vanity'. This is an angular plant that is difficult to grow, but it does have very beautiful flowers. These are large, almost single, and shocking pink. I can never understand why I like this rather cantankerous Hybrid Musk, but it must have something to do with the fact that it has a little more than its fair share of charm, and is willing to share this with me.

The Teas

'Archiduc Joseph'
An outstanding Tea rose, 'Archiduc Joseph' is, like most of its kind, rudely healthy with lots of dark grey-green foliage and few thorns of consequence. Usually grown as a shrub, it will also perform well as a wall climber. It is best positioned where its distinctive fragrance can be appreciated to the full.

The Teas, or Tea-scented roses as they were once called, owe much of their origin to *R. gigantea*, a species that is massive, as its name suggests, and produces flowers in great quantities throughout a long flowering season. In the distant past it is possible that one or more breeders in China, having recognized the garden value of *R. gigantea,* crossed it with a form of *R. chinensis* to raise two of the original stud roses, 'Hume's Blush', also known as 'Odorata', and 'Parks' Yellow' (see p.72); but it is perhaps more likely that these arose through chance fertilization. These two roses, together with other Chinese hybrids, reached Europe in the early 19th century, and after yet further hybridization in the hands of rose breeders, the Teas evolved.

There is no one clearly definable characteristic that makes it possible, at a glance, to identify a Tea rose. To generalize, the blooms are mostly high centred in the early stages, with lots of petals. Their colours embrace the full spectrum and they are almost all fragrant, and they flower continuously through the summer. By no means all are thorny and the majority have glossy foliage.

Most rose books say that the Tea roses acquired their name from their distinctive scent, but nothing in the aroma of these roses reminds me of tea. It may be, of course,

that the smell of tea has changed over time; but is it not just possible that it was the old tea clippers, the ships used to transport the early forms of Tea roses from China to Europe, that gave them their name?

Tea roses soon became very fashionable, as garden plants and as conservatory plants in colder areas. They remained popular for decades until, in the early 20th century, the Hybrid Teas came along in ever increasing numbers. Even today, Tea roses still have a big following in the warmer parts of the world, where winter protection is unnecessary – and rightly so, for they are delightful plants to have around in any garden.

'Clementina Carbonieri'
This full-face close-up shows off the many shades of orange, yellow, and pink found in a single bloom of 'Clementina Carbonieri', one of the most colourful of Tea roses. This rose never gets tall, seldom reaching more than 60cm (2ft) in northern European climates, and so makes an excellent, easy-going pot plant. Although it is perhaps a little brightly coloured for my taste, I never tire of this bubbly little rose.

TEA ROSES FOR THE GARDEN

It is probably correct to say that anyone who gardens above latitude 60°N should avoid growing the Teas in open ground for, north of this line on the map, there will be frosts accompanied by wind-chill, causing serious die-back. This said, the Teas are so beautiful that they are worth growing for their good looks alone, despite the inconvenience of covering them in winter or having to grow them in pots so that they can be moved inside for protection. In northern temperate climates, Tea roses will grow satisfactorily outside as long as they are given a little extra care such as feeding with plenty of potash after flowering, to help them harden off before the winter. Norfolk is one of the coldest counties in the UK, with very little protection from the north and easterly winds that come from the Arctic Circle and Siberia; even so, I grow Teas in my garden at latitude 52°N, never covering them in winter. I also grow them under glass, where their unblemished loveliness can be fully appreciated. If red spider can be kept at bay, the hotter the greenhouse the better they like it. As already mentioned, Teas grown in pots are best kept inside over winter, and moved outside when the risk of frost has passed. Pruning of Tea roses should be kept to the minimum, simply removing older wood when necessary and cutting back lateral shoots to keep the plants in shape. With Teas, good husbandry pays substantial dividends.

Most Tea roses are shrubs but, because of their *R. gigantea* ancestry, some have produced climbing sports from time to time. These old climbing Teas have close affinity to the Noisettes, and I will deal with these two groups of roses later in the book (see pp.152–157).

In all, about 75 varieties of Tea roses are fairly freely available from specialist growers in warmer climates of the world; I have about 50 of these myself, and from these I have selected nine to highlight here. It should be noted that the sizes I quote for each variety can be doubled in warmer climates.

The first is 'Archiduc Joseph' of 1872. This is quite a vigorous rose, growing to 1.5m (5ft), with lots of good, dark greyish green foliage and few thorns of consequence. It freely produces fully double, fragrant flowers all summer through, these being best described as a mixture of pink, purple, orange, and russet shades, with a faint hint of gold in the centre; the overall effect, from a distance, is of a colour on the pink side of crimson. This shrub can also make an efficient climber, especially for walls. There appears to be some confusion in the USA over this rose and 'Monsieur Tillier' (see p.115), but I am convinced that the rose described here is 'Archiduc Joseph'.

My next choice is one of the most colourful Tea roses I know, 'Clementina Carbonieri', which was was introduced in 1913, later than most other Teas. Its fully double flowers are predominantly orange highlighted with touches of yellow and salmon-pink, and they are produced in small clusters on longish stems, amid profuse darkish green, semi-glossy foliage. Not a tall grower in cooler climates, seldom reaching more than 90cm (3ft), this is one of the best Teas for cultivation in pots and for growing under glass.

'Général Schablikine' is another fairly short rose in cooler regions, again growing only to about 90cm (3ft) in good soil; however, I have seen it almost twice this height in both South Australia and southern Italy. The colour of its many semi-double flowers is coppery cherry-red, overlaid pink. They have a mild perfume and are borne all summer long, among healthy foliage. This rose dates back to 1878.

One of the hardiest Teas is a cupped, fragrant rose with many blush-to creamy white petals, each flower

being heavily brushed pink on its outer edges. Called 'Homère', it dates from 1858, a time when Teas were at the height of their popularity. It is another rose that can reach double its size in warmer parts, but attains only about 90cm (3ft) here in chilly Norfolk. Its foliage is plentiful and darkish green in colour; and its stems, like those of so many Teas, have few thorns of any size.

The unfading, golden yellow 'Lady Hillingdon' is a great favourite, even today. It is free flowering and fragrant, and produces many high-centred flowers, similar in form to those of Hybrid Teas. Its stems are plum-coloured, as is its young foliage.

'Monsieur Tillier' is a good, hardy Tea rose that deserves more attention. It has nearly fully double flowers of a very deep red with hints of violet colouring; these are fragrant and produced very freely. Quite a vigorous variety, it forms an open shrub growing to 1.2m (4ft) tall; its foliage is dark green, lush, and plentiful.

Another multi-coloured Tea rose, introduced as late as 1922, is the superb, shapely, almost double, fragrant 'Rosette Delizy'. The pleasing combination of colours takes in pink, buff-apricot, and yellow on the inside of its petals, and orange on the outside. This is a good pot rose, seldom getting taller than 1.1m (3½ft). It has leathery foliage of mid- to bluish green. In Bermuda, I once saw a plant of this rose growing as a wall climber, at least 4m by 4m (12ft by 12ft).

The most yellow of all the Teas, 'Safrano' was introduced in 1839. Its buds are pointed and open to flat, fragrant, saffron-yellow flowers that vary from less than semi-double to fully double in form; these are borne all through the summer and are carried among darkish green, leathery foliage. In cooler regions 'Safrano' usually gets to a height of 90cm (3ft).

Finally, in my choice of Teas I must mention the newest of them all, 'Tipsy Imperial Concubine', which was discovered in a garden in China by Hazel Le Rougetel in 1982. It was sent to me direct from China and, following trials over a number of years, in 1989 I was pleased to introduce what is clearly an old Chinese Tea rose. Its name is an exact translation of the Chinese and it qualifies as an Old rose on account of having been grown in Chinese gardens for many years. Its colour is a subtle mixture of pink, red, and soft yellow. I find that it is completely hardy in the chilly winters of Norfolk; here it grows 60cm (2ft) high, a size that makes it good as a pot plant.

'Tipsy Imperial Concubine'
The latest member of the Tea roses, 'Tipsy Imperial Concubine' is, in fact, probably an old Chinese cultivar. It was found in China by Hazel Le Rougetel in 1982 and introduced by my nurseries in 1989, after seven years of trials. I find both this Tea and its name an absolute delight. It will grow to about 60cm (2ft) tall and is particularly good in pots.

The Older Hybrid Teas

In an earlier chapter (see p.106) I suggested that the cut-off date for Old roses should be moved forward from 1867, the date of the first Hybrid Tea, to 1940. Therefore, I feel it appropriate to include in this part of the book some of the older Hybrid Teas of historical importance, which were introduced between those dates. I will discuss their history and the garden prowess of Hybrid Teas later on (see p.120).

The oldest of all Hybrid Teas is 'La France', introduced in 1867. To be fair, if it were not for its historical significance, this rose would probably be extinct by now. It is a typically shaped, high-centred HT, soft silvery pink in colour, repeat flowering, and scented. Its grey-green foliage, regrettably, is rather prone to mildew.

Introduced some 15 years later than 'La France', 'Lady Mary Fitzwilliam' also has fragrant, pink flowers, but this rose was raised by an Englishman, Henry Bennett. It was rediscovered by Keith Money in 1975, having been thought extinct for many years. A thorny plant with plenty of good foliage, it is slightly taller than 'La France', growing to about 75cm (2½ft), and is less prone to mildew.

'Soleil d'Or' comes next chronologically. One of the first truly yellow Hybrid Teas, it also has some orange in its colouring. It was raised by Joseph Pernet-Ducher of France in 1900, and was grouped with several other yellow HTs under the name Pernettianas; like most of these, 'Soleil d'Or' is very prone to black spot. It grows to about 90cm (3ft) and has rich green, slightly glossy foliage.

In 1912, British hybridizer William Paul exploited the growing market for roses as cut flowers by introducing 'Ophelia', one of the most fragrant roses ever raised. It became very popular very quickly: thousands of plants were soon sold and roses of this type filled florists' shops to overflowing. The colour is soft blush-pink with lemon deep down in the centre of the petals. 'Ophelia' has produced two sports in its time, the first named 'Mme Butterfly', which is a fraction deeper in colour than its parent; the second a much deeper pink named 'Lady Sylvia'.

A very beautiful, single, golden yellow HT called 'Mrs Oakley Fisher' was introduced in 1921, a real eye-catcher with prominent stamens, which fits easily among bright herbaceous plants and shorter flowering shrubs. This lovely rose displays its flowers in large clusters and gives me lots of pleasure each summer.

'Dainty Bess', another beautiful single rose, came out some four years after 'Mrs Oakley Fisher'. This has soft pink flowers, their petals attractively ragged around the edges, with dark stamens. I have never seen this rose taller than 60cm (2ft), which means it fits readily among a wide range of plants within the garden.

'Dame Edith Helen', introduced in 1926, is one of the most double HTs ever raised. It has very fragrant, bright glowing pink flowers, Centifolia-like in both shape and colour, and is tidy in growth, reaching no more than 60cm (2ft). It blooms freely all summer. This is another rose reintroduced from Keith Money's collection in 1975.

Of all the red HTs, 'Crimson Glory' has to be one of the best. It was introduced in 1935 and has one of the strongest perfumes of any rose I know. Growing to about 60cm (2ft) tall, its only real fault is its decidedly weak neck, causing its superbly shaped flowers to hang down, as though bashful, which it certainly should not be. If such reticence can be forgiven, then 'Crimson Glory' is very difficult to fault. This rose brings back pleasant memories to me. I recall being taught to arrange my first ever bowl of roses using this variety, at the Chelsea Flower Show in 1954.

'La France'
This soft silky pink rose was the first ever Hybrid Tea. Introduced in 1867, it took until the early part of the 20th century – 33 years and more – for 'La France' to be taken seriously as the first of a new distinct group. From then on until recently Hybrid Teas ruled the roost in roses.

MODERN ROSES

The Hybrid Teas

The first Hybrid Tea rose, known as 'La France', came into existence in 1867, the result, it is believed, of a secret liaison between an alluring Hybrid Perpetual and a Tea rose with a roving eye. The nurseryman who introduced it, Jean Baptiste Guillot of France, knew at once that there was something different about this foundling rose, especially in the shape of the flower, but it took two decades for it to become officially recognized as the first of a new group. After that, such was the rise in popularity of Hybrid Teas that, by the 1920s, they had become the only roses used for bedding and for exhibition, and breeders responded to the demand by raising hundreds of new cultivars with ever bigger and more shapely blooms.

There are several differences between the Hybrid Teas and the Hybrid Perpetuals they eventually succeeded, the shape of their flowers being perhaps the most obvious. HT flowers are initially high in the centre, opening to usually fully double blooms with outwardly furled petals. Their habit of growth is also different, being rather more upright than the Hybrid Perpetuals; and most are fairly short in stature, seldom growing above 90cm (3ft) tall. Many Hybrid Teas have inherited the fragrances of their parent groups, and most, if not all, produce flowers throughout the summer months, continuing until the first frosts of autumn.

HYBRID TEAS FOR THE GARDEN

Over the last two decades Hybrid Teas have fallen from their pinnacle as the most popular roses of all time. This, though, has more to do with changing fashions in gardening than with any deterioration in their prowess as garden plants. Hybrid Teas today still make excellent bedding plants and look especially good planted en masse. Many settle in comfortably when grown among other shrubs and perennials; and most will thrive in pots, urns, and other containers. All will provide beautiful flowers for cutting. However

they are grown, most Hybrid Teas need to be pruned very hard early each spring if they are to give of their best.

Most good rose nurseries these days list between 70 and 100 Hybrid Teas, which are also known as Large-flowered roses. I will choose just 15 or so of my favourites by colour, starting with the yellow shades.

Peace, undoubtedly the most famous rose of all time, was originally introduced in France by the Meilland family under the name 'Mme A. Meilland', which was subsequently changed to Gloria Dei. It was in 1945, at the end of the Second World War, that this exceptional rose was given the name Peace — and millions were sold throughout the world. Its sweetly perfumed flowers of soft yellow brushed with red are beautiful in the true high-centred, cabbage style, and are borne among dense, thickly textured, glossy, dark green foliage. At about 1.2m (4ft), Peace is rather tall for bedding, but it makes an ideal shrub. Its only fault, if it can be called that, is a slight shyness in producing flowers.

Elina
One of the classic modern Hybrid Tea roses, Elina is delightfully fragrant and very free flowering. Although its many blooms are of exhibition size, it will grow, if allowed to, into a most useful free-standing shrub, a purpose for which I frequently use it.

'Pinta'
One of the first roses I ever introduced, 'Pinta' is an excellent bedding rose and has the captivating fragrance of sweet briar. Although grouped here among the Hybrid Teas, its flowers are produced freely enough for it to qualify as a Floribunda.

Another first-class yellow HT is Elina, originally called Peaudouce. It was raised by Dickson and is one of the classics among Modern roses. Its fragrant, fully double flowers are initially lemon-yellow, paling to ivory when fully open. These are borne on an exuberant plant with healthy, glossy, dark green foliage. If allowed to develop, it will make a superb shrub.

'Grandpa Dickson', known as 'Irish Gold' in the USA, is another Dickson rose. Excellent for bedding, it produces large, exhibition-type blooms of soft yellow. These appear generously among glossy, mid-green foliage. Like Elina, if allowed its head, it will make a well-balanced, upright shrub.

Moving now to the creamy white shades, I start with one of my own, called 'Pinta' (also featured in the Introduction, see p.10). This is a unique blend of pure white and cream and, although each bloom is not large, its petals are scrolled in bud and the flower opens semi-double, with the distinct scent of sweet briar. It is about 60cm (2ft) tall, with dark green foliage.

To me, white roses are very beguiling and I find myself drawn to them whenever I see them in a garden. One, in particular, of which I have become rather fond is Polar Star from Tantau, which was "Rose of the Year" in Britain in 1985. Its scented flowers are shapely, of exhibition form, and as near pure white as is possible, with just a hint of cream at the base of each petal. Its foliage is dark green and healthy. About 90cm (3ft) tall, it will become a little scrawny if allowed to grow too big without any pruning.

Pascali, introduced by Louis Lens of Belgium, is another outstanding creamy white rose. The shapely, high-centred flowers are borne on very strong stems amid dark green foliage. Again about 90cm (3ft) tall, it is good in groups or for bedding.

I now move to the bright orange shades. The first has superb HT-style blooms but, at 1.2m (4ft), it is almost tall enough to be termed a Shrub rose (Grandiflora in the USA). Its name is Alexander, from Harkness. Bright vermilion is probably the best description of its flowers, which are slightly fragrant and borne singly or in small clusters on very long stems. The foliage is abundant and mid- to dark green.

'Just Joey' was introduced by Cants in the same year as Alexander, but its orange colour is quite different, being coppery yellow to golden amber. The shapely, fragrant flowers are carried on a rather angular plant that grows to about 60cm (2ft) high. It is fairly thorny and its foliage is dark olive-green in colour.

Deep copper blended with yellow is the colour of a rose called Remember Me, introduced by Cockers. Its high-pointed buds open to cupped, fully double flowers, carried in quantity above dark green foliage. It is an ideal rose for bedding and provides excellent cut flowers.

It is difficult to know where to start with red HTs. One of the best of all is also from the Cocker nursery, an outstanding rose named Alec's Red. It is very, very fragrant, globular in shape, strong-necked, and dark velvety red in colour. Its stems are thorny and its foliage dark green.

Red roses should always have a fragrance, in my opinion, and Summer Fragrance from Tantau is one that certainly does. It has high-centred, deep red blooms, borne very freely among dark green foliage.

My third choice for a red is Royal William, raised by Kordes and "Rose of the Year" in Britain in 1987. This beautifully formed HT is fragrant, deep velvety red in colour, and held erect on strong, thorny stems with plenty of purplish green leaves. Allowed to grow as a free-standing shrub, it will reach 90–120cm (3–4ft).

Coming to the pink shades, again it is difficult to choose, but one that must be included is 'Silver Jubilee', named by Cockers in 1978 to commemorate Queen Elizabeth's 25 years on the throne. Its flowers are shapely, very fragrant, and freely produced. They are silvery pink to apricot and honey in colour and appear in

'Just Joey'
Rose breeders are always seeking quality orange-coloured roses of all types, but when one is a Hybrid Tea, it is considered a bonus. Although, as I have intimated elsewhere, these colours are not always to my taste, the sheer good looks of 'Just Joey' make it an exception and I have become quite fond of it.

exceptionally large numbers all summer through. Its foliage is glossy, mid-green, and plentiful. 'Silver Jubilee' is best grown in groups or as a bedding rose.

Savoy Hotel, bred by Harkness, is without doubt one of the best pink roses raised during the last two decades or so. Extremely free flowering, it has large, full, perfumed blooms of mid- to soft pink. It makes a good free-standing shrub, to about 90cm (3ft), and has plenty of dark green foliage.

Quite a few HTs over the years have been multicoloured or bicoloured, and one that stands out in my mind from early in my career is Piccadilly, introduced by McGredy in 1960. Thorny and upright in growth, it is still popular in Britain today. Its flowers are a mixture of very bright yellow and red, and they are fragrant.

One of the most popular HTs over the last 25 years or so has been Double Delight. Fragrant and free flowering, it has fully double, high-centred blooms, creamy yellow in colour, with distinct pinkish red paint marks on the edges of the petals. The maximum height of this shrub is about 90cm (3ft). It was introduced by the Armstrong nursery in the USA, and its awards are innumerable.

'Silver Jubilee' (*left*) Introduced in the UK by Cocker of Aberdeen in 1978 to mark 25 years of the reign of Queen Elizabeth II, 'Silver Jubilee' has become a firm favourite. Not without cause either, for over the years it has proved an excellent rose.

Double Delight (*below*) Bicoloured and multicoloured roses come second only to orange roses in popularity today, but they do not suit all tastes. Double Delight, however, seems to appeal to almost everyone, perhaps because it is just a little less garish and not so loud as most of the others.

The Floribundas

Floribundas were, in a way, the natural progression of the Hybrid Teas, the inevitable result of the curiosity of rose breeders who mixed their genes with cultivars of a cluster-flowered nature derived from *R. multiflora*. The first results of these experiments came along at the turn of the 20th century, in the form of a small group called Polypompons. These were followed in the 1920s by a group of compact, multiflowered roses that became known by the name Dwarf Polyanthas; these in turn, were hybridized with Hybrid Teas of the day, thus laying the foundations for what were at first known as Hybrid Polyanthas, to be renamed Floribundas in the early 1950s.

Lilli Marlene (*right*)
This lovely, dark red rose is seen here dominant among a wide variety of perennials, including a bronzy leaved canna, montbretia (*Crocosmia*), and *Sidalcea* 'Croftway Red'. In the background, closer to the hedge, the other red rose in the scene is the single, continuous-flowering, Modern Climber Altissimo.

Sexy Rexy (*below*)
A particular feature of this amusingly named rose is the near perfect layering of its many petals. Other features of significance are its tidy, bushy disposition and its free-flowering nature.

FLORIBUNDAS FOR THE GARDEN

Like Hybrid Teas, Floribundas are tidy, upright plants, seldom taller than 90cm (3ft). All carry their flowers in large clusters (hence they are also called Cluster-flowered roses), and these appear from summer into autumn. Ideal for bedding, Floribundas also make good companions for other shrubs and herbaceous perennials. Many can be used for hedging, and the shorter ones especially are excellent pot plants. The best advice I can give on pruning is to use common sense: if in beds, keep their height even; if among other shrubs, prune less hard and adjust their size to their surroundings.

I have chosen three sizes of Floribundas: short – below 45cm (1½ft); medium – 45–90cm (1½–3ft); and tall – 90cm (3ft) and over. Those under 45cm (1½ft) I prefer to call Compact roses (see pp.210–213); anything taller than 1.2m (4ft) is a Shrub rose (see pp.132–143).

The shorter Floribundas

A beautiful, short-growing rose I have enjoyed for several years is the delicate soft pink 'English Miss', introduced by Cants of the UK. It has large clusters of fully double, fragrant flowers and attractive dark green foliage, and it makes a superb bedding rose.

Another lovely, fully double rose of soft to salmon-pink is Sexy Rexy from

'Lilac Charm'
This is a delightful, single rose from the 1960s, the heyday of the Floribundas. Short and bushy, it mixes well with herbaceous plants of all types, especially those of pastel colours. I consider this to be the most charismatic of all the unusually coloured Floribundas raised by Edward LeGrice, the "Floribunda King" of the 1950s and 1960s.

one of the world's most famous breeders, Sam McGredy, once of Ireland now New Zealand. Always in flower, this cultivar is fragrant, tidy in growth with light green foliage, and superb for bedding.

Bred by Kordes of Germany, Lilli Marlene has very dark red blooms, each one displaying a lovely central boss of golden yellow stamens. The flowers present themselves in large clusters, and retain their colour well. In good soil this rose might get a fraction taller than its normal 45cm (1½ft).

I consider 'Lilac Charm' one of the most beautiful roses ever raised by the late Edward LeGrice. I love this rose: its fragrant, single flowers are a soft pastel mauve, each with a wonderful array of dark honey-coloured stamens.

Earlier I put forward the view that the defining date for Old roses should be moved forward from 1867 to 1940, and this book reflects this principle. However, by virtue of their behaviour and garden-worthiness, a few roses are completely timeless, and two of these I must mention here: 'Grüss an Aachen' and its sport 'Pink Grüss an Aachen'. 'Grüss an Aachen' is a superb rose, introduced in 1909, and one of the best cluster-flowered roses ever raised. Its colour is soft flesh-pink, changing to cream in maturity, and it is fragrant and very free flowering; it is also tidy in habit, and perfect for both bedding and group planting, 'Pink Grüss an Aachen' is a much deeper pink but in all other respects exactly the same, and just as charming. I confess to being one of a number of nurserymen who, until recently, have distributed the pink form erroneously as 'Irène Watts', a mistake I regret but have now rectified.

Medium-height Floribundas

Of the medium Floribundas – those 45–90cm (1½–3ft) tall – I start with probably the most famous, the pure white Iceberg or Schneewittchen. Millions have been planted since its introduction by Kordes in 1958. Its many flowers are carried in sizeable clusters, on relatively thornless stems among light green foliage. Excellent for both bedding and hedging, this is a timeless classic and will go on for ever.

The very fragrant Margaret Merrill, raised in the UK by Harkness, also has white flowers, but these have a soft pink tinge. A superb, multipurpose cultivar, it is rather more upright than Iceberg, with darker foliage.

One of the finest yellow roses ever raised has three names – 'Korresia', 'Friesia', and 'Sunsprite' – and was also raised by Kordes. Its fragrant flowers are almost fully double and are borne continuously through the summer against a background of healthy, dark green foliage. It is excellent for bedding and for grouping among brightly coloured perennials.

Of slightly deeper orange-yellow is the fragrant, free-flowering Amber Queen, a bushy rose that is good as a companion plant among herbaceous perennials, or for bedding. This is yet another excellent cultivar from Harkness.

There is a wide choice of pink Floribundas in this height range. My favourite is 'Pink Parfait', from Herbert Swim of the USA. Made up of many different shades of

Margaret Merrill
Seen here performing one of its most useful roles, providing a mass display, this softly spoken rose is of very tidy disposition, extremely free flowering, and superbly fragrant. Even though it is modern, I could never be without it in my garden, if only for cutting and taking into the house.

'Norwich Castle' (*above*)
This is a rose from the 1970s, but it is still one of the most popular roses grown by my nursery. The keep of the Norman castle and the tall spire of the 11th-century cathedral dominate the skyline of the city of Norwich, capital of my native Norfolk. Over the years I have named roses for both of these historic buildings.

Beautiful Britain
(*right*) A tall Floribunda rose, producing many tomato-red flowers, Beautiful Britain makes a useful bedding rose for those who like strong colours. It was "Rose of the Year" in Britain in 1983, indicating that, for a rose to win prizes, the brighter it is the better – an interesting reflection on modern tastes!

pink, it has a visible touch of yellow deep down in its fully open flowers. A special feature is its furled, high-centred buds.

The background colour of Amanda, introduced by Bees, is yellow but with highlights of orange and red. It keeps on flowering well into autumn, and although it may sometimes get a little taller than 90cm (3ft), it can be contained with judicious pruning. Its foliage is mid-green and semi-glossy.

The taller Floribundas

I start the taller Floribundas – those 90cm (3ft) high and above – with one of my own, 'Norwich Castle'. Its colour is unfading golden honey with underlying coppery tones. The blooms are fragrant and shapely and sit among dark green foliage. Growing to 1.1m (3½ft) tall, it is superb as a hedge, and also looks excellent planted in groups in mixed borders.

Rather taller than 'Norwich Castle' is the fully double, yellow 'Chinatown', raised by Poulsen in Denmark. Its flowers are borne in large clusters and are touched with orange on the outer edges. Upright in growth, it has plenty of foliage, which is rich lime-green in colour. It is excellent for hedging within the garden.

For hedging, of course, I cannot exclude the famous and now ubiquitous Queen Elizabeth, introduced by Lammerts of the USA in 1954. Its almost scentless, silvery pink flowers are produced on long stems, with substantial greyish green foliage. Although now rather dated, this unusually tall cultivar is still one of the best roses ever introduced. Like all roses of this stature and florescence it is listed as a Grandiflora in the USA, a classification not used in Britain.

One of the tallest red Floribundas is Beautiful Britain, from Dickson, which was "Rose of the Year" in the UK in 1983. Its bright tomato-red flowers are borne in large clusters among generous quantities of dark green leaves.

Crazy for You, a Floribunda from Weeks in the USA (where it is known as The Fourth of July), is one of the most colourful roses I have ever seen, a mixture of yellow, orange, and red, as though splashed from an artist's palette. Anyone who likes bright colours should try this one: it is almost dazzling.

Lastly, Escapade from Harkness is a tall, magenta-to-lilac rose with masses of fragrant, semi-double flowers on stems profuse in mid-green foliage. Excellent for hedging and group planting, it mixes well with quieter colours in shrubberies.

The Modern Shrub Roses

The first roses that could be reasonably termed Shrub roses were developed in the early part of the 20th century. They were the Hybrid Musks raised by the Rev. Pemberton and were well ahead of their time (see pp.106–111). It was not until after the Second World War that Modern Shrub roses emerged as a distinct group, with breeders building on Pemberton's work by introducing genes from many different types of rose. While some are hybrids of a range of different species, by and large, Modern Shrub roses are no more than extra exuberant Hybrid Teas and Floribundas. The only consistent factor of recognition is stature; my yardstick is a rose that grows taller than a Hybrid Tea or Floribunda (although there is the occasional exception even to this), but not so tall that it needs supporting in order to remain upright.

MODERN SHRUB ROSES FOR THE GARDEN

As well as having many diverse characteristics, Shrub roses encompass the whole spectrum of colour and are excellent mixers, making themselves at home in situations from wild gardens to the more formal, and from hedging to specimen planting. Some bear hips, others have attractive autumn foliage. In addition, many of the taller varieties can be adapted for use as shorter-growing climbers. Pruning Modern Shrub roses should essentially be an adjustment of the shrub to the space it occupies. This is best done after flowering for cultivars that bloom only once in the season, and in early spring for those that flower repeatedly or continuously.

Following are 35 or so of my favourites, which include, inevitably, some of my own roses and some bred by my daughter. They are grouped by flower form: single, semi-double, and fully double. The Canadian Explorer roses are grouped separately.

Modern Shrub roses with single or almost single flowers

It is not only the Species roses that have single or near single flowers. There are also a number of beautiful single-flowered Modern Shrub roses of all sizes, varying in habit from wide and spreading to upright and bushy. I reserve a special place in my affection for these, for they have a simplicity and sincerity not always apparent in the more complex double cultivars.

I love very much the fragrant, soft golden yellow 'Golden Wings', which blooms all summer. Although it may be possible to increase the number of later flowers by regular deadheading, refraining from doing so will allow a crop of large, round, orange-yellow hips from early autumn onwards.

A much taller, soft creamy yellow, near single Shrub rose is the superb 'Frühlingsgold'. Sadly, its hips are of no great ornamental value; but its fragrance, hardiness, and accommodating nature will always put it high on my list of yellow favourites. Although having only one flush of flowers each year, these come along hard on the heels of spring. Attaining a height of at least 2.5m (8ft), 'Frühlingsgold' can be kept shorter by annual pruning after flowering.

'Frühlingsmorgen' has just five large petals forming each of its beautiful flowers, which are enhanced by a lovely central array of golden stamens. Each petal is soft yellow at the base with a pink overlay, which deepens towards the edges. As a plant, it will grow to 2.5m (8ft) but, like its sister 'Frühlingsgold', it can be contained by pruning after flowering. It is scented and comes into bloom very early in the year, usually towards the end of spring.

Another yellow single, flowering even earlier than the previous two, is 'Canary Bird'. It is always a delight to see the first blooms of this variety coming out in mid-spring; and, if placed in a sunny position in good fertile soil, it will continue to produce a few flowers throughout the summer and into autumn. As well as making a superb Shrub rose of arching habit, with purple-coloured, thorny stems and dense, fern-like foliage, 'Canary Bird' is also good if grown as a gracefully drooping standard rose ("tree rose" in the USA).

'Golden Wings'
To my mind, roses with single or near single flowers have a special appeal and the very beautiful 'Golden Wings' is no exception. In addition, its generosity of blooms and well-apportioned foliage make it one of the best yellows of its kind. Here it is emerging from a blanket of catmint (*Nepeta*).

'Canary Bird'
'Canary Bird' is one of the earliest roses to come into flower each year. A well-grown shrub of this lovely, single rose is truly delightful. Its flowers, seen here at about twice their normal size, have a delicate perfume and are produced on a nicely proportioned plant amid fern-like foliage.

Several other excellent Shrub roses flower at roughly the same time as 'Canary Bird' and are, in their way, equally charismatic. 'Cantabrigiensis', the Cambridge rose, is paler and grows taller than most of the other single yellows, up to 3m (10ft). 'Golden Chersonese' is an upright, medium-sized grower with many thorns and buttercup-yellow flowers. 'Hidcote Gold' is upright, with flowers of the same colour and shape as those of 'Canary Bird'; and 'Helen Knight' produces small, saucer-shaped flowers of clear deep yellow in great abundance in late spring. Most of these roses are especially useful in natural settings, when the richness of their colouring will stand out among dark-coloured foliage.

Another classic single rose is the tall 'Dortmund'. Its flowers are red with creamy white centres and produced in numerous trusses on a healthy plant, well endowed with foliage. Wherever a tall rose is needed to perform well in difficult soil or less than congenial surroundings, then 'Dortmund' is the one to choose. I have seen it growing and enjoying life all over the world.

In the summer of 2000 I was in Oregon, USA, browsing through the seedling beds at Heirloom Roses, when one of the owners, John Clements, mentioned there was a Shrub rose on the other side of the plot that I might like to see. After admiring the rose for a few minutes, John asked if I would like it named after me. Who could refuse? It has very bright red, single blooms with rich golden yellow stamens and a modest perfume. It flowers all summer, and is bushy but not excessively tall, at about 1.2m (4ft), with lots of healthy, dark green foliage.

Another very bright red single is a Gallica hybrid from Kordes known as Scarlet Fire, more often listed as 'Scharlachglut'; the name itself indicates the brightness of its large, single flowers, which are enhanced by a centrepiece of golden yellow stamens. This shrub can be kept within reasonable bounds by regular pruning, but I find it best left to its own devices, to grow tall or scramble up into trees or hedges.

'James Mason' is a lovely fragrant Gallica hybrid that looks single but is actually made up of about two layers of dark velvety red petals, with golden anthers. The plant

'Dortmund'
This rose is a true citizen of the world – no matter which garden I visit in whatever country, I find 'Dortmund' not only growing but thriving. It flowers throughout the summer, and is happy to be used as either a shrub or a small climber.

'Nevada' (above)
A tall, dense shrub, this rose probably has *R. moyesii* in its ancestry. It was raised by Pedro Dot in Spain in 1927. Its uses in the garden are numerous but it is especially good as a specimen shrub, on its own in a lawn. 'Marguerite Hilling', its sport of 1959, does all the same things as its parent but its flowers are soft pink in colour.

Peter Beales (*right*)
This rose is excellent when grown in pots; it also does well mixed with plants of other genera, or even as a short-growing hedge. I cannot resist relating an e-mail received out of the blue recently from a lady I have never met: "When I sniffed your rose, it tickled my nose!"

reaches a height, in maturity, of about 1.5m (5ft). I was asked to name this rose for the British actor James Mason by his wife Clarissa, and he was able to see its first flowers just before his death in 1984.

A very lovely rose of an undemanding nature is 'Hazel Le Rougetel', a cross between *R. rugosa* and *R. nitida*, named after its breeder. It was originally called 'Corylus'. Its mid-pink, single flowers repeat throughout summer and produce oval, red hips from early autumn onwards. This interesting rose has richly coloured autumn foliage and is good for grouping and for ground cover. Unlikely ever to get above 90cm (3ft) tall, it will spread equally as wide.

Modern Shrub roses with semi-double flowers

Of the semi-doubles, one of the best known is 'Nevada', a vigorous rose with plenty of foliage, which grows up to 2.5m (8ft) in good soil. The flowers are large, sometimes 13cm (5in) or more across, and when fully open have about two layers of petals that are ivory-white in colour. Along with its pink sport 'Marguerite Hilling', this rose is a good mixer in shrubberies and woodland gardens; the two also complement each other as specimen plants in lawns and open spaces. Both are in full flower in early summer and may produce an odd flower or two later on.

The lovely flowers of Jacqueline du Pré, from Harkness, are of similar colouring and shape to those of 'Nevada', but have very conspicuous, amber-coloured stamens. As a bush, this will seldom get taller than 1.2m (4ft) and its foliage is soft lime-green.

Westerland is a bright orange, semi-double Shrub rose from Kordes. It is very healthy and robust and bears many flowers in sizeable clusters on strong stems. It is also fragrant. Westerland produced a lovely golden yellow sport called 'Autumn Sunset', which was discovered by Mike Lowe of Nashua, New Hampshire, in the USA. This has since become a popular shrub in its own right. Of medium size like its parent, it grows to no more than 1.2m (4ft).

Bonica '82, bred by Meilland in France, is a rose that tends to be difficult to place: is it a Shrub, a Floribunda, or a Procumbent (ground-cover) plant? I like it best as a Shrub, hence its inclusion here. It is, without doubt, one of the best roses ever raised,

Jacqueline du Pré
This lovely, semi-double rose flowers all summer without taking even a short rest. Here it is enjoying life among catmint (*Nepeta*), with the Procumbent rose 'The Fairy' in the foreground and what is probably the Floribunda 'Pink Grüss an Aachen' just behind.

always in bloom from early summer through to late autumn. Its colour is bright, almost fluorescent pink, and it produces its scented flowers in large clusters. It has many uses, from bedding to hedging or mixing in borders. This is a cultivar of which the Meilland nursery can be very proud.

A hybrid of *R. rubiginosa*, Autumn Fire or 'Herbstfeuer', from Kordes, is a superb semi-double red. This rose flowers freely in early and midsummer, and occasionally blooms again in autumn; its display of elongated-oval red hips is outstanding. I have become very fond of this interesting hybrid Sweet Briar, which will grow to about 1.5m (5ft) without too much effort.

'Sadler's Wells' was introduced by me for the ballet company of that name. It is a very good rose and certainly one of the best cultivars I have ever raised. Its semi-double flowers are silvery pink laced with cherry-red, especially around the edges, these colours intensifying in autumn. The blooms are impervious to inclement weather and last extremely well when cut and placed in water. An upright shrub, with plenty of lush, large foliage, dark green in colour, 'Sadler's Wells' is ideal for hedging and for group planting.

Large, semi-double, and golden yellow best describes the flowers of 'Goldbusch', a tall Shrub rose from Kordes. It is related to the Sweet Briars but I can barely detect the scent of apple in its foliage. Its flowers, however, are very fragrant, with a hint of apple scent coming through. They are freely produced all through summer on a vigorous but relaxed shrub at least 2.5m (8ft) tall. This rose also makes a good, continuous-flowering, short climber.

A relatively new small Shrub rose called Rhapsody in Blue is one of the bluest roses ever introduced. Raised by the British amateur breeder Frank Cowlishaw, it was the "Rose of the Year" in Britain in 2003. Its subtly fragrant, semi-double, purplish mauve flowers are produced in sizeable clusters on an upright shrub, among an abundance of healthy, dark green foliage.

Jacqueline du Pré
Proving that even hybrid roses can be ornamental in winter, these hips stay on the plant right through until they are pruned off in late winter. This is one of the roses that retains its calyces until the fruit falls; in some other hip-bearing roses the calyces drop off long before the hips ripen.

Double-flowered Modern Shrub roses

Perhaps 'Agnes' should have been included among the Rugosas since it has one Rugosa parent, the other being *R. foetida* 'Persiana'. Although introduced in 1922, I always think of it as a Modern Shrub rose, mainly because its soft primrose-yellow colour is unique among the Rugosas. Its flowers spread themselves rather spasmodically through the summer, beginning with a big burst early on. They are fully double and have the texture of crumpled crêpe paper; they are also very fragrant. As a shrub 'Agnes' is rather thorny, with darkish green, wrinkled leaves.

In 1981, I introduced a very highly scented rose named 'Anna Pavlova' (featured in the Introduction, see p.12). I can never quite decide whether it is a Hybrid Tea or a Shrub but, since it can get quite tall, I include it here. Although it is one of the most beautiful of roses, it is not the most reliable and needs lots of loving care to give of its best. Its delicate, soft pink flowers open fully double and shapely and its perfume is stronger than that of any other rose I know. Its foliage is dark green and lush.

A very tall Shrub rose of which I am rather fond is 'Cerise Bouquet', a hybrid from *R. multibracteata*, raised by Kordes. Its colour is in its name. The flowers are fully double and produced in small clusters on long stems. As a plant it is quite capable of growing 4m (12ft) tall and equally wide. Its leaves are small and numerous and its stiff stems have many sharp thorns. As well as being useful as a specimen shrub, when it will tolerate some dappled shade, it will also grow up into trees as a scrambler.

The Macmillan nurses in Britain are wonderful people who care for the terminally ill and, in 1997, HRH Prince Charles suggested to me that they should have a rose named for them; accordingly, the following year we introduced Macmillan Nurse, bred by my daughter Amanda. A very double, many petalled rose, opening flat, its colour is almost pure white with a soft peachy tinge down in among the petals. The strong-stemmed blooms are subtly fragrant, and are borne in large clusters throughout the summer. As a plant, it is compact and short, to a maximum of 90cm (3ft), and it has healthy foliage that is dark, glossy green in colour.

In 1999 we were asked by my then publisher, Christopher MacLehose, if we would name a rose after the American poet Raymond Carver. Carver loved yellow but we did not

Bonica '82 (*right*)
A most prolific rose, Bonica '82 goes on flowering continuously from the beginning of summer through until the first frosts of winter. It is wide growing and scented and I have no doubts about it being one of the best general-purpose Shrub roses ever raised. It is shown here with a clump of *Knautia macedonica* at its feet.

'Anna Pavlova' (*below*)
The delicate soft pink blooms of 'Anna Pavlova' are more fragrant than those of any other rose I know. In cooler climates it is a little sparing with its flowers, but is rather more generous I understand in warmer regions. Each flower is held upright on a strong stem.

Louise Clements
I first met this brightly coloured Shrub rose when visiting John and Louise Clements at their nurseries in Oregon, USA. It is free flowering, and densely bushy in growth. Those who like orange roses will enjoy having this one in their garden, especially since it is also very strongly fragrant.

have a seedling of that colour at that time, so Colin Horner, a well-known amateur breeder, obliged us with a superb, fully double, coppery yellow Shrub rose to name for him. 'Raymond Carver' grows to 1.2m (4ft) and produces its fragrant flowers on long stems with dark coppery green leaves. It is good for hedging and group planting.

When visiting Heirloom Roses in the year 2000 I came upon a beautiful orange-coloured Shrub rose called Louise Clements, named for one of the owners of the nursery. An outstanding rose, it is very fragrant and fully double, opening flat and cushion-like. Free flowering, and with bronze-green, slightly glossy foliage, it makes a good hedge and is superb when grouped among brightly coloured herbaceous plants.

In the early 1990s a terrorist bomb exploded in Bishopsgate in the City of London, destroying buildings all around, among them the church of St Ethelburga, one of the oldest and smallest in the capital. Happily, the church was rebuilt and, in 2003, I was asked to name a rose to commemorate its re-opening as "a place of reconciliation and peace". I chose to give the name to a fully double, cup-shaped, soft pink rose bred by Amanda. A vigorous shrub, to about 1.2m (4ft) high, with dark green, healthy foliage, it flowers continuously and is very highly scented; indeed, St Ethelburga is worth growing in any garden for its perfume alone.

As a present to my mother on her 85th birthday, I named a rose of my own breeding for her, 'Evelyn May'. It is an upright shrub, with large, dark green leaves on very thorny stems, and bears double, bright salmon-orange flowers, with a lovely perfume, all summer through.

have a seedling of that colour at that time, so Colin Horner, a well-known amateur breeder, obliged us with a superb, fully double, coppery yellow Shrub rose to name for him. 'Raymond Carver' grows to 1.2m (4ft) and produces its fragrant flowers on long stems with dark coppery green leaves. It is good for hedging and group planting.

When visiting Heirloom Roses in the year 2000 I came upon a beautiful orange-coloured Shrub rose called Louise Clements, named for one of the owners of the nursery. An outstanding rose, it is very fragrant and fully double, opening flat and cushion-like. Free flowering, and with bronze-green, slightly glossy foliage, it makes a good hedge and is superb when grouped among brightly coloured herbaceous plants.

In the early 1990s a terrorist bomb exploded in Bishopsgate in the City of London, destroying buildings all around, among them the church of St Ethelburga, one of the oldest and smallest in the capital. Happily, the church was rebuilt and, in 2003, I was asked to name a rose to commemorate its re-opening as "a place of reconciliation and peace". I chose to give the name to a fully double, cup-shaped, soft pink rose bred by Amanda. A vigorous shrub, to about 1.2m (4ft) high, with dark green, healthy foliage, it flowers continuously and is very highly scented; indeed, St Ethelburga is worth growing in any garden for its perfume alone.

As a present to my mother on her 85th birthday, I named a rose of my own breeding for her, 'Evelyn May'. It is an upright shrub, with large, dark green leaves on very thorny stems, and bears double, bright salmon-orange flowers, with a lovely perfume, all summer through.

Finally, I have chosen a Shrub rose from 2004, a beautiful, creamy white called Countess of Wessex. It has large, superbly fragrant flowers, opening from pointed buds to become almost fully double, which are borne in clusters on a sturdy, upright shrub that grows to about 1.2m (4ft) tall. It is constantly in bloom throughout the summer and is very healthy. Its foliage is light green and durable. It is another rose bred by Amanda, and I believe it will go far.

The Explorer Shrub roses

Over the last three decades or so a new group of roses known as the Explorer series has come about in Canada, conceived from the need for winter-hardy roses for the colder parts of the world. To achieve this a number of hardy Species roses were used as breeding stock and crossed with some of the hardiest of modern hybrids. This work, carried out by the Horticultural Research and Development Centre, Saint-Jean-Sur-Richelieu, in Québec, has made good progress and around 30 hardy, garden-worthy roses have now been introduced. I have tried and grown several of these and, as a result, will certainly grow more in future. I have selected six of those that I know to be excellent to discuss here.

'Jens Munk' is a superb Shrub rose, good for hedging or group planting. It bears lilac to mauve-pink, semi-double to double flowers among plentiful, wrinkled foliage. Fragrant and very free flowering, it deserves to be much better known.

'John Cabot', like 'Jens Munk', is fully hardy. Its semi-double flowers are sizeable and numerously produced in early summer, rather spasmodically later on. It is slightly fragrant and of a reddish colour, with lovely golden stamens. It is very tall and could well make an excellent climber. The foliage is rugged grey-green.

'Henry Kelsey' is a wonderful bright red, semi-double, with golden stamens. I am reluctant to express a preference for any of these roses, but this is certainly a good one. It grows to 1.5m (5ft) for me, and I have used it successfully as a hedge. Like others of its type, it will also make a small wall plant.

'William Baffin' is a reddish pink, semi-double rose with much to commend it. It is tall, reaching almost 2.5m (8ft), and has plenty of grey-green foliage. It has little or no scent, but makes up for this with its freedom of flower. It is very resistant to black spot and powdery mildew. Like the rest of its group, it is completely hardy, and makes a fine specimen plant in lawns and open spaces.

'George Vancouver' is a short-growing Shrub rose worthy of a place in any garden. Its large, semi-double flowers are very bright red in colour, ageing to softer red, and are borne in large clusters on strong stems. The foliage is dark green.

'Martin Frobisher' was the first ever Explorer rose, introduced in 1968. It is closely related to the Rugosas but does not show much affinity with that group. Upright in growth, it has dark brownish stems with few thorns. Its fully double, medium-sized flowers are almost blush-pink, with a good scent. This is a first-class rose, but a little short of foliage to be truly a classic.

'Henry Kelsey'
This is one of the brightest of the Explorers, an excellent group of hardy roses from Canada. Like most of the others in the series, this one makes a superb shrub but will also double as an accommodating, continuous-flowering climber. Its slight scent adds to its charm.

The New English Roses

Gertrude Jekyll (*right*)
Raised in 1986, this is a
very free-flowering,
strongly fragrant Shrub
rose. I consider it to be
one of the best of the
deeper pink Austin roses.

Constance Spry
(*below*) This tall, once-
flowering rose is highly
scented, some say of
myrrh. It also makes a
good climber. In its way, it
is the first of a race, being
the forerunner of David
Austin's many roses.

A new and fascinating group of roses has emerged over the last 30 or so years. With one or two exceptions, the so-called New English roses are all the lifetime's work of one man, David Austin. The first was the vigorous, highly scented, bright pink Constance Spry, introduced in 1960, followed in 1967 by Chianti, which is a very deep purple. Both flowered only in summer, so remontancy became a high priority in Austin's breeding programme. Compared to other Modern roses, almost all of his roses are composed of many petals, which open cup shaped or flat to form large, cushion-like, fragrant flowers. In other words, they follow the pattern of old European garden roses, except they are in modern colours and are fully remontant.

While I do not grow them all personally, many are extremely beautiful and make very worthwhile garden plants. Most are easy to grow and have the bearing and demeanour to fit comfortably among assorted garden plants. Regrettably, some of the

Graham Thomas
(*above*) Widely regarded as the best ever Austin rose, this lovely yellow rose was named for the late Graham Stuart Thomas, arguably the most influential rosarian of the 20th century. It can be grown as either a dense shrub or a small climber. It cohabits well with most other plants and is seen here in a mixed border associating superbly with *Campanula lactiflora* 'Prichard's Variety'.

Jayne Austin (*right*) Here seen with *Clematis* 'Lasurstern' and biennial clary (*Salvia sclarea*), this old-fashioned style, modern-coloured, medium-growing rose continues to flower all summer. Its raiser tells us it has a close affinity to the old Noisettes.

earlier introductions are rather prone to disease, but the more recent cultivars are much healthier. As I have said elsewhere, I dislike the term "New English roses" since, after all, several other Englishmen, including myself, introduce new varieties. Wherever I go in the world people refer to them as "Austin roses", and in my opinion, this is a much more appropriate name.

NEW ENGLISH ROSES FOR THE GARDEN

From the 100 or so cultivars introduced to date, I have selected nine that I like best to feature here, in alphabetical order. In hotter climates, such as those of California and the Mediterranean, many grow to double the sizes given.

Abraham Darby has a rich fruity fragrance and carries a good crop of large, fully double, cupped, apricot and yellow blooms throughout summer. A vigorous shrub, with dark green foliage, it will grow to 1.5m (5ft), in slightly arching fashion.

Geoff Hamilton is an exceptional commemorative rose for a famous British gardener who died far too young. It is strong growing and very healthy, and produces flowers all summer. Cupped in shape, its pleasantly scented blooms are soft pink in colour with paler edges to the petals. As a plant it will grow to at least 1.5m (5ft) tall, and has plenty of good, darkish green foliage.

Another pink but of a deeper shade is the lovely, fully double Gertrude Jekyll. This cultivar is always in flower and is richly scented. It has ample grey-green foliage and grows reasonably compactly to 1.2m (4ft). It makes a good border plant and is equally good as a hedge.

Named after the childhood home of the late Queen Mother and the setting for Shakespeare's *Macbeth*, Glamis Castle is a superb white rose. It is a quintessential Austin cultivar, cupped to begin with, flat and cushion-like when fully open. It is fragrant and in flower all summer. Its foliage is mid-green and its height a manageable 90cm (3ft).

Most people will agree that Graham Thomas is David Austin's best ever rose, named for one of the world's most famous horticultural authors. Certainly, it is one of the most popular. Its unfading golden yellow, fully double, cupped flowers are borne all through summer.

William Shakespeare
(*above*) The Austin roses cover the whole spectrum of colour and William Shakespeare is one of the darkest reds. It is shapely at most stages of development, but especially so when fully open. The dark green foliage is an excellent foil for the flowers. In the last few years, a superior clone has been developed named William Shakespeare 2000.

Mary Rose (*right*)
This picture illustrates what a free-flowering Shrub rose can do; add fragrance and tidiness of growth and it indicates just how good Mary Rose can be. Since its introduction, this has rightly become one of the most widely grown of the Austin roses.

The foliage is prolific and mid- to bright green. This rose will grow to 1.2m (4ft) in northern Europe, much taller in hotter climates, where it makes a good climber.

The many flowers of Heritage are very double, cupped, and soft silky pink; they are also exceptionally fragrant. In my order of favourites of the Austin roses, this comes second only to Graham Thomas. It is a shrubby plant, which grows to about 1.2m (4ft), with lots of good mid-green leaves.

Jayne Austin is best described as having rosette-shaped flowers, which are large, fully double, scented, and of a soft yellow colour with apricot undertones. It makes a tidy shrub, growing to a height of about 1.1m (3½ft). Its foliage is soft grey-green and it mixes well in borders and shrubberies.

Mary Rose was named back in 1983 to celebrate the lifting of Henry VIII's flagship from the bottom of the sea, after being submerged for 400 years. It is a lovely, mid rose-pink, not quite fully double, with a sweet fragrance, and free flowering. Lots of good foliage completes a robust, shrubby plant, growing to a height of 1.2m (4ft).

Lastly, I come to William Shakespeare, which has fragrant, fully double, shallowly cup-shaped flowers of deep crimson, changing to rich purple with age. In bloom throughout the summer, it will attain a height of 1.1m (3½ft) in good soil. Its dark green foliage complements its flowers, and it makes a superb border plant.

CLIMBING ROSES

The Noisette Roses and Climbing Teas

The first Noisette rose came about in 1802, the result of a cross between the China rose 'Old Blush' and *R. moschata*. This cross, which became very significant and far reaching, was made by John Champneys of Charleston, South Carolina, USA, and was sent to France for introduction by Louis Noisette, who owned a rose nursery there. The rose was named 'Champneys' Pink Cluster', and one of its first seedlings was 'Blush Noisette'. Both went on to become very popular, largely because they flowered continuously, and had tidy, easy-going natures. Other Noisettes were subsequently raised, almost all making their mark as good climbing roses.

The Climbing Teas almost all evolved during the 19th century; some developed as sports of bush forms of Tea roses; others came about through hybridization and so are Climbers in their own right. Like the Noisettes, they enjoyed considerable popularity among the Victorians, especially as greenhouse and conservatory plants. Hardiness is a factor to consider when selecting both Noisettes and Teas. Beautiful though they are, the majority do not enjoy severe winters in northern Europe. In warmer climates, however, they come into their own and are a real pleasure to grow.

Like all climbing roses, Noisettes and Climbing Teas are superb extra-dimensional plants, lending height and width to flat areas of the garden, and perspective to horizons both far and near. Walls and fences, pergolas and archways can all provide support and act as backdrops for them. Because they flower on new wood, they are best pruned in early spring, by removing all unwanted growth and spurring back lateral shoots; also, the stems should be trained as near to the horizontal as possible and twisted as many ways as they will allow without breaking, to encourage the development of new flowering wood each year.

In all, I am familiar with about 30 Noisettes and Climbing Teas and have selected ten to discuss here, chosen mostly for their natural beauty, but also for their capacity to tolerate a wide range of different climates in the open.

NOISETTE ROSES FOR THE GARDEN

One of the original Noisette roses, 'Blush Noisette' is soft pinkish lilac in colour and its small, semi-double flowers are borne in numerous clusters. The plant is almost thornless and is adorned with abundant soft grey-green foliage, which is also soft to touch. In good soil it will attain a height of 2.5m (8ft), even taller on walls.

Iceberg (*previous pages*)
The pure white rose over the arch in this study in white and soft colours is the climbing form of the ubiquitous Floribunda Iceberg. With its relatively few thorns, it is an ideal subject for regularly used archways such as this. The grey foliage in the foreground is that of *Senecio cineraria* 'Silver Dust'.

'Blush Noisette' (*right*)
Free-flowering 'Blush Noisette' has a pleasingly accommodating nature, and will repeat its flowers all through the summer. Here it is clearly enjoying life in the company of the honeysuckle *Lonicera periclymenum* 'Graham Thomas'.

'Alister Stella Gray', also known as 'Golden Rambler', is a completely hardy, vigorous plant that is excellent for arches, trellis, and walls. It will also tolerate some shade. It produces cascading clusters of rather muddled-petalled, soft yellow flowers, with deeper yellow centres; these are reasonably fragrant, and appear continuously throughout summer. The lush, dark green foliage is carried on relatively thornless stems, and the plant will reach 5m (15ft) in height, or even taller if grown into trees.

One of the very best, most beautiful and hardy of the Noisettes is 'Mme Alfred Carrière'. This rose will climb to 5m (15ft), whether into a tree or on a shady, cold wall. Its very fragrant flowers, borne continuously, are initially cupped, opening to loose, double, soft blush to white blooms. Its foliage is lush, slightly glossy, and greyish green and its stems have few thorns. I place this rose high in my top ten of all roses.

A much shorter Noisette, reaching only 2.5m (8ft) in height, is the bright lemon, fully double, continuous-flowering 'Céline Forestier', which has soft, light green foliage, under which some of its many flowers sometimes hide. With so few yellow roses to choose from, it must have been a real hit when first introduced in 1842.

'Crépuscule' is a deep yellow to orange, semi-double rose always in bloom. It is fragrant and carries its flowers in many small clusters. Its petals have a lovely silky

'Alister Stella Gray' (*left*) Repeat-flowering, yellow Climbers such as 'Alister Stella Gray' are few and far between. If they are fragrant so much the better. This picture shows the rose in good shape. It also draws attention to the way the flowers pale to cream, and highlights the sheer quantity of blooms that make up each of its many clusters.

'Mme Alfred Carrière' (*below*) The ability of this lovely Noisette to tolerate hardship, in particular shade, makes it one of the most versatile roses ever introduced. 'Mme Alfred' is seen here doing what she enjoys most – festooning walls and cascading from them. Terracotta containers add extra interest to the scene.

'Aimée Vibert'
A classic Noisette rose from 1828, 'Aimée Vibert' first comes into flower after the summer equinox, demonstrating its close affinity to *R. moschata*. It then goes on producing its tight-knit clusters of flowers on long, drooping branches for the rest of summer and well into autumn.

sheen, which adds considerably to its charm. Its foliage is rich green and plentiful. As a plant, it will grow to 3m (10ft) and, like many Noisettes, its stems have few thorns of consequence. One of its attributes is its density of growth, making it ideal for arbours and the like.

A very old but useful Noisette is the lovely 'Aimée Vibert', which produces small clusters of double, fragrant, pure white flowers at the ends of long, virtually thornless shoots. This rose shows its *R. moschata* heritage by coming into bloom a little later than most others of its kind, but then goes on flowering into autumn. A particularly attractive feature is its profuse light green foliage.

CLIMBING TEAS FOR THE GARDEN

One of the best known Climbing Teas is the classic 'Gloire de Dijon', made famous in Britain as the favourite rose of the Rev. Dean Reynolds Hole, first President of the Royal National Rose Society. Its large, heavily scented, fully double, flat and quartered flowers are a mixture of buff, apricot, peach, and yellow. Following its first main flush, this old cultivar produces a few flowers each autumn. It was introduced in 1853 and, following the example set by Dean Hole, was planted, it would seem, on the walls of almost every Victorian rectory in Britain.

The climbing form of 'Lady Hillingdon' first came onto the scene in 1917. This superb Tea is excellent on a warm wall, where it will grow to 5m (15ft) or more. A very special feature is its almost thornless, purple-coloured wood and luscious plum-coloured foliage. The blooms are rich yellow and described more fully in the earlier chapter on the bush Teas (see p.112).

'Souvenir de Mme Léonie Viennot' is an absolute delight in warm climates and well worth the little extra care it may need in cooler ones. The most lovely example of this rose I have ever seen was at Ninfa in Italy; the blooms on that expansive plant were spectacular and countless. The flower colour is a mixture of primrose and yellow with copper and honey overtones. As a plant, it is healthy and has good foliage.

It is impossible for me to think of Climbing Teas without 'Sombreuil' coming to mind. One of the most beautiful roses ever raised, it has perfect cushion-like blooms that are large, very fragrant, and almost pure white, with hints of soft peachy cream. Its foliage is dark green and its stems a little thornier than most other Teas. It is better on a warm wall than on a trellis but seems to be perfectly hardy here in chilly Norfolk. In my view, 'Sombreuil' is synonymous with the rose distributed as 'Colonial White'.

'Lady Hillingdon'
This sweet-scented, Climbing Tea rose flowers first in early summer and again in early autumn. Its foliage is semi-glossy and plum coloured and its almost thornless stems are also near purple. It is photographed here in the company of the lilac *Syringa x josiflexa* 'Bellicent'.

The Modern Climbing and Pillar Roses

'Aloha'
Although placed here among the Climbers, this superb rose from the USA can also be grown as a sturdy shrub. As well as being very healthy, it has flowers all summer and an intoxicating perfume. I have loved this classic rose ever since it first came to me in the late 1950s.

The Modern Climbers are really no more than exuberant, very large shrub roses, not climbers at all. Rather than sending up true climbing shoots, they produce tall, lax stems that need some form of support if they are to stay upright. These roses are easily trained on obelisks, pillars, and walls but, with a few exceptions, they are less suitable for fixing to arches and pergolas, because their shoots are awkward to manipulate and bend. Most Modern Climbers repeat their flowers, which gives them a considerable advantage over many older, once-flowering varieties and makes them especially useful in smaller gardens. As with the true climbing roses, they are best

pruned in early spring, and their stems bent, twisted, and trained as near to the horizontal as possible to encourage new flowering shoots to develop.

Since the first of the Modern Climbers was raised in the 1950s, at least 100 different cultivars have been introduced throughout the world. I am familiar with about half these and have selected 17, some from each colour, for discussion here.

MODERN CLIMBERS FOR THE GARDEN

One of the best and most sumptuous of the pink Modern Climbers, in fact one of the best of all Climbers, is 'Aloha'. With superb glossy foliage and huge, fully double, high-centred, deep rose-pink flowers, overflowing with fragrance, it is an almost perfect pillar rose. It was raised by Gene Boerner of the USA, and one of its parents is the beautiful 'New Dawn', a continuous-flowering form of 'Dr W. Van Fleet', which has had much influence on the development of the Modern Climbers. 'New Dawn' is discussed under Wichurana Ramblers (see p.182).

Eden Rose '88
This is the English name of a rose that, in other parts of Europe, is known as Pierre de Ronsard. I wish its raiser, Meilland, had never given it a non-French name for I still grow a Hybrid Tea from the 1950s called 'Eden Rose' and this causes much confusion among both staff and customers at my nurseries. Leaving that to one side, Eden Rose '88 is a superb Climber, which provides a succession of large, full blooms all summer long.

Penny Lane, raised by Harkness, is a pink Modern Climber that should be in every garden. Its flowers are reminiscent of Old roses in both shape and fragrance. They start off blush-pink but quickly change to soft peach, with a honey colour deep down in the centre. Always in bloom, it excels as a pillar rose and is also relaxed enough for pergolas and arches. It will grow to 4m (12ft).

Known also as Pierre de Ronsard, Eden Rose '88 is a wonderful cultivar with globular buds that open to large, fully double, cupped flowers. These are creamy white, with pronounced pinkish red markings on the slightly ragged edges of the petals. Raised by Meilland, it is fragrant and always in bloom. For such a full rose it is surprising how impervious it is to wet weather. It will reach a height of 4m (12ft), and its foliage is plentiful, dark green, and leathery in texture.

In the year 2000, to celebrate the 100th birthday of Queen Elizabeth the Queen Mother, we named a rose 'Clarence House', after her London home, at her request.

Raised by my daughter Amanda, it was presented to the Queen Mother at Sandringham Flower Show that year. It produces fully double, creamy white flowers all summer through. A special feature is its strong perfume, described by the Queen Mother herself as citrus. It is vigorous, growing to 4m (12ft), and ideal for trellis, arches, and gazebos. Its foliage is glossy, dark green and provides a lovely foil for the flowers.

'White Cockade' is a shorter, very free-flowering, white cultivar from the Cocker nursery. Its flowers are high centred, cockade shaped, and fully double when open, with a slight scent. Reaching a height of about 2.5m (8ft), with mid-green foliage, it is best as a wall plant or pillar rose.

There are quite a number of good yellow Modern Climbers, one of the most recent of which is Della Balfour, from Harkness. Its colour is on the edge between yellow and orange, with red highlights on the margins of its fully double flowers. Very free blooming and fragrant, this cultivar has lots of glossy foliage and will grow to about 2.5m (8ft) tall.

Another orange rose is Breath of Life, again from Harkness. Rich apricot best describes the colour of its double, fragrant, high-centred blooms, which are borne in large quantities all through the summer. Its leaves are large and mid- to dark green. Growing to about 3m (10ft), this is an excellent pillar rose.

'Maigold', from Kordes, starts to flower earlier than most other climbing roses, probably because of the *R. pimpinellifolia* genes it has inherited. The yellowish burnt-orange flowers are semi-double and carried in smallish clusters, set against a background of healthy, light green, glossy foliage. Another legacy from *R. pimpinellifolia* is its very thorny stems. It will grow to 4m (12ft) even in poor soil.

A beautiful near single rose, 'Meg', sometimes listed as a Climbing Hybrid Tea, was raised by an amateur breeder named Gosset in 1954. Its large flowers are buff-yellow flushed apricot, with pronounced russet-red stamens and a good perfume. Excellent as a pillar rose or even for a wall, it will easily reach 4m (12ft) in height. Its foliage is dense and dark green. This cultivar is a special favourite of mine but requires a little extra mollycoddling to thrive.

'Phyllis Bide' has lots of China rose in its ancestry and, with such lineage, it is not surprising that it blooms continuously through the summer. Its smallish, semi-double, cupped flowers, in a mixture of yellow, cream, and pink, deepening with age, are arranged in large, cascading clusters on slender, pliable, almost thornless stems. Its leaves are light green and, like its flowers, small and numerous. Quite capable of attaining a height of 4m (12ft), it is good trained on most structures, including walls.

Dublin Bay
Red roses are expected to have fragrance and this continuous-flowering, easy-going Modern Climber will not disappoint, although it is by no means intensely perfumed. An ideal pillar rose, a special feature is its lush, darkish green foliage.

An unusually coloured rose, suitable for a variety of uses, 'Bright Ideas' is a new Climber from amateur breeder Colin Horner, which was introduced by my nursery in 2003. Its semi-double, scented flowers are deep cerise-pink, striped and splashed white; they are borne on an upright, bushy plant, reaching a height of 2.5m (8ft), with plenty of dark green foliage.

One of the best Modern Climbers is Dublin Bay from McGredy. Almost constantly in flower, it has fully double, sizeable blooms, which are deep velvety red in colour and slightly fragrant. It is an excellent pillar rose, growing to 2.5m (8ft) high, with lots of darkish green foliage.

Another fine rose always in flower is the almost single, deep crimson to red 'Parkdirektor Riggers', from Kordes. Very vigorous, this cultivar has an abundance of dark green foliage and, even in poor soil, easily grows to 5m (15ft). It is best trained on trellis or pergolas rather than on arches or walls.

'Leverkusen' has semi-double to fully double flowers in soft yellow fading slightly to lemon. These are produced in clusters on a very healthy, densely leaved plant, which grows to a height of 3m (10ft) in good soil. Yet another rose from the Kordes stable, it does especially well trained on trellis or on walls.

Handel (*left*)
The lovely white clematis 'Gillian Blades' here keeps company with Handel, a rose that, I have to be frank, is just a little too pretty pretty for me. This is perhaps rather unkind since, overall, it is a healthy rose, and performs well in most situations.

'Leverkusen' (*below*)
A Modern Climber with lots of personality, 'Leverkusen' is very free flowering all through summer, and it is blessed with an abundance of healthy, bright green foliage. Raised in Germany in 1954, it has proved to be one of the most reliable yellow Climbers ever, and deserves to be much better known.

'Karlsruhe' (*above*)
This is one of the many excellent roses raised in Germany in the early 1950s. Although I realize that this is perhaps a difficult colour to place in the garden, I do not understand why such a good, healthy, free-flowering rose as 'Karlsruhe' is not more widely grown, even in its country of origin.

'Golden Showers' (*right*)
Shown here in all its glory, 'Golden Showers' lives up to its name and demonstrates just what a good climbing rose it can be, providing colour and an added dimension to a red brick wall.

Handel is an excellent Climber raised by McGredy. This rose is an interesting colour, a combination of silvery white overlaid with deep rose-pink, with even deeper markings on the edges of the petals. The flowers are fully double, shapely, and fragrant, and the foliage glossy and dark green; as a plant, its growth is dense and upright, and it will attain a height of at least 4m (12ft).

The very double, old-fashioned style flowers of 'Karlsruhe' are produced continuously throughout the summer, on a vigorous plant that will reach a height of 2.5m (8ft) and spread just as wide. I can never understand why this rose has not been more widely grown; perhaps it is because its colour is shocking bright pink. Raised by Kordes, it is as healthy as any rose I know and it is adorned with plenty of glossy, mid- to dark green foliage.

Finally, in this section, I have chosen 'Golden Showers', perhaps the most popular of all yellow climbing roses. It produces hundreds of ragged, slightly scented flowers all summer; although these start off golden in colour, they change to soft primrose before the petals fall. The upright plant grows to at least 3m (10ft); not over thorny, it has glossy, dark green foliage. It was raised by Lammerts of the USA.

The Climbing Hybrid Teas and Floribundas

M ost Climbing Hybrid Teas and Climbing Floribundas are sports, the result of spontaneous mutation by bush forms of roses of the same name. A few are Climbers in their own right, having been bred by hybridization. All are similar in growth, usually very vigorous, with firm, unyielding stems, which makes them difficult to train on walls or structures; in most instances, however, I can overlook this because they are very free flowering as well as pleasingly fragrant. Most have just one major flush of blooms each summer, although some produce a flower or two late in autumn. For all of these, early spring is the best time to prune.

During the development and expansion of the bush forms of HTs and Floribundas, hundreds of climbing sports have been, and still are being, introduced by many different nurserymen. Some of these revert quickly to bushes; others fail to make the grade in some other way, usually because of a tendency to be rather shy in flowering. For example, a climbing form of Peace, introduced in the 1950s, seldom produces more than a few flowers each year. During my lifetime with roses, I have come to know about 50 good Climbing HTs and about seven good Climbing Floribundas. I have selected eight of the former and two of the latter to discuss in this chapter.

CLIMBING HYBRID TEAS FOR THE GARDEN

'Crimson Glory' was mentioned as a bush in the chapter on Older Hybrid Teas. I include it here because, despite its reputation for hanging its head, it is one of the best red Climbers ever introduced. Indeed, in the climbing form, the weak flower stalks are an advantage since they allow a better view of the velvety, smoky, dark red blooms. These are very highly scented, and borne among dark green foliage on stiff, extremely thorny branches. To get the best from this awkward cultivar, which will reach 5m (15ft) at least, its shoots should be bent and trained in as many directions as possible.

'Cupid' is a most beautiful Climber in its own right (not a sport). Satin-like in texture, its moderately fragrant flowers are large, single, and soft peachy pink. The plant I have conforms to its reputation for being rather shy in flowering, but this weakness is overridden by its sheer good looks. Stiff and a little angular in growth, to about 3m (10ft) tall, it has large leaves that are matt, greyish green in colour.

The climbing form of 'Ena Harkness' is, in my opinion, superior to the bush form. It inherits its weak flower stems from 'Crimson Glory', one of its parents; but so exquisite are its bright velvety red, high-centred, fragrant blooms that I readily forgive it for such a defect. Its thick, firm, upright stems are very thorny and its foliage dark green, but perhaps lacking a little lustre. It makes an excellent wall plant, growing to 5m (15ft) or more.

Another Climbing HT in its own right, in other words not a sport, is 'Guinée', a very dark velvety red. It was raised by Mallerin in France back in 1938. It will reach 4m (12ft) in height, but it is temperamental and often rather difficult to grow. I hope this description does not put too many off, since this is a rose of great beauty with a superb fragrance. Very generous with its first flush, it repeats its flowers intermittently each autumn. Its wood is thorny, and leaves dark green. With a little bit of extra care and a forgiving gardener, it will afford immense pleasure.

Climbing 'Lady Sylvia' has delightfully shaped, high-centred buds, which open to fully double, well-proportioned blooms of bright pink with deeper pink shading and a hint of lemon in the base; their perfume is strong and pervasive. It will attain a height of 5m (15ft). Its inflexible stems are difficult to train but the effort is worthwhile for,

'Mme Grégoire Staechelin'
One of the earliest climbing roses to come into bloom each summer, this delightful Climbing Hybrid Tea from Spain is a wonderful sight in full flush. Although the flowers are fleeting, they always stay fresh in my memory, until they turn into bright orange-red, turnip-shaped hips in autumn and winter.

'Paul's Lemon Pillar'
An almost perfectly shaped Hybrid Tea, 'Paul's Lemon Pillar' dates back to 1915. Although nowadays there are several Modern Climbers of creamy white colour, few have a better temperament than this one. It even occasionally repeats its flowers in autumn, and these are sometimes accompanied by sizeable, orange-coloured hips.

as a result, the plant will produce a very big crop of blooms each summer, repeated to a lesser degree in autumn. Its foliage is leathery and mid- to dark green.

'Mme Grégoire Staechelin' is yet another Climber in its own right. It is also known as 'Spanish Beauty' and beauty it is, with large, curvaceous buds opening to huge, blowsy, fragrant flowers, up to 15cm (6in) across, in heavily veined, bright pink, with a softer pink at the petal edges. It has a prolific crop of blooms early each summer but never repeats them later. It will, however, produce the most wonderful large, turnip-shaped, orange hips, which stay on the plant until well into winter. It has plenty of leaves on the grey side of dark green, and will grow to a height of 5m (15ft).

One of the parents of 'Paul's Lemon Pillar' is the old Hybrid Perpetual 'Frau Karl Druschki', which accounts for its classic, high-centred blooms; its good fragrance comes from its other parent, 'Maréchal Niel'. The large and shapely flowers are lemon-yellow in bud but pale almost to pure white by the time the petals fall. 'Paul's Lemon Pillar' grows to a height of 5m (15ft) and has large, fairly dark green leaves, on strong, thorny stems. It repeats just a few blooms in late summer each year.

Every summer I look forward to the first blooms of Climbing 'Shot Silk'. For one thing, they are superlatively beautiful, being very fragrant, silky textured, and a lovely soft cerise and pink in colour; but they also come in great abundance. The leaves are large, crisp, and mid-green, borne on a vigorous plant that grows to 5.5m (18ft). This rose dates back to 1931, and it is still one of the best Climbers I know.

CLIMBING FLORIBUNDAS FOR THE GARDEN

There can be little doubt that Climbing 'Allgold' is one of the best yellow Climbers. It was introduced in 1961, and there is still no other Climber of such unfading yellow. Its semi-double, slightly fragrant flowers are produced in small to medium-sized clusters. The plant is vigorous, growing to 4m (12ft), and has rather thorny stems; its foliage is dark green and glossy. Although most climbing sports do not repeat their flowers in the autumn, 'Allgold' will do so, albeit with a much reduced crop.

Climbing 'Masquerade' dates back to 1958. At the time of its introduction it was a sensation, being the first rose of any real garden value to have such a wide range of colours in one cluster of flowers. Each semi-double bloom starts off clear yellow and, when fully open, changes first to pink, then to orange, and finally to deep red. 'Masquerade' is a superb climbing rose; not over vigorous, it will grow to about 3m (10ft) tall. Its leaves are darkish green and very healthy.

'Guinée'
This is a most beautiful, dark red Climbing Hybrid Tea, with perfume to match. 'Guinée' prefers not to be on a shady, cold wall but, if it likes the place in which it is planted, it will provide lots of these velvety textured blooms in early summer each year, with a few more later on. Unfortunately, if it does not take to its position, it will sulk and refuse to give of its best.

RAMBLERS AND
SCRAMBLERS

Rambler — as I have explained elsewhere — is the official term for all roses capable of rambling. Scrambler is a description I like to use for the more vigorous Ramblers, those that will climb readily into tall trees and quickly camouflage eyesores such as unsightly buildings. It is not an official classification. The majority of Ramblers and Scramblers owe their lineage to two species, *R. multiflora* and *R. wichurana*, which came to Europe from Asia in the early 1860s. Both have white flowers, borne in clusters, but when crossed with more colourful roses of other types, each species produced its own distinctive group of hybrids. Other Rambler species from various parts of the world have been used for breeding, and these have given rise to a diverse collection of hybrids, all worthy of use in any garden.

Except for some that are slightly susceptible to mildew, the Ramblers grown today comprise some of the healthiest of all roses. Broadly speaking they are very colourful but not very many have any significant fragrance. With a few, very important exceptions, all Ramblers flower only once each summer.

Ramblers differ from Climbers in that they flower only on wood produced in the previous season; they are also much more flexible in growth and so rather easier to train. They are especially suitable for arches and pergolas, the very vigorous ones for growing into trees, and they have a greater affinity with companion plants such as clematis, jasmine, and wisteria than the more unyielding Climbers.

By virtue of their preferred habitat and behavioural patterns, Ramblers and Scramblers can sometimes be difficult to prune; this is not a serious problem, though, as they tend to grow into dense plants whatever their treatment. If pruning is possible, it is best to remove all dead and old wood, usually after flowering each summer, and train all the long young shoots in as many different directions as they will allow. Where colourful hips are produced, pruning should be left until early spring.

'Mannington Mauve Rambler' and 'Rambling Rector' (*previous pages*) These two Multiflora Ramblers are captured here in close embrace. I expect them to continue to intermingle with each other as they grow bigger, and bigger, and bigger, eventually to be contained only by the drastic use of secateurs.

'Lauré Davoust' (*far right*) This attractive Rambler is seen here tumbling over a post and rail fence. It is one of the oldest of the Multiflora Ramblers, having been around since 1843, and is more often seen in France, its country of origin, than anywhere else.

'Emily Gray' (*right*) The Wichurana Rambler 'Emily Gray' provides the backdrop to a group of shrubby and herbaceous plants, among which are *Phlomis* and the rock rose *Cistus x purpureus*; the decorative containers add bold structure to the scene. 'Emily Gray' has particularly shiny foliage and grows quite densely, as can be seen here.

The Wichurana Ramblers and Scramblers

'Albéric Barbier'
Featured here with *Jasminum humile* in a charming study of yellows and greens, 'Albéric Barbier' shows off its full range of colour with blooms of varying ages. A special feature of this Rambler is its plentiful glossy, dark green foliage.

The discovery of *R. wichurana* in Asia and its subsequent arrival in Europe in about 1860 was a most significant happening. The species itself remained hardly noticed for almost 40 years but, at the turn of the century, it was crossed with various hybrid roses of the day, especially Teas, Chinas, and Noisettes, and most of the resulting progeny inherited its propensity to ramble, coupled with brighter flower colours passed on by the pollen parents.

Although only a few breeders made use of this species, the outcome of their work remains with us today, for Wichurana Ramblers play very important roles in the

modern garden landscape. While they do not make natural wall plants, give them an archway, an obelisk, or a trellis and they will thrive with relatively little attention beyond the removal of old wood, after they have finished flowering each summer.

Over my lifetime I have come to know, and enjoy, a good number of Wichurana Ramblers and will discuss about 20 of these, in alphabetical order, in this chapter.

WICHURANA RAMBLERS FOR THE GARDEN

The first, appropriately, is one I consider to be among the very best of its type. Introduced by Barbier in France in 1900, 'Albéric Barbier' is one of an indispensable clutch of Wichurana Ramblers brought out between the end of the 19th century and the 1930s. Its shapely, globular buds open to beautiful, double roses of creamy white flushed lemon and are complemented by lots of dark green, very glossy foliage. A vigorous plant, with sparsely thorned shoots, it looks especially good when grown on gazebos, trellis, and arches, where, if allowed, it will get to at least 6m (20ft).

'Albertine' is one of the world's best loved roses, also introduced by Barbier, in 1921. Its glossy leaves are conspicuously brushed coppery red, and its stems, of similar colouring, are very vigorous and thorny. The scented flowers open from tight buds to

'Albertine'
Since its introduction in 1921, 'Albertine' has become one of the most popular rambling roses in the world, this despite its slight proneness to mildew after flowering. No plant that I know ever gets tired or out of breath, and no one who grows this Rambler will ever tire of having it in their garden.

become rather muddled-petalled; their colour is lobster-pink, with a hint of yellow deep down, and fades with age. After flowering, 'Albertine' becomes prone to mildew, but this feisty rose shrugs off this affliction, continuing to grow bigger and better every year, and reaching a maximum height of about 5m (15ft).

'Alexandre Girault' is yet another rose introduced by Barbier, this time in 1909. It has almost double flowers made up of soft, quill-like petals in shades of cerise, yellow, and pink, giving the overall effect of burnt orange; they have a fruity scent. The growth of the plant is slender and flexible and it has dark green, glossy foliage; it will grow 4m (12ft) high and wide, and is quite amenable to being trained to a much greater width on walls or pergolas, or any structure big enough to accommodate it.

'American Pillar', raised by Van Fleet in the USA in 1902, is one of the most thorny of all Ramblers. The R. setigera genes in its ancestry probably account for its vigour and exuberance. It fills up with flowers in midsummer, each one single and bright pink with a white eye. At peak flush they are so dense as to make it almost impossible to see any of its ample dark green leaves; very occasionally it has a small second flush. It grows very vigorously to 5.5m (18ft) tall and can easily get much wider. A rather coarse, overpowering rose, it fulfils itself perfectly by covering, and even hiding, unsightly buildings and other eyesores.

Yet another Barbier rose is 'Auguste Gervais', raised in 1918, which has masses of medium to large, fragrant, fully double flowers like powder puffs, in coppery yellow suffused salmon, fading to creamy buff with age. Its foliage, like that of so many of Barbier's roses, is glossy, dark green. Its shoots are very pliable and have few thorns, making it easy to train. It will get up to 4m (12ft) high on any form of structure.

Awakening is a most beautiful, fully double rose of blush- to soft pink. Its name is an exact translation of 'Probuzini', its Czechoslovakian name. It was rediscovered in that country by Richard Balfour, who brought it back for me to introduce into Britain in 1988, just before the collapse of the Iron Curtain. I am pleased to have done so for it is an outstanding rose – a sport of 'New Dawn', which is itself one of the best Wichurana

Ramblers (see p.182). Awakening is fragrant and continues blooming well into winter. This rose has lots of small, dark green leaves and can reach up to 3m (10ft) without too much effort.

'Breeze Hill' is another Van Fleet rose, dating from 1926. Its flowers are fully double, scented, and clear pink, lightly brushed with soft peachy buff. It is vigorous, reaching at least 5.5m (18ft), and enjoys the challenge of growing even taller into trees. Its small, dark green leaves are plentiful and very healthy.

'American Pillar' (*right*)
One of the most vigorous and lusty of the Wichurana Ramblers, this rose is capable of performing any task that requires climbing prowess, such as camouflaging unsightly buildings and scrambling up into the branches of trees. Wherever it grows, it will provide a splash of bright colour, especially when set against a greenish background.

Awakening (*below*)
A lovely fully double Wichurana, Awakening is a sport of 'New Dawn' and shares the many attributes of that rose, including flowering continuously through the summer. Another virtue inherited from its parent is a delectable but not overpowering fragrance.

'Debutante'
Because of its pliable nature, the Rambler 'Debutante' is especially suitable for adorning arches and pergolas. On such structures it produces a profusion of small clusters of tousled, rosette-like flowers each summer.

'Debutante' is a lovely soft lilac-pink rose with a good fragrance. It produces many cascading clusters of small, tousled, rosette-like flowers amid an abundance of small, dark green leaves. Growing to 4m (12ft), this rose is particularly attractive on obelisks, arches, and trellis. It was raised by Walsh in the USA in 1902. In view of what little interest has been shown by breeders in Wichurana Ramblers in recent times, I find it fascinating that, 100 or more years ago, both Barbier in France and Walsh in the USA should, independently, work on breeding them at that same time.

Now known all over the world, by name at least, 'Dorothy Perkins' came from Jackson and Perkins, in the USA, in 1901. It produces large cascades of small, clear pink, almost double, fragrant flowers in midsummer, when it is a fabulous sight to behold. The plant is very pliable, with mid-green leaves aplenty, and it will grow comfortably to 5m (15ft). Its one weakness is a proneness to mildew, usually after its flowers are over; although unsightly, this affliction never seems to affect the quality or quantity of the next season's blooms. A similar rose, but deeper pink in colour, is 'Minnehaha', which is rather less prone to mildew.

The very vigorous 'Dr W. Van Fleet', raised in the USA, dates back to 1910. As well as being robust and expansive in growth, it is fairly thorny and has lots of dark green foliage. Scrolled in bud, its flowers open blowsy, semi-double, and blush-pink. This rose is excellent for growing into trees or covering large buildings, when it will easily get to well over 6m (20ft).

I am never quite sure where 'Easlea's Golden Rambler' fits into the scheme of things. On the one hand it has many large, fragrant, golden yellow blooms like those of a Hybrid Tea; and on the other, copious, large, shiny green leaves, which rather places it here among the Wichuranas. Mr Easlea, its raiser, obviously thought it a Rambler, otherwise he would not have named it so. It dates back to 1932 and to complicate its

'Minnehaha'
This rose will make itself comfortable anywhere where it can ramble and scramble without hindrance. It is clearly at home here, although soft pink Grouse, normally a prostrate rose, is coming up from beneath and surreptitiously beginning to invade 'Minnehaha's space, with the intention of taking over if not curtailed soon.

designation even more, its parentage is not recorded. One thing, though, is certain: it will always flower profusely in midsummer. It will grow to at least 6m (20ft) in a very short time.

One of the most striking features of 'Emily Gray', raised by Williams in Britain in 1918, is the superb, dark green, glossy foliage, which complements the golden yellow flowers exquisitely. These are semi-double, fragrant, and produced in considerable numbers in midsummer, followed by one or two blooms later on. If allowed its head, it will easily grow to 5m (15ft).

'Ethel' is a very thorny, vigorous, rather uncharacteristic Wichurana, bearing clusters of cupped, semi-double, soft blush-pink flowers, with robust, dark green foliage. Raised by Turner in Britain in 1912, it will grow up to 6m (20ft) tall.

'Evangeline' has great character. Its small, almost single flowers are pinkish white with slightly deeper markings on the petal edges; they are produced freely amid glossy, dark green leaves for about three weeks in midsummer, seldom longer. Easily growing to 5m (15ft), it is an excellent tree climber. It was raised in 1906 by Walsh in the USA.

'Excelsa', another Walsh rose, introduced in 1909, is sometimes called 'Red Dorothy Perkins'. This is because these two Ramblers have much in common, in particular cascading clusters of bloom, comparably sized flowers, and dense foliage. 'Excelsa', though, is bright reddish crimson. In good soil, this Rambler will reach a height of 5m (15ft). It will grow up into trees, but its flowers, being red, tend to become lost to view through leaves and branches.

A really lovely and free-flowering Wichurana hybrid is 'François Juranville'. Its colour is lobster-pink, similar to 'Albertine's, but its flowers are more double and more shapely than those of 'Albertine' and its shorter stalks hold them closer to the foliage. Raised by Barbier in 1906, this is a dense plant, growing to about 5m (15ft).

One of the most appealing of the Ramblers is the shapely, double, soft creamy yellow 'Gardenia'. Its abundant flowers are scented and quite impervious to weather, except that they fade slightly in the sun. Its dense foliage is bronze-green and it grows to 6m (20ft) tall, its flexible stems making it useful for many purposes, such as adorning obelisks, trellis, and pergolas. 'Gardenia' was introduced by Manda of the USA in 1899. I found this delightful rose in 1985 on a cottage wall on the island of Jersey. It was thought extinct in Britain at that time and I have had the pleasure of growing it and offering it to rose growers ever since.

'Easlea's Golden Rambler' (*above*)
This is one of the most vigorous of roses, quite capable of exceeding the height of a house, as can be seen here. Its foliage is glossy, dark green, and durable, hanging on well into winter.

'Alexandre Girault' (*left*)
Seen here on a trellis, the Wichurana 'Alexandre Girault' is doing a fantastic covering act. Covertly showing through is a small cluster of 'Paul's Himalayan Musk' – and if it has its way, it will soon take over. Introduced in 1909, 'Alexandre Girault' quickly became popular, for there were few other Ramblers of such bright colouring at that time.

The many colourful flowers of 'Léontine Gervais' are a mixture of deep salmon, yellow, and orange, with hints of pink. They are semi-double and fragrant. Semi-vigorous only, it needs lots of care to grow taller than 4m (12ft), for me at least. Its foliage is dark green and glossy. Raised by Barbier, it first appeared in 1903.

'New Dawn', the deluxe version of 'Dr W. Van Fleet', is one of the best known Ramblers of all time, and will always be in my top ten of all roses. It produces many semi-double, blush-pink, distinctly scented flowers all through the summer and well into autumn. Its leaves, although small, are greyish green and abundant. It was introduced as a sport from 'Dr W. Van Fleet' in 1930. In good hands and good soil it will attain a height of 3m (10ft), and is effective wherever a climbing or rambling rose is required, from walls to arches, and from pergolas to obelisks.

An old but most useful Wichurana is 'Paul Transon', yet again raised by Barbier, in 1900. It is difficult to tell this rose apart from 'François Juranville', but it is a little tidier in habit and its peachy buff blooms are more orange-salmon deep down. They are, however, just as double, if not more so, and produced in equally large numbers; and they are well scented. This cultivar has very dark green, glossy foliage, and it will grow to about 5m (15ft).

'Sanders' White Rambler' is the only pure white of the Wichuranas. Its small, double, cascading flowers are fragrant, and seldom tarnished by inclement weather. Its foliage is glossy, mid-green and comes in liberal quantities. Its shoots are flexible and its growth vigorous, to 4m (12ft). Raised by Sanders in Britain in 1912, it is an excellent rose for arches, obelisks, and pillars.

'Excelsa' (*right*) 'Excelsa' is a rose with the willpower to ramble over almost anything that provides it with enough support. It is also very capable of scrambling into trees. The dark red colouring of its flowers makes it less visible from a distance than, for example, some of the white Ramblers, but this dry stone wall sets it off perfectly.

'New Dawn' (*far right*) This charming association of 'New Dawn' and *Clematis* 'Comtesse de Bouchard' works superbly in terms of colour, form, and timing. The rose will go on flowering through the summer, together with the clematis. Since its introduction in 1930, 'New Dawn' has been, along with 'Albertine', one of the most popular of all Ramblers worldwide.

The Multiflora Ramblers and Scramblers

'Rambling Rector'
Give this rose the chance to show off its ability to scramble and it will rise to the challenge without a murmur of protest. It is especially happy growing into trees, and will cover walls and buildings with the greatest of ease. Its deliciously fragrant blooms are semi-double, unlike those of 'Seagull', with which it is sometimes confused, which are single.

The species *R. multiflora*, as I have said earlier, is these days rather frowned upon as a weed in some parts of the world. However, when we look back into the ancestry of our Modern roses, especially those with cluster flowers, this species has played a major part in their development. The Rev. Joseph Pemberton harnessed some of its qualities in his Hybrid Musks in the early 20th century; but long before him, Ramblers such as *R. multiflora* 'Carnea', *R. multiflora* 'Platyphylla', and 'Lauré Davoust' had already made their marks. Not that they were effectively utilized, for only in the 1920s did such roses start to be trained on trellis and other structures as a matter of course.

Two features the Multiflora Ramblers have in common with the Wichuranas are their relative vigour and, by and large, their glossy foliage. While there are several differences between the two groups, the most important and I suppose the most obvious is that the Multifloras come into flower two to three weeks earlier in summer. Multifloras tend not to be quite so relaxed in their habit of growth as the Wichuranas and, generally speaking, their hips are more conspicuous in autumn.

I have come to know many different Multiflora Ramblers over the last 50 years. I will embrace those I like best, alphabetically, in the following pages.

MULTIFLORA RAMBLERS FOR THE GARDEN

'Astra Desmond' is a little-known Multiflora Rambler, introduced by Hilliers in the UK in the early 20th century. It is probable that it is the same rose as that grown by other nurseries as 'White Flight'. The flowers of this rose

are small, semi-double, and pure white with a hint of green, borne in huge trusses that cascade down from a vigorous plant of about 6m (20ft). Its foliage is healthy and light green. The more I see of this rose, the more I like it. Astra Desmond was an opera singer, at her peak in the 1930s.

Only a few purple-coloured Ramblers have ever been raised, all belonging to the Multiflora group. One of the best is 'Bleu Magenta', of obscure origin but probably dating back to about 1900. Its small, fully double, rich purple flowers cascade from a mature plant like large bunches of grapes, and look very effective when grown with white Ramblers such as 'Astra Desmond', 'Rambling Rector', or 'Seagull'. It has dark green foliage and will grow as tall as 4m (12ft). Sadly it has little or no scent; apart from that, and a little mildew after flowering, it is faultless.

A rose that quickly became popular when introduced in Edwardian times is 'Blush Rambler', from Cants in the UK, and it was made even more famous by Gertrude Jekyll, who used it on structures in some of her garden schemes. It is very vigorous, sending up strong, thick shoots after flowering every year. It blooms quite early compared to some others of its kind. The flowers are slightly more than single and blush-pink in colour with deeper pink markings; they are borne in large, upright clusters and look good against its numerous light green leaves. 'Blush Rambler' has

'Astra Desmond'
Here growing amicably with common honeysuckle (*Lonicera periclymenum*), 'Astra Desmond' is about to burst forth with a multitude of its almost single, fragrant, milk-white flowers. A special feature is its abundant, fresh, light green foliage. If required this rose will easily climb as high as 6m (20ft).

'Bleu Magenta' (*above*)
Seen here cascading down
into a group of Armenian
cranesbills (*Geranium
psilostemon*), 'Bleu
Magenta' is perhaps the
most vigorous of the older
purple-coloured Ramblers,
growing dense and tall, up
to 5m (15ft).

'Bobbie James' (*far right*)
Just the bottom part of a
huge plant of 'Bobbie
James' is seen here, with
the top part, no doubt,
romping away off camera.
In the foreground are
delphiniums, lilies, and the
broad-leaved or perennial
pea (*Lathyrus latifolius*).
Quite apart from its
floriferousness and vigour,
a particularly fine feature of
'Bobbie James' is the lush,
glossy, light green foliage.

'Blush Rambler' (*right*)
Few Ramblers flower in
early summer with more
exuberance than 'Blush
Rambler'. It will attain
heights of up to 5m
(15ft) and, in doing so,
will provide dense cover
for camouflaging eyesores
of all types.

little or no fragrance. The plant, as a
whole, will grow to 5m (15ft).

Introduced by Graham Thomas while
he was at Sunningdale Nurseries in the
1960s, 'Bobbie James' is an orphan, with
enough Multiflora qualities to qualify for
inclusion here. For me, it is one of the
loveliest foundlings ever introduced. Its
foliage is superb, being healthy, plentiful,
slightly coppery green, and glossy. Its
sweetly fragrant flowers are made up of
about two layers of pure white petals,
with golden yellow stamens, and they
form large, drooping trusses. This is a
truly good Scrambler, growing to at least
10m (30ft) tall.

'Francis E. Lester' was introduced
by the Lester Rose Gardens, in the USA,
in 1946. It is a fairly distant relative of
R. multiflora, being a seedling from 'Kathleen', a Hybrid Musk. Its small, single flowers
are blush-white with deeper pink highlights; they are held upright in large clusters,
each of which may have as many as a hundred blooms. Their scent is strongly
reminiscent of a bowl of fruit salad. An excellent rose for pergolas and trellis, it is
very robust and can grow 5m (15ft) high; its foliage is dark green touched maroon.

A variety that can be treated either as a small rambling rose or as a large shrub,
'Ghislaine de Féligonde' is a very good
garden plant. It will grow to 2.5m (8ft)
and continue to flower without a pause
throughout summer. Its blooms are a soft
apricot colour, fading fairly quickly to
creamy buff; rather short on perfume,
they are fully double, opening up to show
off yellow stamens. They are displayed in
small clusters among dense, light green
foliage. One minor problem is that, in
hot weather, this rose is susceptible to
downy mildew; but this can be kept to
the minimum by regular watering to its
roots, never from over head. This rose
dates back to 1916 and was introduced
by Turbat of France.

'Francis E. Lester'
This relatively young plant
of 'Francis E. Lester' looks
to be struggling to cope
with the fierce competition
from golden hop
(*Humulus lupulus*
'Aureus'). Someone will, no
doubt, soon intervene with
secateurs on behalf of the
rose. A few foxgloves
(*Digitalis*) stand
dispassionately beneath.

'Goldfinch' is a charming rose. Its almost semi-double flowers are bright yellow, but quickly fade to cream. The late Graham Thomas described their scent as that of oranges and bananas. Borne in large clusters among mid-green, semi-glossy foliage, the flowers go on for about three weeks, during which time the display is magnificent. 'Goldfinch' would be hard pressed to exceed 2.5m (8ft). Its growth is spreading, if rather inflexible, making it ideal as a companion for similarly sized purple clematis or the Rambler 'Violette' (see p.190). It was introduced by Paul in the UK in 1907.

'Lauré Davoust' was raised by Laffay of France in 1843 and dates right back to the beginning of the development of the Multiflora hybrids. It is a splendid rose. Its foliage and growth are not altogether typical of the Multifloras, but it is probably best placed among them. Its almost thornless shoots are flexible, easy to train, and well furnished with soft mid-green leaves. In France, I have seen this rose covering arches 3m (10ft) high with no difficulty. Its pleasantly fragrant flowers are fully double, rosette shaped, and of soft lilac to lavender-pink; they fade a little with age, so each cluster is composed of blooms of varying colours.

Over the last few years I have come to know a superb mauve rose called 'Mannington Mauve Rambler', which was discovered by Lord Walpole in the gardens of Mannington Hall in Norfolk in 1998. It is said to be a sport of 'The Garland' (see p.190) and, certainly, it has many of the right characteristics to be so. Its colour is a glowing pinky mauve. It is an upright-growing plant with lots of good foliage. It was shown by us at Chelsea Flower Show in 2003, and was well received. I have seen the original plant only recently, growing on an archway 2.5m (8ft) tall. It will probably double this size in quite a short time.

'Goldfinch' is a charming rose. Its almost semi-double flowers are bright yellow, but quickly fade to cream. The late Graham Thomas described their scent as that of oranges and bananas. Borne in large clusters among mid-green, semi-glossy foliage, the flowers go on for about three weeks, during which time the display is magnificent. 'Goldfinch' would be hard pressed to exceed 2.5m (8ft). Its growth is spreading, if rather inflexible, making it ideal as a companion for similarly sized purple clematis or the Rambler 'Violette' (see p.190). It was introduced by Paul in the UK in 1907.

'Lauré Davoust' was raised by Laffay of France in 1843 and dates right back to the beginning of the development of the Multiflora hybrids. It is a splendid rose. Its foliage and growth are not altogether typical of the Multifloras, but it is probably best placed among them. Its almost thornless shoots are flexible, easy to train, and well furnished with soft mid-green leaves. In France, I have seen this rose covering arches 3m (10ft) high with no difficulty. Its pleasantly fragrant flowers are fully double, rosette shaped, and of soft lilac to lavender-pink; they fade a little with age, so each cluster is composed of blooms of varying colours.

Over the last few years I have come to know a superb mauve rose called 'Mannington Mauve Rambler', which was discovered by Lord Walpole in the gardens of Mannington Hall in Norfolk in 1998. It is said to be a sport of 'The Garland' (see p.190) and, certainly, it has many of the right characteristics to be so. Its colour is a glowing pinky mauve. It is an upright-growing plant with lots of good foliage. It was shown by us at Chelsea Flower Show in 2003, and was well received. I have seen the original plant only recently, growing on an archway 2.5m (8ft) tall. It will probably double this size in quite a short time.

R. multiflora 'Carnea' is a classic example of a Multiflora Rambler. It came from China in 1804. The plant will grow to a height of around 6m (20ft), both into trees and on structures. Its small, globular, semi-double flowers are blush-white but heavily flushed with soft lilac-mauve; they are scented, and borne in large, cascading clusters on relatively thornless stems. The foliage is darkish green and dense.

Introduced in 1913, but of unknown provenance, the delightful 'Rambling Rector' is described by some as Shakespeare's musk rose, which is pure conjecture since it certainly does not display any *R. moschata* characteristics. To me, it seems to be very much a Multiflora hybrid, both in growth and flower, the former being very vigorous and thorny with lots of grey-green, soft-textured foliage; admittedly, its many thorns are not typical of *R. multiflora*. The flowers, produced in huge clusters in early summer, are semi-double and white, with an overwhelming fragrance. 'Rambling Rector' is really too robust and invasive to be grown on trellis, arches, or arbours. It should, however, be seen growing over every unsightly building in the world and also up into the branches of every undistinguished tree. It will easily make 10m (30ft) in height and 5m (15ft) wide. In the autumn a further delight is a good crop of yellow-coloured hips, turning to orange as the season gives way to winter.

'Ghislaine de Féligonde'
This small Rambler, seen here effectively covering an old outhouse, is in no way aggressive and will continue flowering throughout summer. Peeping through here and there are a few blooms of the climbing Bourbon 'Blairii No. 2', which is a much more demanding rose and will continue to grow when 'Ghislaine' has stopped at about 2.2m (7ft). Beneath are Jerusalem cross (*Lychnis chalcedonica*) and *Phlomis russeliana*.

Another very good purple Rambler is 'Rose-Marie Viaud', raised by Igoult in France in 1924. Its smallish, fully double flowers are rich purple and borne in large, drooping clusters; they are fragrant and, like all the purple Ramblers, harmonize superbly with those of other Multifloras in white, cream, or soft yellow – 'Goldfinch' for example. 'Rose-Marie Viaud' is vigorous, grows to about 5m (15ft), and has lots of light green foliage. It has a slight problem with powdery mildew, but usually only after its flowers are finished in late summer.

'Seagull' is very much like 'Rambling Rector' in most respects. Its flowers, though, are pure white and single, and show off fine golden stamens; they are intoxicatingly scented. When in full flush, their sheer numbers completely blanket the plentiful, soft, greyish green foliage, and they are followed by small, orange hips. This rose will easily attain 8m (25ft). Its authenticity is sometimes challenged, but I need convincing that the one I have is not true to name.

The most thorny Multiflora Rambler is probably 'The Garland', raised by Wills in Britain in 1835. It is actually a cross between *R. moschata* and *R. multiflora*. It has semi-double, sweetly scented, white daisy-like flowers held in large, upright clusters, its leaves often hidden by the mass of blooms. It is very vigorous, growing up to 6m (20ft). I have a plant on the wall of our cottage that is allowed to have its head for three years – the time it takes it to reach the eaves; I then cut it down, almost to the ground, and it starts all over again, otherwise it would take over the house completely.

'Veilchenblau' is perhaps the best known of the purple shades mentioned here. It dates back to 1909 and was raised by Schmidt of Germany. Its small, scented flowers are semi-double, rather ruffled, and purple-violet in colour with white markings; they are borne in clusters on an almost thornless plant, with lots of light to mid-green foliage. It will grow to a substantial size, but by the time it reaches 4m (12ft) it will be in need of pruning.

A more delicate Multiflora Rambler is 'Violette', its semi-double, deep violet flowers beautifully enhanced by golden stamens. The blooms are borne in small clusters. This is a wiry plant, which is good trained on walls, mixing well with other white Ramblers, white wisteria, or white clematis. Its leaves are dark green and perhaps a little sparse. Notwithstanding this minor fault, 'Violette' is a good reliable Rambler from Turbat, France, dating back to 1921. Planted in good soil on a warm wall it will attain, at most, 4m (12ft).

'Veilchenblau' (*right*)
Probably the best known of all the bluish Ramblers, 'Veilchenblau' is extremely free flowering for about three weeks each summer. Accommodating in size, it loves to grow on arches, trellis, and pergolas. Here it has campanula and ferns growing up from beneath, making this a lovely study in blue.

'Rose-Marie Viaud'
(*below*) On a structure such as a trellis, 'Rose-Marie Viaud' will grow as tall as 5m (15ft). This young plant here, however, will probably well exceed this size as it spreads along the iron fence.

Miscellaneous Ramblers and Scramblers

A number of Ramblers and Scramblers fall into groups other than the Wichuranas and Multifloras, almost all of which deserve attention as worthwhile garden plants. In fact, some should be far better known and more widely grown. They are diverse in origin, evolving all around the northern hemisphere. Their characteristics are disparate: some are sprawling and thorny, others upright and smooth stemmed; a few are evergreen; and several bear a worthwhile crop of hips. By and large, they fulfil much the same roles in the garden as do members of the better-known groups; it is simply because of their relative obscurity that they tend not to be as well used as the Wichuranas and Multifloras, not through any failing in appearance or performance.

Over my lifetime, I have grown or seen upwards of 40 varieties from this mixed collection. The 20 or so that follow are those I consider the best, placed in alphabetical order according to classification.

MISCELLANEOUS RAMBLERS FOR THE GARDEN

The Ayrshires are hybrids of *R. arvensis*, the British native field rose. These are medium-sized Ramblers and, like their progenitor, will tolerate some shade; they are also very easy to grow. Various accounts have it that the group name Ayrshires arose because the

R. x l'heritierana
Closely related to *R. pendulina*, this out of the ordinary, Boursault rose has several uses within the garden. No more than 2.5m (8ft) tall, it can be used either as a free-standing shrub or as a small wall plant. Its foliage is soft to touch, and its stems reddish brown and completely free of thorns.

first double form was found in the village of Orangefield in Ayrshire, Scotland, having been brought there by a circuitous route from Canada via Yorkshire. As I have said before, this book is not the forum to discuss the authenticity of such things. The Ayrshire cultivar 'Dundee Rambler' is seldom seen these days, but it is an excellent, medium-grower, reaching 6m (20ft) high. Its pure white flowers are fully double and, when it blooms, it really does so with a vengeance, producing many smallish clusters against a foil of very dark green leaves. It was bred by a Mr Martin of Dundee around 1850.

Another Ayrshire, which can be useful either as a medium Rambler, to 5m (15ft) tall, or as a ground-cover plant, is 'Venusta Pendula', an old cultivar rediscovered in Germany in 1928 and introduced by Kordes soon after. It has shapely, milky white flowers, heavily overlaid pink, which are borne in great abundance every summer. In spite of having little or no perfume, they will justify the presence of this rose in any wild, woodland-style garden.

'Ramona' (*left*)
This beautiful single rose came about in the USA in 1913, the result of a sport from the soft pink 'Anemone Rose'. Both Ramblers have close affinity with *R. laevigata*, an old Chinese species that became naturalized in the southern states of the USA at the end of the 19th century, and is now known worldwide as the Cherokee rose.

I now move on to two roses of a small group known as the Boursaults, all of which are hybrids of *R. pendulina*, a central European species. The first of these, which gave rise to the remainder, is a near species called *R. × l'heritierana*. This rose goes back to before 1820 and has deep pinkish, almost red flowers, which occasionally repeat. Its reddish brown stems are completely free of thorns; its foliage is plum to dark green; and it will grow to 2.5m (8ft) tall. Like *R. pendulina*, it has slim, oval hips.

Without doubt, one of the loveliest of the Boursaults is the fully double 'Mme de Sancy de Parabère', introduced by Bonnet, in France, in about 1874. When fully open,

'Cooper's Burmese' (*left*)
The delightfully pure, single, fragrant flowers of this vigorous Rambler are displayed to advantage against a background of copious leathery, dark green foliage in midsummer each year. It is dense in growth and, when fully mature, prickly enough to deter intruders, especially those of the human kind.

'Paul's Himalayan Musk' (*above*) One of the world's most vigorous roses, 'Paul's Himalayan Musk' is seen here as a large clump ready to begin scrambling into the tree just visible behind it. The setting is Elsing Hall, Norfolk, home to one of the finest collections of Old roses in the UK.

'Félicité Perpétue' (*right*) This superb Rambler is one of a group of hybrids of *R. sempervirens* known as Evergreen roses. Its growth is pliable and it produces large quantities of shapely flowers (shown here at least four times their natural size), which burst forth in clusters towards midsummer each year.

its rich pink flowers appear like flat, fluffed-up cushions. As a plant, it can attain a height of at least 5m (15ft), and it has darkish green foliage, which is soft to touch. I must confess I have a big soft spot for this superb variety.

'Mermaid' is the result of a speculative cross between *R. bracteata* and an unknown yellow Tea rose, made by William Paul in the UK in about 1918. It has sizeable, single, soft yellow flowers with conspicuous stamens; they are deliciously fragrant and, after an early first flush, appear continuously throughout the summer. The leaves are large, glossy, and mid-green, and are borne in profusion on strong, brittle stems armed with vicious, hooked thorns. 'Mermaid' is a Scrambler; by regular pruning, it can be contained to 3m (10ft) or thereabouts, but given its head, it can easily reach 10m (30ft), even more in warmer climates. This rose, with all its thorns, planted against a house wall will deter the most purposeful of burglars. If it has a fault it is that one or two shoots will die back for no apparent reason; also, in the most severe of winters, it may succumb to frost, recovering again in spring with another enthusiastic crop of long, thorny shoots.

A native of China, *R. laevigata*, the Cherokee rose, was mentioned in an earlier chapter (see pp.28–29) in respect of its escape into the wild from gardens in the southern states of the USA. In 1895 'Anemone Rose' was born, the result of a cross made by Schmidt of Germany between *R. laevigata* and an unknown Tea rose. It bears the botanical name *R. anemonoides*. Its large, single flowers are soft pink, heavily veined deeper pink, and they have a lovely array of delicate, creamy yellow stamens. Each flower is borne singly on this angular, rather thorny plant, which has dark green,

'Adelaïde d'Orléans'
This Sempervirens hybrid is a delight grown on arches and gazebos, from which its wiry-stemmed flowers can pour down. The photo shows the rose at about twice its normal diameter.

glossy foliage. It grows vigorously and profusely, maturing at about 3m (10ft). In 1913, in the USA, 'Anemone Rose' produced a deeper pink, almost red sport, which was named 'Ramona'. Some rose devotees consider this to be the better form; my preference, though, is for the softer pink. Both roses have a slight scent.

'Cooper's Burmese', or *R. cooperi*, is no more than a hardier form of *R. laevigata*. It is equally thorny, but its brown stems are slightly more polished and its leaves a darker green. It has large, single, white flowers and makes a useful, dense shrub to a height of about 5m (15ft). Of uncertain provenance, it dates back to 1927.

A very useful hybrid of the musk rose, *R. moschata*, is that most rampant of all roses 'Paul's Himalayan Musk'. This eager giant will easily reach 12m (40ft) if allowed its head to scramble up into the branches of tall trees or ramble over sheds, outhouses, and banks. Its small, semi-double flowers are fragrant, soft blush to lilac-pink in colour, and very freely produced. As a plant it is fairly free of thorns and is very, very healthy. No one is quite sure of its date, but it is probably a foundling introduced by William Paul in the late 19th century.

In Victorian times hybrids of *R. sempervirens* were known as the Evergreen roses and this collective name, although not in common use nowadays, is still appropriate since most of them never shed their leaves, or at least not until new ones come to replace them each spring. Almost all of the Evergreens were raised by a Frenchman named Jacques between 1826 and 1850. Despite their relative old age, they are all, even now, very important garden roses. One of the best is 'Adelaïde d'Orléans', which has lots of small, rosette-like, semi-double, white to soft pink flowers. These cascade down from a wiry, almost thornless plant, which can reach 5m (15ft) in height and is ideal for arches, pillars, and obelisks. This rose was first introduced in 1826.

'Félicité Perpétue', dating from 1827, is probably the best known and the most widely grown of the Evergreens. It is much less wiry in growth than 'Adelaïde d'Orléans', and its many stems are better clothed with dark green foliage. The small, fully double, rosette-like flowers are soft creamy white with hints of pink; they emerge from deep ruby-red, tight little buds, and are borne in cascading clusters in early and midsummer each year. This lovely rose is ideal for tall structures such as pergolas and arches and will easily reach a height of 5.5m (18ft). In 1879 a bush form of 'Félicité Perpétue' was discovered in the USA; it is called 'White Pet' and features in the chapter on Compact Floribundas (see p.213). 'Félicité Perpétue' is sometimes

'Chevy Chase'
I first found 'Chevy Chase' in the Cranford Rose Gardens, which are part of Brooklyn Botanic Gardens, New York. When it is in flower in midsummer, no other red Rambler can outshine it. Seen here in my mother and sister Rosemary's garden in north Norfolk, it has two companions, growing alongside and for the time being beneath: cream 'Albéric Barbier' and golden yellow 'Emily Gray'. Before too long, both of these will intermingle with 'Chevy Chase'.

erroneously referred to as the seven sisters rose. The true seven sisters, however, is *R. multiflora* 'Platyphylla', a much coarser-growing rose with larger leaves and fully double, fragrant flowers, each a different shade of pink within the same cluster.

There has been some controversy over recent years about the true identity of two very lovely hybrids of *R. sempervirens*, both raised by M. Jacques of France in 1829; these are 'Princesse

Louise' and 'Princesse Marie'. I grow both, and if they are not true to name, I have no idea what they could be. 'Princesse Louise' is similar in colour and vigour to 'Félicité Perpétue', and again bears its flowers in cascading clusters, but the blooms themselves are larger and slightly more cup shaped at first; as a plant it reaches a height of 5m (15ft). 'Princesse Marie' produces larger, similarly shaped flowers, again in cascading clusters; these are pinkish lilac in colour and held on a less vigorous plant.

A pink species from the USA is *R. setigera*. Known as the prairie rose, it is an extremely healthy shrub, growing to about 1.8m (6ft), and tolerant of most soils. This species has produced several hybrids, one of the most beautiful being 'Baltimore Belle', raised by Feast, in the USA, in 1843. It should, perhaps, be classified as a Climber. It is extremely vigorous in growth, with darkish green leaves similar to those of *R. setigera*; interestingly, its pollen parent was a Gallica hybrid. Its slightly scented flowers are silky clear pink in colour, initially globular but opening cupped and fully double, and are held on wiry stalks in small, drooping clusters. This is a rose that has no difficulty in reaching 5m (15ft) in height.

'Long John Silver', another *R. setigera* hybrid, was raised by Horvath of the USA in the 1930s, and this is a rose I have come to enjoy very much. It will easily grow to 5m (15ft) or more and is very healthy, with durable, matt, light green foliage. Only slightly thorny, its stems are strong and robust. The flowers of this rather oddly named rose are of the old-fashioned style, sizeable, opening flat, and held in closely arranged clusters. They are pure white in colour, but regrettably have no scent.

R. sinowilsonii, mentioned earlier among the Species roses (see p.41), has produced just one seedling of consequence: 'Wedding Day', a foundling by Sir Frederick Stern in Britain in 1950. Smelling sweetly of citrus, its many small, single flowers begin life as soft yellow buds; as they open, they quickly fade through soft lemon to milky white, and they have prominent golden stamens. Although its foliage is a little sparse for my taste, this rose will grow and grow to reach at least 10m (30ft) up into trees. If I am absolutely honest, 'Wedding Day' has probably won more friends because of its name, than for its performance or good looks.

'Baltimore Belle' (*above*) This is a famous old American rose, which dates back to 1843. Its foliage is darkish green and its growth rather spindly, with few thorns. Rudely healthy, it is a cross between *R. setigera* and a Gallica rose; with this parentage, of course, it will never repeat its flowers.

'Wedding Day' (*left*) This picture illustrates clearly the prolific flowering habit of 'Wedding Day', a rose that can sometimes be a little sparing with its foliage. Its milky white blooms are sweetly perfumed of citrus. The best purpose to which this rose can be put is scrambling up into the branches of trees, but it also enjoys cavorting on trellis, obelisks, and gazebos.

'Sir Cedric Morris' is a foundling rose, introduced by my nursery in 1979. Sir Cedric himself had discovered it at his home in Suffolk, growing among a batch of seedlings of *R. glauca* (then *R. rubrifolia*). When I first saw it, just a few years later, the plant was huge, at least 10m by 6m (30ft by 20ft) and – not surprisingly, since its pollen parent is thought to have been the very vigorous *R. mulliganii* – it was completely smothering an old apple tree. A superb Scrambler, its foliage is glaucous-grey in colour, and its stems are thorny, thick, and rather unyielding. Its flowers, which waft scent all around, are small, single, and pure white, with golden stamens; they are produced in large clusters, and are followed by a multitude of small, very conspicuous, orange-red hips.

One of my favourite wild roses is *R. soulieana* from China. Between 1912 and 1960 a trio of excellent Ramblers came forth from this species, the best known of which is probably 'Chevy Chase'; until recently, this was more often seen in the USA than in Britain. In full flush, from early to midsummer, this spectacular rose shows off masses of bright red, fully double, pompon-like flowers, arranged in large clusters. Sadly, these are almost scentless. 'Chevy Chase' has profuse, mid-green foliage and virtually thornless, pliable stems. It is quite capable of scrambling 6m (20ft) up into trees, and considerably higher if the tree is big enough. It is named, I believe, after a small town in the area of Washington DC.

My second *R. soulieana* hybrid is 'Kew Rambler', a very vigorous rose introduced by Kew Gardens to Britain in 1912. When fully mature it displays thousands of single, mid-pink flowers, paling to creamy white in the centre; these are scented and followed by equal numbers of bright red hips in autumn and winter. Perhaps best growing up into a tree, where it will reach 5m (15ft), this Rambler can also be used on walls or structures, but it is not easy to train because of its stiff, extremely thorny stems.

'Wickwar' (*far right*)
A very thorny rose, like 'Kew Rambler' (*right*), 'Wickwar' is equally free flowering. Although it is a foundling, it is clearly out of *R. soulieana*. Here it harmonizes with a variety of perennials, among them Armenian cranesbill (*Geranium psilostemon*), a double form of meadow cranesbill (*Geranium pratense* 'Plenum Violaceum'), and *Selinum wallichianum*.

'Kew Rambler' (*right*)
This lovely, single rose looks quite innocuous in this picture, but it is one of the thorniest of all the Ramblers, making it a useful deterrent to burglars when trained onto the wall of a house. Apart from its spiteful thorns, it is a very tasteful, free-flowering Rambler.

My final rose in this selection is the third of the *R. soulieana* hybrids; it is another foundling, 'Wickwar', named after the English village in which it was discovered by Keith Steadman in 1960. In many ways this easy-going Rambler is similar to its parent, with greyish green foliage, ample thorns, and slightly larger, single, pure white flowers, enhanced by lovely golden yellow stamens. This is not a rose to plant too near a path or on an archway, for it will grab at every woollen garment that passes by. Nevertheless it is ideal for use on walls and trellis, where it has no problem attaining a height of about 4m (12ft).

PROCUMBENT AND
COMPACT ROSES

The Procumbent Roses

'The Fairy' (*previous pages*) Initially introduced in 1932 as a Polyantha, this delightful Procumbent rose always enjoys the company of other plants. Here it mingles successfully with lavender.

Berkshire (*below*) This wide-growing rose is one of the most agreeable of its type. It has larger flowers than many other Procumbents and produces them in very large numbers. A special feature, just visible in the picture, is copious, glossy, dark green foliage.

The term Procumbent embraces all roses that grow broader than tall. I consider it a more accurate appellation than Ground Cover, since not all wide-growing roses form an impenetrable blanket that suppresses weeds (which is what we demand of a ground-cover plant). Prostrate would be an equally good term.

The advantage of using Procumbents, especially in a large garden, is that fewer plants are needed to cover a given area, making them much more cost effective than upright varieties. They can be used as underplanting in shrubberies, or for concealing unsightly objects such as manhole covers and tree stumps, and they are useful as bedding roses in positions where too much height is undesirable; they also look good when cascading down banks and drooping from pots, tubs, and urns. In addition, most Procumbents make superb small Ramblers, several being continuous flowering, others bearing hips. There are now some 50 varieties generally available from rose specialists and garden centres. I will discuss about half this number in alphabetical order.

PROCUMBENT ROSES FOR THE GARDEN

Over these past few years I have come to know an English garden in Japan, called Barakura, which belongs to the Yamada family. In 1998, we named a rose 'Barakura', to help cement the relationship between my garden and theirs. Growing to about 60cm (2ft) tall and twice as wide, it is a densely spreading plant with healthy, light green foliage. Its fully double, rosette-like flowers are soft pink to blush-white and carried in large, crowded clusters.

Several Procumbent roses introduced over the past few years have been given the names of English counties, and they are known collectively as the County series. Berkshire, from Kordes, is one of my favourites. Its semi-double flowers

are quite large, bright pinkish red, and lightly fragrant; borne in clusters on strong, thorny stems, they rise above the prostrate plant, which grows to a height of about 60cm (2ft). The foliage is exceptionally healthy and dark green in colour.

Cambridgeshire, also from Kordes, is one of the most colourful of the County series, its flowers a mixture of yellow, orange, and bright pink. They are semi-double and arranged in many medium-sized clusters, which are produced continuously throughout the summer. The foliage is mid-green and glossy, and the plant grows to almost 90cm (3ft) high and 1.2m (4ft) wide.

Somewhat different in character is a wide-spreading, rather more than semi-double rose called Cardinal Hume, from Harkness. The flowers, of reasonably large size, are fragrant and beetroot-red to purple in colour. Reaching up to 90cm (3ft) high in good soil, Cardinal Hume will also grow to 1.2m (4ft) wide. Its foliage is dark green and crisp in texture; its growth is dense and thorny. Excellent as a low, wide hedge or as a bedding rose, it will need deadheading regularly if it is to repeat its flowers.

'Dunwich Rose' is the procumbent form of *R. pimpinellifolia* (see p.29). Since its discovery on the sand dunes of Dunwich, on the east coast of England, in the 1950s, it has rightfully become a very well used garden plant. With its fern-like foliage and single, creamy white flowers, borne in late spring and followed by a good crop of colourful hips, it has all the good characteristics of a Pimpinellifolia rose, with the added attribute of spreading to cover an area twice its height of 90cm (3ft).

Ferdy from Suzuki, Japan, is an unusual rose bearing small, semi-double, bright salmon-pink flowers with a light fragrance. Its strong, very thorny branches, which are inclined to arch downwards, are covered in tiny, mid-green leaves. Ferdy will flower just once each summer with the occasional haphazard repeat. Capable of growing to 1.5m (5ft) tall, even more on a wall, it will normally get to 90cm (3ft) and roughly twice as wide. It does best, though, if regularly pruned to a more manageable size of about 60cm (2ft) high.

Ferdy
Taken in my garden, this picture shows a group of three Ferdy in full flush. By removing the long, non-flowering shoots clearly seen here soon after the plants have flowered, it is possible to keep these roses at roughly this height and shape for years. Ferdy will also make itself comfortable when grown against a wall; in this situation it should simply be left to grow, unpruned, each year.

Fiona
The term semi-procumbent would, perhaps, better describe the normal posture of Fiona, seen here enjoying life with *Geranium wallichianum* 'Buxton's Variety'. As the picture shows, this rose produces its many flowers in good-sized clusters.

Fiona is a semi-prostrate rose and I am never quite sure whether to treat it as a Shrub rose or a Procumbent. Growing to 90cm (3ft) tall and 1.2m (4ft) wide, it is certainly useful for filling gaps in borders and shrubberies and will not encroach upon other plants around it. Introduced by Meilland of France, it has sizeable clusters of slightly more than semi-double blooms, shapely in bud and very bright red in colour, which are borne in regular succession each summer. If not deadheaded, it will produce a magnificent crop of red hips in the autumn.

One of a small series of roses named after game birds, Grouse bears clusters of small, single, blush to white flowers from early to midsummer. These are fragrant and occasionally recur later on. Its foliage is small, light green, and dense. This is a very broadminded rose and can be kept as low as 60cm (2ft). If allowed its head, however, it will make a huge plant for growing up into the branches of trees or hedges; in my own garden I have one 3m (10ft) tall and equally wide growing into a beech hedge.

Introduced by Jackson and Perkins in the USA in 1994, Magic Carpet was hailed at that time as being the healthiest of all roses and, indeed, it is very free of disease. Its flowers are semi-double and bright pink, with a hint of lavender showing through. Its perfume is spicy and its foliage glossy, dark green. It will grow to about 60cm (2ft) high and up to 1.2m (4ft) wide.

Norfolk, from Poulsen of Denmark, is one of the rare Procumbent roses with bright yellow flowers. Fully double and rosette-like, these are borne extremely freely all

summer, among small but numerous, dark green leaves. A rose that can be relied upon to fulfil the role of spreading without intrusion, Norfolk grows to 90cm (3ft) wide without getting taller than 60cm (2ft). It is exceptionally good as a pot plant.

Although many fine roses have been produced in Japan over the years, only a few of these are in general cultivation in other parts of the world. Ferdy is one I have already discussed, but the best known and most successful of the Japanese Procumbents is 'Nozomi', raised by Onodera. In early summer, this rose bears an abundance of single, star-like, soft pink flowers, held on short stems close to the many small, dark green leaves. Its shoots are thin and very thorny. As a shrub 'Nozomi' will grow to 90cm (3ft) tall and 1.8m (6ft) wide. It is excellent cascading from tall urns or pots; it is also good as a weeping standard ("tree rose" in the USA).

Another rose that is difficult to classify is the lovely Pearl Drift, but since it is broader than tall, I place it here among the Procumbents. Its flowers are milky white with honey-coloured stamens and are larger than those of most other wide-spreading cultivars. Pearl Drift will attain a height of 90cm (3ft) and spread to 1.2m (4ft), and it has good, leathery, semi-glossy leaves. This is an ideal rose for planting in groups. It was raised by Edward LeGrice in 1980, the result of an unusual cross between 'Mermaid' and 'New Dawn'.

Pheasant is one of the gamebird series from Kordes, with slightly fragrant, semi-double flowers of rich, clear pink, repeated throughout much of the summer. As a plant, it can get quite big if allowed to grow untouched by secateurs. I have seen one 2.5m (8ft) high and equally as wide, but it can easily be kept to one third of this size. Its leaves are large for a Procumbent but dark green and healthy.

Three roses that are fine ground-covering plants are Pink Bells, Red Bells, and White Bells. Their flower colours are in their names. All three were introduced by Poulsen and they are all fairly similar. They have dense growth spreading close to the ground, and their leaves are small, dark green, and plentiful. Their double flowers, too, are small, and borne in clusters; and they bloom profusely in early summer, but only occasionally do they repeat. Never getting taller than 60cm (2ft), each will spread to twice this width with ease.

Queen Mother is a bright pink cultivar with masses of semi-double flowers borne in sizeable clusters. Its foliage is dark green and glossy, and it grows to

Pink Bells
A true ground-covering rose, Pink Bells will suppress all but the most determined of weeds once it is established. Fulfilling a taller ground-covering role behind is the Multiflora rose 'Rambling Rector' which, in this position in my garden, is allowed to ramble at will and is then brought back within bounds by the removal of all over ambitious rambling shoots after flowering has finished each year. At that time the spent blooms must not be removed otherwise no hips will form.

about 30cm (1ft) tall and twice this width. Raised by Kordes, it makes an excellent bedding rose, but is also very useful in pots and urns. It is superbly healthy, although I must confess I find it a little lacking in personality. I struggle to understand quite why it should bear this name.

'Raubritter' was raised in 1936, the year I was born, and I am pleased to have arrived in such good company. This is a very lovely rose; the fact that it flowers only in early summer is of little importance. It has dark grey-green foliage and long, arching, thorny stems, bearing copious, cascading clusters of cup-shaped, almost double flowers. These are clear silvery pink in colour and rich in fragrance. 'Raubritter' will grow as tall as 90cm (3ft) and 2.5m (8ft) wide. Both foliage and thorns are particularly prone to mildew, but this seldom takes hold until the flowers are over. In fact, I always ignore its penchant for mildew, knowing that all of us born in that year have our little idiosyncrasies, and use it for a variety of purposes, from tumbling down banks to training into small trees and hedgerows. It especially thrives if grown close to water.

A rose that more than lives up to its name is Red Blanket, from Ilsink, of the Netherlands. This cultivar, if grown as a normal shrub, will get to about 90cm (3ft) tall and at least twice as wide. However, just like my grandson, if it finds itself next to a tree, it will attempt to climb it. I have one in my garden that suddenly appeared 6m (20ft) up in the branches of a nearby twisted willow. Wherever it grows, though, Red Blanket produces clusters of rather more than single, bright red flowers with paler centres, set among dark green foliage. Although perhaps a little coarse, this rose tolerates poor soil and even thrives on neglect.

Red Max Graf, from Kordes, is a spreading rose of proportions even larger than those of Red Blanket. As well as being robust and adventurous in its behaviour, it is one of the brightest red roses I know. Its name is a little misleading in that 'Max Graf' is several generations removed in its ancestry. The flowers are single and borne in large clusters on strong, thorny stems; if regularly deadheaded, blooms will appear intermittently all through summer. If this is not done, however, a good crop of bright red hips will ensue. The foliage is healthy and dark green. Rather bright for my taste, this rose will make a big splash, especially if planted in large groups in a mixed shrubbery.

Two roses bred by my daughter Amanda and introduced by my company in 1994 are 'Summer Sunrise' and 'Summer Sunset'. Both have Bonica '82 as a parent, crossed with 'New Dawn' to produce 'Summer Sunrise' and with Robin Redbreast to produce 'Summer Sunset'. Both have healthy, glossy foliage and bear rather more than single, candy pink flowers, which are mildly fragrant. Normally they grow to a maximum height of 45cm (1½ft) tall, with a spread of up to 1.2m (4ft). As well as good Procumbent roses, both are very useful as small climbers, when they will attain heights of 2.5m (8ft) on walls and trellis. If deadheaded regularly, they will continue flowering all through the summer; but if the spent flowers are left on the plant, a lovely crop of red, oval hips will form, to give a good display in the autumn.

Sussex, from Poulsen, is very colourful, with rather ragged, semi-double flowers of bright apricot-orange, changing to bright pinkish buff in maturity. These are borne in sizeable clusters on a relaxed plant 60cm (2ft) tall and 90cm (3ft) wide. Its foliage is dark green and shiny. This is a bright and cheerful rose, which looks good in modern garden settings, especially when grown in pots, urns, and their like.

Another rose that I am never sure where to place is Tall Story, from Dicksons, but since it is considerably wider than tall, it is best included here among the Procumbents. This rose will easily get to 90cm (3ft) tall and 1.2m (4ft) wide. Quite beautiful at every stage, its fragrant, semi-double flowers are deep yellow in bud and soft creamy white when fully open. Tall Story always seems to be in flower and never adversely affected by wet weather. It is good as a shortish rose in shrubberies and as a companion to herbaceous plants in beds or borders.

'The Fairy' is yet another rose difficult to designate, but I place it here since it is inclined to grow quite a bit broader than it is tall, reaching a height of no more than 45cm (1½ft) and spreading about 75cm (2½ft) wide. This is an excellent rose for bedding or grouping among perennials. It has small, semi-double, soft pink flowers, displayed in very large clusters. Introduced by Bentall in England in 1932, this lovely little rose fell from favour for a time, but it is now back in fashion as one of the best and most popular of its kind.

A fine rose in the Kordes County series, Wiltshire has initially cupped flowers that open to almost double, but not quite. Fragrant and reddish pink in colour, they are freely produced all summer in large clusters, on stems with lots of dark green foliage. Reaching a maximum height of 60cm (2ft), Wiltshire spreads to 1.2m (4ft).

'Raubritter'
As expected from a rose of this superb colour and shape, 'Raubritter' has a lovely perfume. It also produces its flowers in very large numbers over a period of about three weeks in early summer. Dense in growth, it spreads expansively over the ground. It tends to be prone to mildew after it has finished flowering each year, but I always forgive it this minor flaw.

The Compact Floribundas and Miniature Roses

Apart from a few very good ones that I have come to know rather well, Compact Floribundas and Miniatures are the roses I know least about – but they are, without doubt, indispensable in many modern gardens. Compact Floribundas are more commonly called Patio roses but, in my view, this name undervalues them, and has led to a tendency for them to be associated only with patios. I much prefer to use the name Compact Floribundas which, to my mind, fully characterizes these roses and embraces their potential for wider use in the garden. For a rose to qualify for Compact Floribunda status it should never get taller than 45cm (1½ft). The term Miniature of course speaks for itself and embraces all roses that are diminutive in stature, foliage, and flower size, growing, at the very most, to 30cm (1ft) tall. Such roses are superb in small containers; they are happy in greenhouses and conservatories but, if grown in the house, will need to be placed on window-sills with plenty of natural light.

In my experience, there is usually a correlation between the vigour of a rose and the degree of difficulty encountered in growing it, so these small, short cultivars will all need good, fertile soil and regular feeding if they are to flourish. They will also appreciate regular watering throughout summer to help sustain healthy growth.

Hundreds of Compact Floribundas and Miniature roses have been introduced by rose breeders over the years, but my choice is restricted to those I know or have seen growing, covering about 20 in all.

COMPACT ROSES FOR THE GARDEN

I start with 'Baby Albéric', a little-known but superb Compact Floribunda that is a diminutive version of the Rambler 'Albéric Barbier', containing itself to no more than 45cm (1½ft) tall and approximately the same width. Its lightly fragrant, creamy white flowers are much the same size as those of the Rambler, and are produced continuously throughout summer. The foliage, too, is similar to that of its parent, being shiny, dark green. This rose is an absolute delight. It came to me initially from David Ruston of Australia, but I have also seen it growing and flourishing in the USA.

'Dresden Doll' is a Miniature Moss rose, an introduction by Ralph Moore of the USA. Continuity of flower is just one of its many attributes; the small, cup-shaped, blooms are slightly fragrant, soft pinkish buff in colour, and produced in clusters on a compact bush to about 30cm (1ft) tall. Its stems and buds are covered in moss, as are some of its young leaves. This is an ideal novelty rose for growing in pots.

Regensberg
The brightly coloured blooms of this Compact Floribunda rose always seem to have perfect symmetry, whether in bud form or fully open. Even though its colour is not entirely to my taste, Regensberg has many good points, freedom of flower and excellent health being just two of them.

A delightful soft yellow rose, which I happened upon by chance in the gardens of John and Louise Clements of Oregon, USA, is a pocket-sized form of 'Mermaid', appropriately called 'Happenstance', with all of its parent's characteristics except that of size. Despite my suspicions that it might not be fully hardy, I have grown this rose successfully here in Norfolk for the past three years. Growing to 45cm (1½ft) high and spreading a little wider, it is inclined to send up long shoots to about 60cm (2ft), but these are the exception not the rule, and they are best cut off.

'Maude Elizabeth' is a neat and tidy, free-flowering rose, which never grows over 38cm (15in), although it does spread a little wider. An ideal rose for pots or small gardens, it produces masses of single, deep red flowers, with golden yellow stamens; these are held close to the many dark green leaves. It was introduced by us in the year 2000, named by the successful bidder in a radio auction to raise money for charity.

'Mr Bluebird' came about as a self-cross of 'Old Blush', making it almost pure China. It bears clusters of almost single, lavender-mauve flowers and is constantly in bloom. Growth is robust for a Miniature, and its foliage greyish green.

Orange Sunblaze (also known simply as Sunblaze) is one of the Sunblaze group of Compact Floribundas, which also includes Pink Sunblaze and Yorkshire Sunblaze. All are

Robin Redbreast
Short and upright, this Compact Floribunda always seems to be in bloom. I like it because it is single, and for the way it flaunts its beautiful array of golden stamens against a background of unfading, bright red petals.

superb, neat little roses, ideal for the modern garden. Their flowers are bright, semi-double, and freely produced among plenty of foliage.

'Perla de Montserrat' was raised in Spain in 1945, and still crops up from time to time in rose catalogues. Its fully double, shapely, soft blush-pink flowers are borne in clusters, not unlike those of 'Cécile Brünner', one of its parents. This rose is a true Miniature, upright and bushy, and no more than 23cm (9in) tall.

Red Ace is considered one of the best Miniatures ever raised. It has deep red, fully double, shapely flowers, borne in small clusters on an upright plant, which reaches a maximum height of 30cm (1ft). This rose is excellent in containers, perhaps crowded with several other pot-grown plants in a window-box.

Regensberg, one of the best Compact Floribunda roses, came from McGredy of New Zealand in 1979 and has remained popular ever since. It has superb, glossy foliage, and large, fully double, cherry-pink flowers, with silvery white markings. No more than 45cm (1½ft) high, this makes a good, short bedding rose or a pot plant for patios or terraces.

I can never quite decide whether Robin Redbreast is a Floribunda or a Compact Floribunda; but since it seldom if ever exceeds 45cm (1½ft), it is probably the latter. It is a most beautiful little rose, producing bright red flowers with creamy yellow centres, on upright, thorny stems among mid-green foliage. Normally I am not too fond of such bright colours but this is one I can and do live with, in my own garden.

A rose that cannot be left out of this chapter is 'Rouletii', the primogenitor of all Miniature roses. It is said to have been discovered in Switzerland by a Major Roulet in 1918, and introduced to the world four years later. Its influence is still apparent in Miniatures to this day. The flowers are small, semi-double, and a little ragged, and deep rose-pink, very slightly streaked white; the leaves are small, healthy, and dark green. As a plant 'Rouletii' will never get much taller than 30cm (1ft).

A charming, very free-flowering Miniature is Snowball which, as its name suggests, has many tight, snowball-like blooms. This is a tidy little plant, only 23cm (9in) tall, and has dense, light green foliage. It came from McGredy of New Zealand and, in my opinion, is still one of the best white Miniatures.

One of the most popular Compact Floribundas of recent times is Sweet Dream from Fryer, in the UK. A bushy plant, up to 45cm (1½ft) tall, it bears fully double, peachy apricot flowers all through summer, and is well endowed with mid-green foliage. This is a useful rose for bedding and for pots.

Sweet Magic is an upright, rich golden yellow Compact Floribunda with good dark green foliage. Its slightly fragrant flowers are semi-double and held in erect clusters. It is ideal for bedding or grouping among low-growing herbaceous plants.

I must include a little Miniature Rose called 'Tom Thumb' or 'Peon'. Raised in the Netherlands in 1936, it is seldom seen today, but is important because it features in the pedigrees of many modern, and not so modern, Miniatures. Its semi-double flowers are deep red with white centres; its foliage is dark green; and it makes a free-flowering bush not more than 23cm (9in) tall.

In 1996 my company celebrated 25 years of exhibiting at the Chelsea Flower Show. To mark the occasion we introduced a lovely red Compact Floribunda named Twenty-fifth. When fully open, its semi-double flowers show off golden yellow stamens and, if kept deadheaded, will appear throughout summer. At 45cm (1½ft) high, this is a good, compact bedding rose; its foliage, although small, is dense and dark green.

One of the most adorable garden roses of all time is 'White Pet' or 'Little White Pet', as it is often called. It was introduced in 1879, when it was classified as a Polypompon, and is actually a reverse sport – a bush form of the Rambler 'Félicité Perpétue'; normally such mutations occur the other way about. Its white pompon-like flowers emerge from reddish pink buds arranged in large clusters, which go on appearing all summer. Growing only 45cm (1½ft) high and wide, it has dark green foliage and is a perfect rose for mass display or pot culture.

Sweet Dream
This is a bushy Compact Floribunda which, as can be seen from the photograph, is very free flowering. The small, old-fashioned blooms usually last for several days without shattering. It is ideal for growing in pots.

DIRECTORY

The Way The Directory Works

This Directory covers, in concise terms, all of the roses discussed in the main body of the book, along with a handful of others that, through lack of space alone, could not be included there. It is not in any way intended to be a comprehensive encyclopaedia of roses. I believe my choice of species and cultivars reflects my own tastes, which are admittedly rather eclectic. All those described here are known by me personally. Any derogatory remarks I may have made about any rose are simply an expression of opinion and, hopefully, will not offend any reader.

Classification

Each rose has been placed in its class according to one of the three worldwide classification systems. First, that of the American Rose Society, as published in *Modern Roses XI*. Second, the World Federation of Rose Societies' system. Third, the system devised by the British Association Representing Breeders. This Directory is not the medium through which the merits of each of these systems should be discussed, except to say that the first is based on assumed or proven ancestry, the second relies upon descriptions of either growth or flowering type, and the third is a combination of the other two. No system is infallible, but there is clearly a need in rose circles to work towards one simplified classification. Some roses, in my humble opinion, are non-conformist so I have placed them in the Directory where I think they fit best.

Nomenclature

The name most commonly used in Britain is given as the first name for every rose described. When a rose is known by a different name in another country, that name is also given. Other known synonyms and common names are also recorded, in order of common usage. Modern roses often have both a trade or selling name (the one most commonly used) and a code name (the registered name); in the Directory, both are given and are styled as follows: Westerland ('Korwest'); in the main body of the book, only the selling name is given. As regards Species roses or close Species roses, the botanical name appears first, followed by any synonyms and common names.

Raisers, Introducers, and Parentage

Where known, the name and location of the raiser or introducer is listed immediately below the name of the rose, as is the year of introduction. This is followed by the parentage if known – seed parent first, then pollen parent. With Species roses, and some of the older rose groups, place of origin is given, followed where known by the year in which the rose was first discovered or first introduced as a garden plant in Europe and/or North America.

Descriptions of Colours

Outside the primary ones, describing colours is very subjective. If any colour described is not as the reader sees it, I cite as my defence "it is as I see it".

Fragrance of the Roses

Degree of fragrance is probably even more subjective than colour. Over the years I have learned that there are "roses for noses" and "noses for roses". It is second nature to put my nose into a rose, and I have without exception sniffed every one mentioned in this book. My fragrance rating is based on my opinion only; I accept that it may not always concur with everyone else's.

Dimensions of the Roses

Dimensions of both height and width are, by no means, uniformly the same the world over. So many factors influence size – such as climate, soil type, aspect, degree of pruning, and good husbandry. Therefore, all I can state is an approximation of ultimate size, as drawn from my own experience.

Awards and Prizes

Around the world many roses are entered into trials for appraisal of their worthiness. While I appreciate that to receive an award at trials usually indicates a good cultivar, I do not believe that this necessarily reflects superiority of any one rose over another, especially after what may be a relatively short test period. No specific awards are therefore mentioned, except when it seems appropriate in passing.

Key to Symbols

◑	Tolerant of partial shade
✿	Prefers sun or sheltered position
♦	Slight fragrance
♦♦	Moderate fragrance
♦♦♦	Strong fragrance
C	Continuous flowering
R	Repeat flowering
S	Summer flowering only
Sp	Spring flowering only
☉	Rather disease prone

'Harry Maasz' and 'Mozart' (*previous pages*) This is an unusual combination of roses differing in both growth habit and flower size, but it somehow seems to work. 'Harry Maasz' is a Procumbent that ultimately grows twice as wide as it is tall, and has small clusters of rather less than semi-double blooms. 'Mozart', a Hybrid Musk, is dense and bushy with huge clusters of much smaller, single flowers. Both roses are scented, 'Harry Maasz' the more so.

Species and Close Species

R. alba
Origin Europe **First noted** Ancient
Single, fragrant, pure white flowers enhanced by yellow stamens. Moderately thorny growth, with greyish green foliage. Narrow oval, bright red hips set fairly freely in autumn. Not unlike *R. canina* in flower size and growth habit. Seen from time to time in the wild in western Europe, mostly in hedgerows.
❍ ♦♦ S H 2.2m W 1.2m (7 x 4ft) Zone 5

R. arvensis (Field rose)
Origin Europe **First noted** 1750
Single, lightly fragrant, pure white flowers with gold stamens, followed by oval, dark red hips, not over conspicuous among subdued, dark green foliage. In the wild, a hedgerow creeper and scrambler; a perfect rose to run wild in a woodland garden.
❍ ♦ S H 3m W 3m (10 x 10ft) Zone 6

R. banksiae banksiae (*R. banksiae* 'Alba Plena')
Origin China **First noted** 1807
Large clusters of small, semi-double to double, pure white flowers in late spring. Lovely fragrance. A very vigorous, thornless plant with light green foliage. Hips small and inconspicuous.
☼ ♦♦ Sp H 10m W 10m (30 x 30ft) Zone 7

R. banksiae 'Lutea' (Lady Banks' rose)
Origin China **First noted** 1824
A vigorous, thornless plant with small, dense clusters of fully double, bright yellow flowers in late spring. Fragrant. Shiny, light green foliage. Inconspicuous hips. The best known of the Banksian roses.
☼ ♦ Sp H 10m W 10m (30 x 30ft) Zone 7

R. banksiae 'Lutescens'
Origin China **First noted** 1870
Single, fragrant flowers of deep yellow in late spring. A very vigorous, thornless plant with lots of soft coppery green foliage. Hips small and inconspicuous.
☼ ♦ Sp H 10m W 10m (30 x 30ft) Zone 7

R. banksiae normalis
Origin China **First noted** *c.*1877
Thought to be the wild form of the Banksian roses. Clusters of single, fragrant, white flowers in late spring, followed by small, inconspicuous hips. Very vigorous, thornless growth. Foliage soft light green.
☼ ♦♦ Sp H 10m W 10m (30 x 30ft) Zone 7

R. blanda (Smooth rose, Meadow rose, Hudson Bay rose, Labrador rose)
Origin USA **First noted** 1773
Similar in most respects to *R. canina* but with fewer thorns and marginally larger, single flowers of slightly deeper pink. Foliage greyish green. Fruit plump and pear shaped.
❍ ♦ S H 1.5m W 90cm (5 x 3ft) Zone 4

R. bracteata (Macartney rose)
Origin China **First noted** 1793
A dense shrub or wall plant with many khaki-coloured stems and thorns. Foliage dark green. Large, single, slightly fragrant flowers, soft primrose-yellow with golden stamens, borne through summer into autumn. Orange hips.
☼ ♦ C H 3m W 3m (10 x 10ft) Zone 8

R. brunonii (Himalayan musk rose)
Origin Himalayas **First noted** 1822
Dense corymbs of small, single, white flowers among drooping, greyish green foliage. Light fragrance. Rather inconspicuous, oval, orange-red hips. One of the most vigorous of all Species roses.
❍ ♦ S H 12m W 10m (40 x 30ft) Zone 6

R. californica
Origin North America **First noted** *c.*1878
A tall, upright shrub bearing masses of small to medium, single flowers of soft pink with golden stamens. Mild fragrance. Foliage is plentiful and soft darkish green. Spherical red hips. 'Plena' is a very attractive form with semi-double to double flowers.
❍ ♦ S H 3m W 1.8m (10 x 6ft) Zone 5

R. canina (Dog rose)
Origin Europe **First noted** Ancient
Medium-sized, single, lightly scented, soft pink flowers on a shrubby, thorny plant with abundant grey-green foliage. Many oval, orange-red hips. Once used as an understock. Common in hedgerows.
❍ ♦ S H 3m W 1.8m (10 x 6ft) Zone 5

R. canina 'Andersonii'
Origin Europe **First noted** 1912
Parentage *R. canina* x *R. gallica*
Large, single flowers, a deeper pink than those of *R. canina* (probably the influence of *R. gallica*). Mild fragrance. Slightly less vigorous than *R. canina*, with soft grey-green foliage, hooked thorns, and oval, orange-red hips.
❍ ♦ S H 2.5m W 1.5m (8 x 5ft) Zone 5

R. chinensis spontanea (China rose, Bengal rose, *R.* x *odorata*, *R. indica*, *R. simnica*, *R. nankiniensis*)
Origin China **First noted** *c.*1885
More confusion surrounds this rose than any other wild rose. Behaves erratically, varying in height and in petal numbers (from single to fully double). Lightly fragrant blooms are soft pink to cerise, and borne continuously. Foliage slightly glossy, darkish green. This form brought back from China by Roy Lancaster *c.*1980. Not to be confused with 'Odorata'.
☼ ♦ C H 0.9–2m W 90cm (3–6½ x 3ft) Zone 6

R. davidii (Father David's rose)
Origin Tibet **First noted** 1808
A useful, slightly later flowering rose, with medium-sized, single, clear soft pink flowers followed by a good crop of large, flagon-shaped, red hips. Mild fragrance. Leathery, dark green foliage, slightly glossy. Stems biscuit coloured and thorny. Healthy.
❍ ♦ S H 3m W 1.5m (10 x 5ft) Zone 5

R. x *dupontii* ('Dupontii')
Origin Europe **First noted** Pre-1596
Parentage Possibly *R. gallica* x *R. moschata*
Soft pink buds open to large, single, blush to white flowers with a lovely array of golden stamens. Fragrant. Growth tall and bushy. Stems with few thorns; foliage grey-green; small, bright red hips.
❍ ♦♦ S H 2.5m W 2.2m (8 x 7ft) Zone 6

R. ecae
Origin Afghanistan **First noted** 1880
A small, branching shrub with chocolate-brown stems and many thorns. Small, single, cupped flowers are bright buttercup-yellow, borne in early summer. Foliage fern-like and dark green. Fruit numerous, very small, dark red when ripe.
❍ S H 90cm W 90cm (3 x 3ft) Zone 5

R. elegantula 'Persetosa' (*R. farreri persetosa*)
Origin China **First noted** 1900
Small, single, star-like, soft lilac-pink flowers, on a wide-growing, arching shrub in early summer. Stems are bristly but not thorny, with lots of small, fern-like, soft-textured, darkish green leaves. Sets fruit spasmodically. Ideal for mixed shrubberies.
❍ S H 1.5m W 1.5m (5 x 5ft) Zone 6

R. banksiae banksiae

R. brunonii

R. canina

R. x *dupontii*

R. foetida 'Bicolor'

R. gentiliana

R. helenae

R. hibernica

R. fedtschenkoana
Origin Central Asia **First noted** 1876
One of a very few repeat-flowering species. Now thought to have played a part in the early ancestry of roses. A large shrub with soft-textured, light grey-green foliage. Sizeable, single, white flowers with golden stamens, only a few of which set elongated, red hips. Fragrance unappealing.
○ R H 1.5m W 1.5m (5 x 5ft) Zone 4

R. filipes 'Kiftsgate'
Introduced Murrel, UK 1954
Large trusses of single, fragrant, white flowers on a very thorny, vigorous plant, followed by masses of small, reddish hips. Healthy, mid-green foliage. This form more common in gardens today than *R. filipes*.
○ ◆◆ S H 10m W 10m (30 x 30ft) Zone 6

R. foetida (Austrian briar)
Origin Asia Minor **First noted** Pre-1600
Sizeable, single, rich golden yellow flowers, with a pungent smell, in early summer. Dark green foliage. Firm and brittle, chocolate-coloured stems with lots of sharp thorns.
☼ S H 1.5m W 1.2m (5 x 4ft) Zone 4

R. foetida 'Bicolor' (R. lutea punicea, Austrian copper)
Origin Asia Minor **First noted** 16th century
Parentage Sport of *R. foetida*
Identical to *R. foetida* except for dazzling bright orange flowers. Colour sometimes reverts to yellow.
☼ S H 1.5m W 1.2m (5 x 4ft) Zone 4

R. foetida 'Persiana' (Persian yellow)
Origin Asia Minor **First noted** 1835
Double, cupped flowers of bright yellow with an unpleasant smell. Otherwise similar to *R. foetida*.
☼ S H 1.5m W 1.2m (5 x 4ft) Zone 4

R. forrestiana
Origin China **First noted** 1918
A sturdy shrub with stout, thorny, mahogany-coloured stems. Medium-sized, single, deep pink flowers, lightly fragrant, and numerous oval, orange hips ripening to red. Foliage blue-green.
○ ◆ S H 2.5m W 2.2m (8 x 7ft) Zone 6

R. gallica (R. rubra, French rose, Rose of Provins)
Origin Europe **First noted** Pre-1600
A low-growing shrub with slightly spreading, bushy growth, few thorns, and dark green foliage. Single flowers are deep pink, bordering on red. Light fragrance. Progenitor of all Gallica hybrids.
○ ◆ S H 90cm W 90cm (3 x 3ft) Zone 5

R. gentiliana (R. polyantha grandiflora)
Origin China **First noted** *c.*1907
Single, fragrant, creamy white flowers borne in large clusters, followed by roundly oval, orange-red hips. An attractive, vigorous scrambler with thick, firm stems and very large, shiny, coppery green leaves. Moderately thorny.
○ ◆◆ S H 6m W 6m (20 x 20ft) Zone 6

R. gigantea (R. x odorata gigantea)
Origin Burma, China **First noted** 1890s
A vigorous scrambler or wall climber with long, thorny, arching branches of bronze-green and similarly coloured foliage. Large, single, creamy white flowers, with yellow stamens, produced continuously. Delicate fragrance. Hips yellow and plumply pear-shaped. Naturalized in southern states of USA. Can be slightly tender in northern Europe.
☼ ◆ C H 6m W 6m (20 x 20ft) Zone 8

R. glauca (R. rubrifolia)
Origin Eastern Europe **First noted** 1814
Arching, moderately thorny, reddish purple stems with a greyish bloom. Foliage plum-purple. Flowers small, single, star-like, and soft pink. Hips oval, dark red, mahogany coloured when ripe.
○ ◆ S H 1.8m W 1.8m (6 x 6ft) Zone 4

R. gymnocarpa
Origin North America **First noted** 1893
Smallish, single, soft lilac-pink flowers in small clusters among plentiful greyish green foliage. Mildly fragrant. Graceful shorter growth. Hips small, whiskery, oval, and bright red.
○ ◆ S H 1.2m W 90cm (4 x 3ft) Zone 5

R. helenae
Origin China **First noted** 1907
A vigorous scrambler, one of the most beautiful of its kind. Fairly thick, brownish stems, the bark flaking with age. Grey-green foliage. Distinctively scented flowers, single and creamy white, packed into superb, long corymbs followed by many red hips the size of redcurrants. In my view there is only one true *R. helenae*, not several as some believe.
○ ◆◆ S H 6m W 6m (20 x 20ft) Zone 5

R. hemisphaerica (R. sulphuria, Sulphur rose)
Origin Western Asia **First noted** 1625
Not a true species. A densely growing shrub with lots of soft-textured, light green foliage. Large, double, rancid-smelling, sulphur-yellow flowers in midsummer each year.
☼ S H 1.5m W 1.2m (5 x 4ft) Zone 5

R. hibernica
Origin Europe **First noted** 1795
A medium-sized shrub with flowers of similar size to those of *R. canina* and much the same colour. Light fragrance. Thorny, upright growth and darkish green foliage. Bears a good crop of sizeable, globose, red hips each autumn. A useful hedging rose.
○ ◆ S H 1.5m W 1.5m (5 x 5ft) Zone 5

R. x kochiana
Origin North America **First noted** 1869
A short-growing shrub with good, bright green foliage and single, mauve-pink flowers with creamy yellow stamens. Mild fragrance. Small, plump, oval hips. Perhaps not a true species, possibly a cross between *R. pimpinellifolia* and *R. virginiana* or *R. carolina*.
○ ◆ S H 90cm W 60cm (3 x 2ft) Zone 4

R. laevigata (Cherokee rose)
Origin China **First noted** 1759
An evergreen scrambler with broad, sharp thorns and dark green foliage. Bears a succession of large, single, lightly scented, creamy white flowers with golden stamens. Naturalized in the southern states of the USA.
☼ ◆ C H 5m W 4m (15 x 12ft) Zone 7

R. longicuspis
Origin China **First noted** 1915
Masses of light green foliage and small, single, white flowers in corymbs, with a banana-like fragrance. Small, inconspicuous hips. The true form of this lovely rose is seldom seen today. (*R. mulliganii* has been distributed wrongly under this label over several years.)
☼ S ◆◆ H 6m W 5m (20 x 15ft) Zone 6

R. x macrantha
Origin France **First noted** 1923
Not a true species. A shrub with an arching, rather relaxed habit and dark green foliage. Medium-sized, single, lightly scented flowers with pronounced stamens are pink in bud, maturing blush-pink then white. Dark red hips. Rather prone to mildew but only when flowers have gone.
○ ◆ S ◉ H 1.2m W 2.2m (4 x 7ft) Zone 5

R. macrophylla
Origin Himalayas **First noted** 1918
A tall shrub with dark mahogany-coloured wood and dark green foliage. Single, lightly fragrant flowers of good size, deep pink to red. Large, pendulous, red hips. Seen more often in gardens these days in the forms 'Doncasterii' and 'Master Hugh'.
○ ◆ S H 2.5m W 1.2m (8 x 4ft) Zone 4

R. x micrugosa
Origin France **First noted** 1905
Parentage R. roxburghii x R. rugosa
Dense, thorny growth with single, papery textured, soft blush-pink flowers throughout summer. Slightly scented. Leaves crinkled and mid-green. Small, spiky, chestnut-like hips. 'Alba' is a pure white form.
○ ◆ C H 1.2m W 1.2m (4 x 4ft) Zone 4

R. moschata (Musk rose)
Origin Asia Minor, Mediterranean Europe
First noted Pre-16th century
Large clusters of single, fragrant, white flowers on a tallish shrub with soft, greyish green foliage. Growth bushy, slightly thorny. A few hips ripen with late flowers in autumn. Also makes a good climber. One of the progenitors of other rose groups.
✿ ◆ C H 2.5m W 1.8m (8 x 6ft) Zone 7

R. moyesii
Origin China **First noted** c.1890
An outstanding species. Sturdy, angular growth with brownish stems, mid-green foliage, and many sharp thorns. Single, slightly scented, clear crimson flowers with pronounced yellow stamens followed by drooping, flagon-shaped, orange-red hips. Parent to several good hybrids including 'Geranium'.
○ ◆ S H 3m W 2.5m (10 x 8ft) Zone 5

R. mulliganii
Origin China **First noted** 1917
A vigorous rose with profuse dark green foliage. Very thorny, flexible stems. Single, slightly fragrant, white flowers in clusters. Small, orange hips borne profusely. Until recently widely distributed erroneously as R. longicuspis.
○ ◆ S H 6m W 3m (20 x 10ft) Zone 6

R. multiflora
Origin Japan, Korea **First noted** 1862
A relatively thornless species with lots of mid-green foliage. Vigorous. Slightly fragrant flowers, small, single, and white, borne in large corymbs in early summer, followed by masses of tiny hips. Important in the genealogy of many roses including 'Carnea' and 'Platyphylla'.
○ ◆ S H 5m W 3m (15 x 10ft) Zone 5

R. nitida
Origin North America **First noted** 1807
A short-growing, dense shrub well armed with prickles. Papery textured flowers are single and clear mid-pink, followed by small to medium, orange-red hips. Very little or no scent. Feathery, mid-green foliage. Ideal for dense planting schemes, effectively covering ground.
○ S H 90cm W 90cm (3 x 3ft) Zone 4

R. nutkana
Origin North America **First noted** 1876
A medium to tall, upright shrub, with good dark grey-green foliage, and few thorns. Lots of sizeable, single, lightly fragrant flowers of soft lilac-pink with pronounced stamens, followed by plump, oval, orange-red hips. 'Plena' is a lovely double form.
○ ◆ S H 1.8m W 1.8m (6 x 6ft) Zone 5

R. omeiensis pteracantha (R. sericea pteracantha)
Origin China **First noted** 1820
A tall, upright shrub, rather rugged, with large, wedge-shaped, translucent, red thorns. Small, grey-green leaves. Bears single, white flowers with only four petals, and small, drooping, orange-red hips.
○ Sp H 3m W 1.8m (10 x 6ft) Zone 5

R. pendulina (R. alpina, Alpine rose)
Origin Central Europe **First noted** 1794
A medium to tall shrub with reddish purple, thornless stems and dark green foliage. Single, deep mauve-pink flowers with prominent, soft yellow stamens. Slim, flask-like hips of reddish orange.
○ S H 1.8m W 1.2m (6 x 4ft) Zone 3

R. phoenicia
Origin Turkey **First noted** 1885
Slender, darkish green stems with profuse greyish green leaves. Lightly fragrant flowers, in corymbs, are single and white, followed by oval, red hips.
✿ ◆ S H 2.5m W 1.2m (8 x 4ft) Zone 6

R. pimpinellifolia (R. spinosissima, Burnet rose, Scotch rose)
Origin Europe **First noted** Ancient
Beautiful, single, mildly fragrant, soft creamy yellow to white flowers in late spring, followed by drooping, mahogany to black hips. Fern-like, mid- to bright green foliage on very prickly stems. Several clones exist, including 'Grandiflora' (also known as 'Altaica'), which is taller with larger flowers, and 'Harison's Yellow', which is very double.
○ ◆ Sp H 90cm W 90cm (3 x 3ft) Zone 4

R. primula (Incense rose)
Origin China **First noted** 1910
A short to medium shrub with dense, fern-like, dark green foliage and single, fragrant, soft yellow flowers in spring; both smell strongly of incense. Sets a few small, orange hips.
○ ◆◆ Sp H 90cm W 90cm (3 x 3ft) Zone 5

R. x richardii (R. sancta, Holy rose, St John's rose)
Origin Ethiopia **First noted** Ancient
Single, pink to blush flowers amid good dark green foliage. Light scent. Lots of hips, but many remain unripe. A useful procumbent rose for mass planting.
○ ◆ S H 90cm W 1.2m (3 x 4ft) Zone 6

R. roxburghii normalis (Burr rose, Chestnut rose)
Origin China, Japan **First noted** 1908
Dense, fern-like, mid-green foliage on brown shoots, the bark flaking with age. Single, mildly fragrant, soft mid-pink flowers. Yellow-orange fruit, distinctively spiky like chestnut husks. A good hedging rose.
○ ◆ S H 1.8m W 1.5m (6 x 5ft) Zone 6

R. roxburghii 'Plena' (R. roxburghii roxburghii)
Origin China, Japan **First noted** 1824
In most respects the same as R. roxburghii except flowers are deep lilac-pink and very double in form.
○ ◆ S H 1.8m W 1.5m (6 x 5ft) Zone 7

R. x macrantha

R. nutkana

R. pendulina

R. phoenicia

R. setigera

R. stellata mirifica

R. villosa

R. virginiana

R. rubiginosa (R. eglanteria, Sweet briar, Eglantine rose)

Origin Europe **First noted** Ancient

A close relative of *R. canina*. Single, strongly fragrant, soft pink flowers followed by many oval, whiskery, red hips in autumn. Shrubby growth with lots of sharp prickles and apple-scented, grey-green foliage.

○ ♦♦♦ S H 3m W 2.5m (10 x 8ft) Zone 5

R. rugosa

Origin Japan, Korea, China **First noted** 1845

A popular hedging rose, very thorny and upright in habit. Leaves coarse and dark green. Single, very fragrant flowers of mid- to deep pink. Lots of round, bright orange hips ripening to red. There are several forms, including a lovely pure white called 'Alba'. Used intensively in hybridization; Rugosa genes are inherent in many Modern Shrub roses.

○ ♦♦♦ C H 2.5m W 1.8m (8 x 6ft) Zone 3

R. sempervirens

Origin Mediterranean, North Africa
First noted 1629

A rampant, evergreen scrambler with glossy, dark green foliage and single, fragrant, white flowers in large corymbs. Hips tiny and bright red. Has given rise to several very good hybrids, including 'Félicité Perpétue', 'Adelaïde d'Orléans', and 'Princesse Marie'. Can be slightly tender in northern Europe.

○ ♦♦ S H 6m W 6m (20 x 20ft) Zone 8

R. setigera (Prairie rose)

Origin North America **First noted** 1810

Single, lightly scented, deep pink flowers produced on a vigorous plant among plentiful, large, dark green leaves. Hips are medium-sized but not conspicuous. Growth spreading and wide.

☼ ♦ S H 1.8m W 1.8m (6 x 6ft) Zone 4

R. setipoda

Origin China **First noted** 1895

A vigorous, stout-stemmed rose with vicious thorns. Foliage dark green. Single, bright clear pink flowers, with paler centres and large bosses of yellow stamens. Light fragrance. Hips large, flagon shaped, and whiskery, dark red in colour.

○ ♦ S H 4m W 3m (12 x 10ft) Zone 5

R. sinowilsonii

Origin China **First noted** 1904

A very vigorous scrambler with exceptionally large, glossy, bright green leaves. Large, showy trusses of single, slightly scented, white flowers followed by elliptical, red hips. Said to be tender in northern Europe but never a problem for me.

☼ ♦ S H 6m W 6m (20 x 20ft) Zone 8

R. soulieana

Origin Western China **First noted** 1896

A superb, vigorous, arching species with profuse greyish green foliage. Can be grown as a shrub or a rambler. Single, mildly fragrant, pure white flowers in large, cascading clusters. Hips small and orange-red. Said not to be fully hardy in northern Europe but fine with me.

○ ♦ S H 5m W 3m (15 x 10ft) Zone 7

R. stellata mirifica (Sacramento rose, Gooseberry rose)

Origin North America **First noted** 1916

One of the shortest-growing species. Looks like a gooseberry bush when dormant. Long spines in profusion among blue-green foliage. Flowers small, single, lilac-pink, very freely produced. Light scent. Spiky, gooseberry-like hips borne close to foliage.

☼ ♦ S H 90cm W 90cm (3 x 3ft) Zone 7

R. villosa (R. pomifera, Apple rose)

Origin Europe **First noted** 1771

A sturdy, spiny species with soft, greyish green shoots and leaves. Flowers are single, slightly fragrant, and mid-pink. Hips are large for size of flowers, globular, bristly, and red. 'Duplex' or Wolley-Dodd's rose is a double form.

○ ♦ S H 1.8m W 1.2m (6 x 4ft) Zone 5

R. virginiana

Origin North America **First noted** 1817

A dense shrub, with plenty of light green leaves. Medium-sized, single, lightly scented, pink flowers in midsummer, followed by plump, round, red hips. Very colourful autumn foliage. Superb for hedging.

○ ♦ S H 1.2m W 1.2m (4 x 4ft) Zone 4

R. virginiana 'Plena' (Rose d'Amour, St Mark's rose)

Origin USA **First noted** 1820

Similar in many respects to *R. virginiana* but with shapely, semi-double, deep pink flowers. Autumn foliage not so colourful as in *R. virginiana*.

○ ♦ S H 1.8m W 1.2m (6 x 4ft) Zone 5

R. webbiana

Origin Himalayas, Afghanistan **First noted** 1879

A vigorous, arching if slender shrub with yellow prickles on blue-green wood. Glaucous grey-green foliage. Small, single flowers are soft rosy pink, with light fragrance. Bottle-shaped, red fruit.

○ ♦ S H 1.8m W 1.5m (6 x 5ft) Zone 5

R. wichurana (R. wichuraiana)

Origin Japan, Korea, China **First noted** 1860

Vigorous rose for ground cover or scrambling into trees. Glossy, dark green foliage in great profusion, almost evergreen. Few thorns. Single, slightly scented, white flowers in clusters, followed by small, dark red hips ripening late in autumn. Has played a major role in the genealogical development of many superb Ramblers.

○ ♦ S H 3m W 6m (10 x 20ft) Zone 6

R. willmottiae

Origin China **First noted** 1904

A superb, arching shrub with fern-like, grey-green foliage and numerous sharp prickles. Single, lightly fragrant, bluish pink flowers. Hips roundly oblong and drooping. Excellent as a specimen plant.

○ ♦ S H 1.5m W 1.5m (5 x 5ft) Zone 5

R. woodsii fendleri

Origin North America **First noted** 1888

An all-round good shrub with plenty of darkish green foliage. Flowers single, lightly fragrant, and lilac-pink with golden yellow stamens. Sizeable fruit are oval, plump, and red. A good hedging rose.

○ ♦ S H 1.5m W 1.5m (5 x 5ft) Zone 4

R. xanthina (Manchu rose)

Origin China **First noted** c.1900

Single, faintly scented, deep yellow flowers in mid-spring among profuse fern-like, dark green foliage. Fruit small and inconspicuous. There are several clones of this species. 'Canary Bird' is closely related.

○ ♦ Sp H 1.8m W 1.8m (6 x 6ft) Zone 5

R. xanthina hugonis (R. hugonis, Father Hugo's rose, Golden rose of China)

Origin China **First noted** 1899

A distinctive, tallish, upright rose with dense, prickly growth and fern-like, dark green foliage. Sizeable, single, soft yellow flowers, slightly scented, borne in mid-spring. Sets small, bright red hips intermittently.

○ ♦ Sp H 2.2m W 2.2m (7 x 7ft) Zone 5

Old Garden Roses

The Albas

'Celestial' ('Celeste')
Origin Europe **First noted** Ancient
Parentage Not recorded
Flowers semi-double, cupped, and silky pink, exuding an "expensive" perfume. Foliage is soft grey-green and ample. Sometimes sets hips but never in quantity. Very beautiful.
○ ♦♦♦ S H 1.8m W 1.2m (6 x 4ft) Zone 5

'Chloris' ('Rosée du Matin')
Origin Europe **First noted** Ancient
Parentage Not recorded
Seldom seen these days. A fully double rose of soft satiny pink. Very fragrant. Shoots comparatively thornless. Foliage matt grey-green.
○ ♦♦♦ S H 1.5m W 1.2m (5 x 4ft) Zone 5

Félicité Parmentier'
Introduced Parmentier, Belgium c.1828
Parentage Not recorded
Fully double, blush-pink blooms with a soft tissue-paper quality, freely produced in clusters. Dark leaden grey-green foliage. Highly scented and healthy. The plant is well proportioned.
○ ♦♦♦ S H 1.2m W 90cm (4 x 3ft) Zone 5

'Great Maiden's Blush' ('Cuisse de Nymphe', 'Incarnata', 'La Virginale', 'La Séduisante', 'Cuisse de Nymphe Émue')
Origin Europe **First noted** 15th century or earlier
Parentage Not recorded
A sophisticated rose, one of the most beautiful of its group. Very double blooms are of soft blush-pink and have a seductive perfume. Grey-green foliage. Usually at the top of my list of favourites.
○ ♦♦♦ S H 1.8m W 1.2m (6 x 4ft) Zone 5

'Jeanne d'Arc'
Introduced Vibert, France 1818
Parentage Not recorded
Double flowers are attractively disarranged with both infurled and reflexing petals, cream in colour, fading to white in hot sun. Scented. Grey-green leaves on an upright shrub.
○ ♦♦ S H 1.8m W 1.5m (6 x 5ft) Zone 5

'Königin von Dänemark' ('Queen of Denmark')
Introduced Booth, Denmark 1826
Parentage R. alba x unknown Damask hybrid
Clusters of very double, highly scented, mid-pink flowers, somewhat smaller than those of most other Albas; also the stems more heavily populated with thorns. Grey-green foliage. This Alba has much to commend it.
○ ♦♦♦ S H 1.5m W 1.2m (5 x 4ft) Zone 4

'Maxima' ('Alba Maxima', Jacobite rose, Bonnie Prince Charlie's Rose, White rose of York, 'Great Double White', Cheshire rose)
Origin Europe **First noted** 15th century or before
Parentage Possibly R. canina x R. gallica
Double, infurled blooms of white with a slight blush, freely produced in medium-sized clusters. Superb fragrance. Grey-green, typical Alba foliage. A beautiful rose with the purity one associates with this group.
○ ♦♦♦ S H 2.2m W 1.5m (7 x 5ft) Zone 4

'Mme Legras de St Germain'
Origin Europe **First noted** Early 19th century
Parentage Not recorded
Fully double, rather pompon-like, pure white flowers borne in large clusters amid soft-textured, soft leaden-grey leaves. Perfumed. Blooms can cope well with both damp and hot weather. A good shrub and also makes a pleasing climber, especially on a wall.
○ ♦♦ S H 2.2m W 1.8m (7 x 6ft) Zone 5

'Mme Plantier'
Introduced Plantier, France 1835
Parentage Not recorded
Clusters of fully double, scented, pure white flowers with muddled-looking petals. Foliage greyish green, and stems with few thorns. A vigorous rose, happy in an informal or mixed border; also good climbing against a wall. Although best classified as an Alba, it probably has some R. moschata in its make-up.
○ ♦♦ S H 4m W 2.5m (12 x 8ft) Zone 4

'Pompon Blanc Parfait'
Introduced Verdier, France c.1876
Parentage Not recorded
Small clusters of fully double, pure white blooms, with reflexed petals forming small pompons. Fragrant. Complemented by soft grey-green foliage. Growth is neat and compact.
○ ♦♦ S H 1.2m W 90cm (4 x 3ft) Zone 5

'Semi-Plena' ('Alba Semi-Plena', R. alba 'Suaveolens', R. alba 'Nivea')
Origin Europe **First noted** Pre-15th century
Parentage Not recorded
Semi-double, very fragrant, pure white flowers displaying superb yellow stamens when fully open. A tall, upright, thorny bush with leaden grey-green leaves. Sets a few hips occasionally. Good for wild gardens and informal hedging. (Some authorities treat 'Semi-Plena', 'Suaveolens', and 'Nivea' as three distinct varieties; I feel that there is just one variety, its clones having varying numbers of petals.)
○ ♦♦♦ S H 2.5m W 1.5m (8 x 5ft) Zone 4

The Damasks

R. x damascena (Damask rose, Summer Damask)
Origin Middle East **First noted** Very ancient
Parentage Possibly R. gallica x R. phoenicia
Seldom seen today. My plant produces dense clusters of very double, highly perfumed, soft to deep pink flowers. Growth upright and thorny, clothed in soft-textured, grey-green foliage. Hips small and inconspicuous.
☼ ♦♦♦ S H 1.5m W 90cm (5 x 3ft) Zone 5

'Belle Amour'
Discovered Lindsay 1950
Parentage Not recorded
Double, fragrant blooms with crinkled petals of soft pinkish salmon and golden stamens. Stems prickly. Foliage grey-green and soft to touch. This rose has an affinity to the Albas and should be better known.
☼ ♦♦ S H 1.5m W 90cm (5 x 3ft) Zone 5

'Blush Damask'
Origin Unknown **First noted** Ancient
Parentage Not recorded
A vigorous, dense shrub, flowering very freely in early summer. Medium-sized, double, mid-pink flowers paling to soft pink at the edges. Very fragrant. Dark green foliage plentiful, but rather coarse. Excellent for hedging.
○ ♦♦♦ S H 1.2m W 90cm (4 x 3ft) Zone 5

'Königin von Dänemark'

'Mme Legras de St Germain'

'Mme Plantier'

'Semi-Plena'

'Ispahan'

'Kazanlik'

'De Meaux'

'Duchesse de Rohan'

'Celsiana'

Origin Probably Europe **First noted** Pre-1750
Parentage Not recorded
Clusters of almost fully double, highly scented flowers of clear pink, fading to blush with age, with golden anthers. Foliage light greyish green. Growth medium and slightly arching.
○ ♦♦♦ S H 1.5m W 1.2m (5 x 4ft) Zone 5

'Hebe's Lip' ('Reine Blanche', 'Rubrotincta')

Introduced Paul, UK 1912
Parentage Probably *R. x damascena* x *R. rubiginosa*
Flowers rather more than single, off-white with red edges to each petal. Very fragrant. Thorny shrub with coarse, dark green foliage, said to be scented but difficult to detect. Sometimes listed as a Sweet Briar.
○ ♦♦♦ S H 1.2m W 1.2m (4 x 4ft) Zone 5

'Ispahan' ('Rose d'Isfahan')

Origin Middle East **First noted** Pre-1832
Parentage Not recorded
Fully double, very fragrant, rich pink flowers, shapely at all stages. Fairly upright stems with sparse thorns and attractive mid-green foliage. One of the most beautiful of its group.
☼ ♦♦♦ S H 1.2m W 90cm (4 x 3ft) Zone 5

'Kazanlik' ('Trigintipetala')

Origin Middle East **First noted** Very ancient
Parentage Not recorded
A vigorous rose, whose flowers are used for the manufacture of perfume in Bulgaria. Blooms a little more than semi-double, rather shaggy, and warm pink. Foliage is mid- to dark green and rather coarse looking; very thorny growth is relaxed and lanky.
☼ ♦♦♦ S H 1.5m W 1.2m (5 x 4ft) Zone 4

'La Ville de Bruxelles'

Introduced Vibert, France 1849
Parentage Not recorded
Large, fully double, pure deep pink flowers with incurving centres. Very fragrant. Growth strong, vigorous, and upright. Coarse, mid-green leaves.
☼ ♦♦♦ S H 90cm W 90cm (3 x 3ft) Zone 5

'Leda' (Painted Damask)

Origin Europe
First noted Probably 19th century
Parentage Not recorded
Fully double, soft blush flowers, opening cushion-like, with red brushmarks around petal edges. Very fragrant. Foliage dark green. Growth bushy, dense.
☼ ♦♦♦ S H 90cm W 90cm (3 x 3ft) Zone 5

'Mme Hardy'

Introduced Hardy, France 1832
Parentage Not recorded
One of the most beautiful of all roses. Fully double, highly fragrant, pure white flowers. Foliage is soft to touch and light grey-green. Stems upright and darkish green.
☼ ♦♦♦ S H 1.5m W 1.5m (5 x 5ft) Zone 5

'Omar Khayyám'

Origin Middle East **First noted** Ancient
Parentage Not recorded
A short-growing rose with fully double, scented, silvery pink flowers and rather sparse, grey-green foliage. Blooms mainly in summer, but occasionally produces a few flowers in autumn.
☼ ♦♦ R H 90cm W 90cm (3 x 3ft) Zone 5

'Quatre Saisons' (Autumn Damask, *R. x damascena bifera*, *R. x damascena semperflorens*)

Origin Middle East **First noted** Ancient
Parentage Possibly *R. gallica* x *R. moschata* x *R. fedtschenkoana*
Modern genetic fingerprint technology casts doubt on the accepted parentage of this rose. Double, soft pink flowers in short-stemmed, dense clusters. Highly fragrant and repeat flowering. Has darkish green foliage and fairly thorny, downy stems.
☼ ♦♦♦ R H 1.2m W 90cm (4 x 3ft) Zone 5

'St Nicholas'

Introduced James, UK 1950
Parentage Possibly Damask x *R. gallica*
An unusual rose. Short growing with downy, grey-green foliage. Vicious spines. Fragrant, bright pink flowers, not quite single, with prominent golden stamens; mainly in summer, with a few in autumn.
☼ ♦♦ R H 90cm W 90cm (3 x 3ft) Zone 5

'York and Lancaster' (*R. x damascena versicolor*)

Origin Unknown **First noted** Pre-1550
Parentage Possibly a sport of 'Kazanlik'
Semi-double, shaggy flowers of mid-pink with random white stripes. Occasionally white blooms in a cluster of pink. Fragrant. Thorny, arching growth. Mid-green foliage is soft to touch.
☼ ♦♦ S H 1.5m W 1.2m (5 x 4ft) Zone 4

The Centifolias

R. x centifolia (Cabbage rose, Provence rose)

Origin Europe **First noted** Pre-16th century
Parentage Not recorded
Fully double, cabbage-like, strong bright pink flowers opening flat and quartered. Very fragrant. Shoots thorny and foliage coarse greyish green. Inclined to sprawl. Good as a small climber, especially on a wall. Slightly prone to mildew.
☼ ♦♦♦ S ☉ H 1.8m W 2.2m (6 x 7ft) Zone 4

'Blanchefleur'

Introduced Vibert, France 1835
Parentage Not recorded
Clusters of fully double flowers opening flat, in blush-white with pink tints. Very fragrant. Stems thorny; soft-textured foliage greyish green in colour. Tidy for a Centifolia.
○ ♦♦♦ S H 1.5m W 1.2m (5 x 4ft) Zone 5

'Bullata' (Lettuce-leaf rose)

Origin Unknown **First noted** Pre-16th century
Parentage Not recorded
Flowers identical to those of *R. x centifolia*, as is growth habit. Differs mainly in its foliage, which is large and crinkled like the leaves of a lettuce.
☼ ♦♦♦ S H 1.8m W 2.2m (6 x 7ft) Zone 4

'De Meaux' ('Rose de Meaux')

Origin Unknown **First noted** Pre-1790
Parentage Not recorded
A short, upright bush with lots of greyish dark green foliage. Small, fully double, soft pink, dianthus-like flowers. Scented. Especially rewarding in pots. There is also a white form, identical in all other respects.
☼ ♦♦ S H 60cm W 60cm (2 x 2ft) Zone 5

'Duchesse de Rohan' ('Duc de Rohan')

Origin Unknown **First noted** *c.*1860
Parentage Not recorded
Fully double flowers of rich warm pink paling to lavender. Highly scented. Unusually for a Centifolia, occasionally repeats its flowers. Thorny stems; grey-green foliage. Mixes well with herbaceous plants.
○ ♦♦♦ R H 1.5m W 1.2m (5 x 4ft) Zone 5

'Fantin-Latour'

Origin & parentage Unknown
A very beautiful example of its type. Fully double, very fragrant, soft pink flowers opening cushion-like. Growth moderately thorny; foliage plentiful, soft to touch, and grey-green. Mixes well with other shrubs.
○ ♦♦♦ S H 1.5m W 1.2m (5 x 4ft) Zone 5

'Juno'

Origin Unknown **First noted** 1832
Parentage Not recorded
An arching, small to medium-sized shrub, moderately thorny with dark green foliage. Globular, white flowers blushed soft pink open fully double and cushion-like. Very fragrant.
○ ♦♦♦ S H 1.2m W 1.2m (4 x 4ft) Zone 5

'Petite de Hollande' ('Pompon des Dames', 'Petite Junon de Hollande')

Origin Holland **First noted** 1800
Parentage Not recorded
A compact shrub producing many, smallish, fully double flowers, clear pink when fully open. Growth fairly thorny; foliage mid-green. Ideal in groups of three among perennials.
○ ♦♦ S H 90cm W 90cm (3 x 3ft) Zone 5

'Pompon de Bourgogne' (*R. burgundica*, Burgundian rose, 'Parvifolia')

Origin Unknown **First noted** Pre-1664
Parentage Not recorded
One of the smaller Centifolias, upright in growth with grey-green foliage closely packed on thinnish, relatively thornless stems. Slightly fragrant, pompon-like flowers, rosy pink to claret, in small clusters. Superb in pots or in groups.
☼ ♦ S H 60cm W 60cm (2 x 2ft) Zone 5

'Robert le Diable'

Origin France
Parentage Not recorded
Sizeable, fully double, fragrant flowers on the crimson side of red, with lilac and grey highlights, each with a small, green eye. Freely produced on a tidy, fairly compact plant with dark green foliage. Looks good with white herbaceous plants.
☼ ♦♦ S H 90cm W 90cm (3 x 3ft) Zone 6

'Rose des Peintres' ('Centfeuille des Peintres', *R.* x *centifolia* 'Major')

Origin & parentage Unknown
Beautiful flowers similar to those of *R.* x *centifolia*, but more refined and a brighter pink. Highly scented. Plant rather sprawling and thorny, with ample dark green foliage. Best if given support.
☼ ♦♦♦ S H 1.8m W 1.5m (6 x 5ft) Zone 5

'Spong'

Introduced Spong, France 1805
Parentage Not recorded
A rose of medium stature with many dianthus-like, scented, rich rose-pink flowers, appearing a little earlier than others of its kind, occasionally with the odd bloom later on. Growth bushy and upright. Produced in pots for selling in Paris street markets in the early 19th century.
☼ ♦♦ R H 90cm W 90cm (3 x 3ft) Zone 5

'Tour de Malakoff' ('Black Jack')

Introduced Soupert & Notting, Luxembourg 1856
Parentage Not recorded
Loose, fully double, magenta-purple flowers fading to lilac-grey. Very fragrant. Darkish green foliage. Growth rather thorny and lanky, needing support. Looks good grown as a short climber, with white clematis.
○ ♦♦♦ S H 2.5m W 1.5m (8 x 5ft) Zone 5

'Unique Blanche' (White Provence, 'Vierge de Cléry')

Origin UK **First noted** 1775
Parentage Probably a sport of another Centifolia
Very beautiful, double, pure white flowers of silky texture, in small clusters. Very fragrant. Growth relaxed, bushy, and thorny, with soft to touch, greyish green foliage. Excellent in shrubberies.
○ ♦♦♦ S H 1.2m W 1.2m (4 x 4ft) Zone 4

'Village Maid' ('Belle des Jardins', 'La Rubanée', *R.* x *centifolia* 'Variegata')

Origin France **First noted** 1845
Parentage Not recorded
A very vigorous, thorny rose, upright in growth, with good grey-green foliage. Very free flowering. Highly scented flowers are globular, double, and soft creamy white, streaked and striped purplish pink.
☼ ♦♦♦ S H 1.5m W 1.2m (5 x 4ft) Zone 5

The Gallicas

'Agatha'

Origin France **First noted** *c.*1818
Parentage Possibly *R. gallica* x *R. pendulina*
Beautiful. Fully double, fragrant, deep raspberry-pink flowers with paler edges. Irregular petal formation gives loose, quartered effect, the texture reminiscent of crêpe paper. Dense, relaxed growth, with dark green foliage.
○ ♦♦ S H 1.5m W 1.2m (5 x 4ft) Zone 5

'Alain Blanchard'

Introduced Vibert, France 1839
Parentage *R.* x *centifolia* x *R. gallica*
Large, open, semi-double, scented blooms are crimson smudged purple, with prominent golden stamens. Growth bushy and dense with dark green foliage. Looks good among soft pink and white roses.
○ ♦ S H 1.2m W 1.2m (4 x 4ft) Zone 5

'Anais Ségales'

Introduced Vibert, France 1837
Parentage Not recorded
Fully double, bright pinkish to soft crimson flowers in small clusters. Fragrant. Growth tidy and bushy. Foliage profuse, grey-green. Good as a pot plant.
○ ♦♦ S H 90cm W 90cm (3 x 3ft) Zone 5

'Belle de Crécy'

Introduced Hardy, France 1829
Parentage Not recorded
Flowers fully double, opening cushion-like, a mixture of purple, mauve, pink, and grey. Very fragrant. Upright, fairly thorn-free growth. Foliage grey-green, plentiful, and coarse to touch. Can be slightly temperamental and prone to mildew.
☼ ♦♦♦ S ⊙ H 1.2m W 90cm (4 x 3ft) Zone 5

'Belle Isis'

Introduced Parmentier, Belgium 1845
Parentage Not recorded
Flowers open flat and almost fully double, delicate soft pink, and very fragrant. Growth tidy and bushy. Foliage dark green. Makes a nice hedge.
○ ♦♦♦ S H 1.2m W 90cm (4 x 3ft) Zone 5

'Pompon de Bourgogne'

'Village Maid'

'Agatha'

'Belle de Crécy'

'Charles de Mills'

'De la Maître d'École'

'Duchesse d'Angoulême'

'Rosa Mundi'

'Camaieux'
Introduced Vibert, France 1830
Parentage Not recorded
Almost fully double blooms of good size, in silvery pink overlaid with irregular stripes of purplish crimson, becoming more lilac-purple with age. Lovely scent. Arching stems carry the blooms well against healthy, grey-green foliage. A compact, bushy plant.
○ ♦♦ S H 90cm W 90cm (3 x 3ft) Zone 5

'Cardinal de Richelieu'
Introduced Parmentier, Belgium pre-1847
Parentage Not recorded
A delightfully symmetrical rose, the outer petals slightly reflexed, the inner ones infurled towards the centre. Double, soft-textured, rich purple blooms, lightly scented. Growth relaxed but bushy. Plentiful dark green foliage, sometimes edged maroon.
○ ♦ S H 1.2m W 90cm (4 x 3ft) Zone 5

'Charles de Mills' ('Bizarre Triomphant')
Introduced Roseraie de l'Haÿ Collection, France
Parentage Not recorded
Large, very double, cushion-like flowers in a mixture of magenta-red to purple and deep pink, displaying a green eye when fully open. Sadly, no fragrance. Blooms in abundance in early summer. Typical dark green Gallica foliage without gloss. Relaxed growth.
○ S H 1.2m W 1.2m (4 x 4ft) Zone 5

'Complicata'
Origin Unknown
Parentage Possibly *R. gallica* x *R. canina* or *R.* x *macrantha*
Large, saucer-like, single blooms are bright pink with paler centres and golden stamens. Flowers once only but is flamboyant. Growth broad and arching, with greyish dark green foliage. May be used against a wall, among other shrubs, or climbing into trees.
○ ♦♦ S H 3m W 1.8m (10 x 6ft) Zone 5

'Conditorum'
Origin France **First noted** Ancient
Parentage Not recorded
Fully double, fragrant, ruby-red to cerise flowers. A bushy, upright, relatively thornless plant with good fresh green foliage.
○ ♦♦ S H 1.2m W 90cm (4 x 3ft) Zone 5

'De la Maître d'École'
Introduced Coquereau, France 1836
Parentage Not recorded
Large, fully double, flat, quartered blooms, mainly pink with highlights of lilac and magenta. Infurled central petals surround a green eye. Fragrant. Flowers borne in trusses on arching, relatively thornless branches with dark grey-green leaves.
○ ♦♦ S H 90cm W 90cm (3 x 3ft) Zone 5

'Duchesse d'Angoulême' ('Duc d'Angoulême')
Introduced Vibert, France c.1835
Parentage Not recorded
Almost fully double, scented, soft blush-pink flowers with golden stamens. Growth relaxed, bushy. Foliage crisp, bright green. Mixes well with perennials.
○ ♦♦ S H 1.2m W 90cm (4 x 3ft) Zone 5

'Duchesse de Montebello'
Introduced Laffay, France 1829
Parentage Gallica x China
Flowers very double, soft powder-pink, with an almost translucent quality, infurled at the centre with a green eye and opening flat. Pleasing fragrance. Foliage healthy and dark green. Good in pots.
○ ♦♦ S H 1.2m W 90cm (4 x 3ft) Zone 5

'Empress Josephine' ('Impératrice Joséphine', *R.* x *francofurtana* 'Empress Josephine')
Introduced Descemet, France pre-1815
Parentage *R. gallica* x *R. majalis*
A sumptuous rose. Almost double, slightly ragged flowers with loosely arranged petals of deep pink, heavily veined with softer pink and lavender highlights. Somewhat sprawling stems well clothed with dark green foliage; relatively free of thorns.
○ ♦♦ S H 1.5m W 1.2m (5 x 4ft) Zone 5

R. gallica officinalis (Apothecary's rose, Red rose of Lancaster, Rose of Provins)
Origin Europe, Southwest Asia **First noted** Ancient
Parentage Not recorded
Semi-double, light crimson blooms with prominent yellow stamens. Highly perfumed. Dense, firm-textured, grey-green foliage on a well-proportioned plant. Much valued for its scent by the apothecaries of the Middle Ages. Excellent for hedging.
○ ♦♦♦ S ☉ H 90cm W 90cm (3 x 3ft) Zone 5

'Gloire de France'
Introduced Bizard, France 1828
Parentage Not recorded
Medium-sized, very double flowers of pale pink with deeper pink centres, paling almost to white in hot sun. Bushy growth with crisp, dark green foliage. Makes a dense, wide-growing specimen shrub.
○ ♦♦ S H 90cm W 1.2m (3 x 4ft) Zone 5

'Hippolyte'
Origin Unknown **First noted** Pre-1842
Parentage Probably Gallica x China
Small, double flowers of purple and magenta, delightfully formed with inwardly furled inner petals but reflexing outer petals. Perfumed. Borne in clusters on thin, willowy, almost thornless, arching stems. Foliage smooth, dark green, and plentiful.
✿ ♦♦ S H 90cm W 1.2m (3 x 4ft) Zone 5

'La Belle Sultane' (*R. gallica* 'Violacea', 'Violacea')
Introduced Dupont, France pre-1811
Parentage Not recorded
Blooms a little more than single, mottled soft violet to purple-red, with golden stamens. Fragrant. Freely produced on a shrub of upright stature with coarse, grey-green foliage.
○ ♦♦ S H 1.5m W 1.2m (5 x 4ft) Zone 5

'Président de Sèze' ('Mme Hébert')
Introduced Hébert, France 1828
Parentage Not recorded
Double flowers of lilac-magenta with softer shades at the petal edges. Grey-green foliage on slightly thorny, arching wood. A beautiful, very fragrant rose.
○ ♦♦♦ S H 1.2m W 90cm (4 x 3ft) Zone 5

'Rosa Mundi' (*R. gallica versicolor*)
Origin Unknown **First noted** Ancient
Parentage Sport of *R. gallica officinalis*
A famous and striking rose. Semi-double flowers are striped and streaked in crimson and white. Coarse, grey-green foliage on a well-proportioned shrub. An excellent hedging rose. A little prone to mildew.
○ ♦♦ S ☉ H 90cm W 90cm (3 x 3ft) Zone 5

'Tuscany' (Old velvet rose)
Origin & parentage Unknown
Lovely, semi-double, dark red flowers with a good array of golden stamens and strong scent. Growth upright with lots of rather crinkled, dark green leaves. Useful as a hedge. A little prone to mildew.
○ ♦♦♦ S ☉ H 1.2m W 90cm (4 x 3ft) Zone 5

'Tuscany Superb'
Introduced Paul, UK 1848
Parentage Possibly a sport of 'Tuscany'
A very beautiful rose. Double blooms are deep dusky red with a velvet texture, often dusted with yellow pollen from stamens. Very strongly scented. Fairly upright in growth with large, dark green leaves. Excellent in herbaceous borders and for hedging.
○ ♦♦♦ S H 1.2m W 90cm (4 x 3ft) Zone 5

'Velutinaeflora'
Origin Unknown **First noted** Possibly 19th century
Parentage Not recorded
Single, deep pink, heavily veined flowers with pronounced golden stamens opening from pointed buds with soft, downy sepals. Fragrant. Large, dark green leaves densely populating a thorny shrub. Slightly prone to mildew.
○ ♦♦♦ S ⊙ H 90cm W 90cm (3 x 3ft) Zone 5

The Pimpinellifolias

'Burnet Double Pink'
Origin & parentage Unknown
Small, double, cupped flowers, a delicate shade of pink with yellow stamens, profusely borne. Buds globular. Fragrant. Growth very bushy and thorny with fern-like, dark green foliage. Fruit drooping, spherical, mahogany to black. Excellent for hedging.
○ ♦♦ S H 90cm W 90cm (3 x 3ft) Zone 5

'Burnet Double White'
As above, except flowers are pure white.
○ ♦♦ S H 90cm W 90cm (3 x 3ft) Zone 5

'Burnet Irish Marbled'
As Burnet Double Pink, except flowers soft purple-mauve marbled and streaked white and soft pink.
○ ♦♦ S H 90cm W 90cm (3 x 3ft) Zone 5

'Burnet Marbled Pink'
As Burnet Double Pink, except flowers are pink marbled and streaked white
○ ♦♦ S H 90cm W 90cm (3 x 3ft) Zone 5

'Falkland'
Introduced UK, early 19th century
Parentage Not recorded
Delightful semi-double, slightly fragrant flowers, opening from globular buds, are lilac-pink to mauve, paling to soft pink. Foliage fern-like and dark green. Growth prickly. Hips globose, maroon to black.
○ ♦ S H 90cm W 90cm (3 x 3ft) Zone 5

'Glory of Edzell'
Introduced UK, early 19th century
Parentage Not recorded
Single, fragrant, clear bright pink flowers with paler centres and prominent stamens, produced in late spring. Growth dense and prickly. Dark green, fern-like foliage. Hips maroon.
○ ♦♦ Sp H 1.2m W 1.2m (4 x 4ft) Zone 5

'Mary Queen of Scots'
Origin Unknown **First noted** Early 19th century
Parentage Not recorded
Attractive single flowers, white heavily marked lilac and purple, with golden stamens; borne in late spring, followed by small, mahogany hips. Slight fragrance. Growth thorny and upright. Foliage grey-green. Superb in groups of three in shrubberies.
○ ♦ Sp H 90cm W 90cm (3 x 3ft) Zone 5

'Mrs Colville'
Origin Unknown **First noted** Early 19th century
Parentage Not recorded
Single, fragrant, deep red to magenta flowers with soft yellow stamens. Prolific in early summer. Foliage fern-like, and darkish blue-green. Growth dense and thorny. Fruit maroon. Excels as a pot plant.
○ ♦♦ S H 1.2m W 90cm (4 x 3ft) Zone 5

'Old Yellow Scotch'
Origin Unknown **First noted** Late 18th century
Parentage Not recorded
A robust plant with many thorny stems. Flowers slightly more than semi-double, fragrant, deep yellow. Foliage coarse, fern-like, and dark greyish green. Good for hedging.
○ ♦♦ Sp H 1.2m W 90cm (4 x 3ft) Zone 4

'Single Cherry'
Origin Unknown **First noted** Early 19th century
Parentage Not recorded
Sizeable, single, scented, bright cherry-red flowers with soft yellow stamens. Growth bushy and prickly with abundant fern-like, darkish green foliage. Deep maroon hips. Mixes well with herbaceous plants.
○ ♦♦ S H 90cm W 90cm (3 x 3ft) Zone 5

'Stanwell Perpetual'
Introduced Lee, UK 1838
Parentage 'Quatre Saisons' x *R. pimpinellifolia*
Large, fully double flowers, opening quartered, soft silky pink, very fragrant. Blooms all summer. Growth bushy, slightly arching. Leaves small, numerous, and grey-green, but sometimes mottled greyish purple.
○ ♦♦♦ C H 1.5m W 1.5m (5 x 5ft) Zone 4

'William III'
Origin Unknown **First noted** Early 19th century
Parentage Not recorded
Semi-double, cup-shaped, maroon flowers, paling with age to magenta. Scented. Compact growth with thorny stems and dark green foliage. Hips chocolate coloured. Good in pots or among herbaceous plants.
○ ♦♦ S H 90cm W 90cm (3 x 3ft) Zone 5

'Williams' Double Yellow'
Introduced Williams, UK 1828
Parentage *R. pimpinellifolia* x *R. foetida* 'Persiana'
A bushy plant with many sharp thorns and rough, fern-like, dark green foliage. Semi-double, clear yellow flowers freely borne in late spring. Fragrant.
○ ♦♦ Sp H 1.2m W 90cm (4 x 3ft) Zone 4

The Moss Roses

'Alfred de Dalmas' ('Mousseline')
Introduced Laffay, France 1855
Parentage Of Damask origin
Flowers semi-double, slightly cupped, creamy pink, borne all summer. Fragrant. Growth stocky, upright. Foliage mid-green. Foliage, calyces, and young stems covered with bristly, khaki-coloured moss. Slightly prone to black spot.
○ ♦♦ C ⊙ H 60cm W 60cm (2 x 2ft) Zone 5

'Blanche Moreau'
Introduced Moreau-Robert, France 1880
Parentage 'Comtesse de Murinais' x 'Quatre Saisons Blanc Mousseux'
Beautiful, fully double, pure white flowers on an upright plant with good darkish green foliage. Scented. Stems, buds, and young foliage covered with bristly, maroon moss. Rather mildew prone. Occasionally gives one or two blooms in autumn.
☼ ♦♦ R ⊙ H 1.2m W 90cm (4 x 3ft) Zone 5

'Mrs Colville'

'Single Cherry'

'Stanwell Perpetual'

'Alfred de Dalmas'

'Common Moss'

'Comtesse de Murinais'

'Jeanne de Montfort'

'Mme Louis Lévêque'

'Capitaine John Ingram'
Introduced Laffay, France 1855
Parentage Not recorded
A very good Moss rose with much character. Medium-sized, fully double, fragrant, reddish to purple flowers. Slightly sprawling. Pine-scented, purplish brown moss on buds and stems. Foliage dark green.
○ ♦♦ **S H** 1.2m **W** 90cm (4 x 3ft) Zone 5

'Chapeau de Napoléon' (Crested Moss, R. x centifolia 'Cristata')
Introduced Vibert, France 1826
Parentage Probably a seedling of R. x centifolia
Fully double, highly scented flowers of deep silvery pink; each bud with a crest of moss on its calyx, resembling the outline of a cocked hat, hence its name. Growth rather sprawling; foliage grey-green.
✿ ♦♦♦ **S H** 1.5m **W** 1.2m (5 x 4ft) Zone 4

'Common Moss' (Old pink Moss, 'Communis')
Origin France **First noted** Pre-1700
Parentage Improved form of R. x centifolia 'Muscosa'
Fully double, bright deep pink flowers emerge from heavily mossed buds. Very fragrant. Wide growing and robust. Young shoots also well covered with mid-green, pine-scented moss. Mid-green foliage.
○ ♦♦♦ **S H** 1.2m **W** 1.2m (4 x 4ft) Zone 4

'Comtesse de Murinais'
Introduced Vibert, France 1843
Parentage Not recorded
Cushion-like, fully double flowers of soft pink to cream. Very fragrant. Lanky, spreading growth with plentiful mid-green leaves Buds and young shoots heavily mossed with bristly, aromatic, light green moss. Needs support to give of its best.
○ ♦♦♦ **S H** 1.5m **W** 1.2m (5 x 4ft) Zone 5

'Deuil de Paul Fontaine'
Introduced Fontaine, France 1873
Parentage Not recorded
Large, fully double, fragrant, very dark red flowers in midsummer, and sometimes a few later on. Growth bushy. Foliage and moss reddish green, changing to mid-green. A little prone to mildew.
✿ ♦♦ **R** ⊙ **H** 90cm **W** 90cm (3 x 3ft) Zone 7

'Duchesse de Verneuil'
Introduced Portemer, France 1856
Parentage Not recorded
A medium to tall Moss rose. Bright pink flowers open fully double, flattish, and cushion-like. Very fragrant. Mid- to light green foliage on strong, upright stems. Moss dense, aromatic, and dark green.
○ ♦♦♦ **S H** 1.5m **W** 90cm (5 x 3ft) Zone 5

'Général Kléber'
Introduced Robert, France 1856
Parentage Not recorded
Densely moss-covered buds open to fully double, soft sugary pink flowers. Very fragrant. Tidy and easy-going, with light green foliage. Moss bright green and strongly aromatic. One of the best Moss roses.
○ ♦♦♦ **S H** 1.2m **W** 1.2m (4 x 4ft) Zone 5

'Gloire des Mousseux'
Introduced Laffay, France 1852
Parentage Not recorded
Very large, fully double, soft blush-pink flowers open from well-mossed buds. Strongly scented. Foliage and stems dark green; moss very dark green. Growth rather lax. Inclined to mildew late in the season.
○ ♦♦♦ **S** ⊙ **H** 1.2m **W** 1.2m (4 x 4ft) Zone 5

'Henri Martin' (Red Moss)
Introduced Laffay, France 1863
Parentage Not recorded
Medium to large, fully double, fragrant, bright red flowers in large clusters. Buds and flower stalks thickly covered in reddish tan moss. Healthy, bright green foliage. Superb with support.
✿ ♦♦ **S H** 1.5m **W** 1.2m (5 x 4ft) Zone 5

'James Mitchell'
Introduced Verdier, France 1861
Parentage Not recorded
A densely growing rose. Large quantities of semi-double, fragrant, mid-pink flowers, with mossy buds and stems. Foliage dark green and crisp. Purplish moss also crisp.
○ ♦♦ **S H** 1.2m **W** 1.2m (4 x 4ft) Zone 5

'Jeanne de Montfort'
Introduced Robert, France c.1851
Parentage Not recorded
A tall Moss rose with fully double, clear rose-pink flowers produced in large, heavy clusters. Fragrant. Crisp, maroon moss, scented like pine needles. Dark green foliage. Needs support to flourish. Rather mildew prone, but still has much to recommend it.
○ ♦♦ **S** ⊙ **H** 2.5m **W** 1.5m (8 x 5ft) Zone 5

'Mme Louis Lévêque'
Introduced Lévêque, France 1898
Parentage Not recorded
Sizeable, cup-shaped, fully double flowers of soft, warm pink with a good scent and silky texture. Leathery, mid- to dark green foliage. Growth sturdy and upright. Moss soft, pinkish green, and dense. A little prone to mildew.
○ ♦♦♦ **S** ⊙ **H** 1.2m **W** 90cm (4 x 3ft) Zone 5

'Mrs William Paul'
Introduced Paul, UK 1869
Parentage Not recorded
A strong-growing, bushy plant with mossy flowerbuds and stems. Well clothed with bright, mid-green leaves. Flowers almost fully double, bright pink with reddish highlights and a good scent. Repeated intermittently in late summer.
○ ♦♦ **R H** 1.2m **W** 90cm (4 x 3ft) Zone 5

'Nuits de Young' ('Old Black')
Introduced Laffay, France 1845
Parentage Not recorded
Large clusters of small, fully double, highly scented flowers of deep maroon, almost black, with moss only a few shades paler. Foliage dark green, crisp to touch. Growth rather lax. Good in groups of three or five. Slightly mildew prone.
○ ♦♦♦ **S** ⊙ **H** 1.2m **W** 90cm (4 x 3ft) Zone 4

'Quatre Saisons Blanc Mousseux'
Introduced Laffay, France pre-1837
Parentage Sport of 'Quatre Saisons'
Of Damask origin, this rose produces fully double, highly fragrant, pure white flowers, repeated intermittently after a rewarding first flush. Moss dark green to plum coloured. Foliage dark green. Susceptible to mildew.
○ ♦♦♦ **R** ⊙ **H** 1.2m **W** 90cm (4 x 3ft) Zone 5

'René d'Anjou'
Introduced Robert, France 1853
Parentage Not recorded
Fully double flowers, opening flat, in a superb shade of soft pink. Well scented. Growth tidy and contained. Dark green foliage. Moss bronzy dark green and aromatic. A good rose for smaller gardens.
○ ♦♦♦ **S H** 1.2m **W** 90cm (4 x 3ft) Zone 5

'Robert Léopold'
Introduced Buatois, France 1941
Parentage Not recorded
Semi-double, lightly fragrant flowers in a blend of pinks with conspicuous yellow centres when fully open. Repeats flowers spasmodically in autumn. Ginger-coloured moss, dense on calyces and stems. Upright growth with durable, dark green foliage.
○ ● R H 1.8m W 90cm (6 x 3ft) Zone 5

'Salet'
Introduced Lacharme, France 1854
Parentage Not recorded
Clusters of fully double, flat, strongly fragrant, deep pink flowers, emerging from buds with sparse ginger moss. Rough, mid- to dark green foliage. Tidy, easy-going. Suitable for pots and smaller gardens.
○ ●●● S H 90cm W 90cm (3 x 3ft) Zone 5

'William Lobb' ('Duchess d'Istrie', Old velvet Moss)
Introduced Laffay, France 1855
Parentage Not recorded
Huge clusters of semi-double, fragrant flowers, cloudy mauve-purple with grey and pink highlights, on long, bendy, pleasantly coloured stems. Moss is soft and pinkish green; foliage greyish green. Best with support or as a climber.
○ ●● S H 2.5m W 1.5m (8 x 5ft) Zone 5

The Chinas

'Arethusa'
Introduced Paul, UK 1903
Parentage Not recorded
Double, lightly scented, soft yellow flowers, with shades of orange deep down. Opening informally, slightly ragged, and in clusters. Foliage shiny, darkish green. Growth bushy.
☼ ● C H 90cm W 90cm (3 x 3ft) Zone 8

'Bloomfield Abundance' (USA 'Spray Cécile Brünner')
Introduced Thomas, USA 1920
Parentage 'Sylvia' x 'Dorothy Page-Roberts'
Large clusters of miniature HT-shaped flowers of soft shell-pink. Lightly scented. Foliage coppery green, a little sparse. Growth upright, tall for a China. Flowers make exquisite buttonholes.
☼ ● C H 1.8m W 1.2m (6 x 4ft) Zone 6

'Cécile Brünner' (Sweetheart rose, Maltese rose, Mignon rose)
Introduced Ducher, France 1881
Parentage Polyantha x 'Mme de Tartas'
Delightfully shapely, soft shell-pink flowers, in clusters on a tidy plant. Mild fragrance. Lovely as buttonholes. Growth spindly but bushy. Foliage sparse, purplish green.
☼ ● C H 75cm W 60cm (2½ x 2ft) Zone 6

'Cécile Brünner' Climbing
Introduced Hosp, USA 1904
Parentage Sport of 'Cécile Brünner'
Flowers identical to the bush form, in early summer with an occasional bloom in some autumns. Growth very vigorous, almost rampant. Plentiful purple-green foliage, nearly evergreen. Good climbing into trees.
○ ● S H 10m W 6m (30 x 20ft) Zone 6

'Cécile Brünner' White
Introduced Fauque, France 1909
Parentage Sport of 'Cécile Brünner'
As 'Cécile Brünner' in all respects except colour.
☼ ● C H 75cm W 60cm (2½ x 2ft) Zone 6

'Comtesse du Cayla'
Introduced Guillot, France 1902
Parentage Seedling of ('Rival de Paestum' x 'Mme Falcot') x 'Mme Falcot'
Sizeable, semi-double flowers, opening to appear almost single, bright orange-pink with yellow at the base. Fragrant. Growth rather angular but bushy. Foliage dark green and glossy. Lovely in pots.
☼ ●● C H 90cm W 90cm (3 x 3ft) Zone 7

'Cramoisi Supérieur' (USA 'Agrippina')
Introduced Coquereau, France 1832
Parentage Seedling of 'Slater's Crimson'
Bushy, compact rose bearing many small clusters of initially cupped flowers opening to slightly more than semi-double; crimson-red in colour, sometimes faintly striped. Light fragrance. Foliage dark green, semi-glossy. A superb pot plant.
☼ ● C H 90cm W 60cm (3 x 2ft) Zone 6

'Cramoisi Supérieur' Climbing
Introduced Couturier, France 1885
Parentage Sport of 'Cramoisi Supérieur'
A superb Climber with crimson-red flowers like those of the bush form. Mildly scented. Unlike most Climbers, repeats in late summer. Slightly glossy, dark green foliage a little sparse. Best on walls.
☼ ● R H 4m W 2.5m (12 x 8ft) Zone 6

'Fellemberg' ('La Belle Marseillaise')
Introduced Fellemberg, Germany 1857
Parentage Not recorded
Semi-double to double, initially cupped flowers opening to rather ragged blooms of bright crimson to cerise. Light fragrance. Stems upright, thorny; foliage plentiful, dark green. A useful rose for shrubberies.
○ ● C H 2.2m W 1.2m (7 x 4ft) Zone 6

'Grüss an Teplitz'
Introduced Geschwind, Hungary 1897
Parentage ('Sir Joseph Paxton' x 'Fellemberg') x ('Papa Gontier' x 'Gloire de Rosomanes')
A complex hybrid but clearly a China. Large, shapely, very double, deep red flowers in quantity. Modest fragrance. Stems bend, allowing blooms to droop. Growth vigorous. Mid-green foliage a little sparse and slightly prone to mildew.
☼ ● C ◉ H 1.8m W 1.2m (6 x 4ft) Zone 5

'Hermosa' ('Armosa', 'Mélanie Lemaire', 'Mme Neumann')
Introduced Marcheseau, France 1840
Parentage Not recorded
Globular, fully double, fragrant, deep silvery pink flowers in great profusion. A short, thorny plant with ample healthy, mid-green foliage. Excellent by a wall, at the front of shrub borders, or in containers.
○ ●● C H 90cm W 60cm (3 x 2ft) Zone 6

'Irène Watts'
Introduced Guillot, France 1896
Parentage Seedling of 'Mme Laurette Messimy'
Very double, fragrant, blush-pink flowers borne in sizeable clusters. A typical China, with semi-glossy, mid- to dark green foliage on a twiggy, compact, thorny bush. Good as a pot plant and for bedding.
☼ ●● C H 45cm W 45cm (1½ x 1½ft) Zone 7

'Le Vésuve'
Introduced Laffay, France 1825
Parentage Not recorded
Shapely, pointed buds open to loosely double, mildly fragrant flowers of silvery pink with deeper highlights. Growth loose and bushy. Foliage mid-green, semi-glossy. Does well under glass and in pots.
☼ ● C H 90cm W 90cm (3 x 3ft) Zone 7

'Arethusa'

'Cécile Brünner' White

'Fellemberg'

'Le Vésuve'

'Louis Philippe'

'Papillon'

'Sanguinea'

'Comte de Chambord'

'Louis Philippe'
Introduced Guérin, France 1834
Parentage Not recorded
Many loosely double flowers in small clusters, crimson to purple, with paler edges and white flecks. Light scent. Takes a rest between flushes. Growth angular, bushy. Foliage greyish green, semi-glossy. Needs good soil to flourish.
☼ ♦ R H 60cm W 60cm (2 x 2ft) Zone 6

'Louis XIV'
Introduced Guillot, France 1859
Parentage Possibly seedling of 'Général Jacqueminot'
One of the darkest of all red roses. Flowers open to semi-double from tight, round buds. Slightly fragrant. Growth angular with sparse, dark green foliage. Well worth growing but in any other colour this rose would probably have been lost in the wilderness long ago. Temperamental.
☼ ♦ C H 60cm W 60cm (2 x 2ft) Zone 7

'Mme Laurette Messimy'
Introduced Guillot, France 1887
Parentage 'Rival de Paestum' x 'Mme Falcot'
Semi-double flowers are bright pink to salmon with touches of yellow. Light fragrance. Growth bushy and upright with ample durable, glossy, dark green foliage. Ideal where an out-of-the-ordinary bedding rose is required.
☼ ♦ C H 60cm W 60cm (2 x 2ft) Zone 7

'Mutabilis' ('Tipo Ideale', *R. turkestanica*)
Introduced 1932 but certainly much older
Parentage Not recorded
An outstanding and interesting rose. Single, initially buff-yellow flowers age through pink shades to deep blood-red. Very little fragrance. Produced in large clusters or singly on an angular shrub. Sparse, smallish, dark green leaves. Erratic in behaviour, sometimes growing taller than stated height.
☼ ♦ C H 90cm W 60cm (3 x 2ft) Zone 7

'Odorata' ('Hume's Blush', *R.* x *odorata*)
Introduced Fa Tee Nurseries, China 1810
Parentage Possibly *R. chinensis* x *R. gigantea*
Double flowers in blush-white, with a touch of cream. Very fragrant. Vigorous growth. Foliage dark green, glossy. (In my book *Classic Roses* I listed this among the Teas. I now believe it is better placed here in the Chinas.)
☼ ♦♦♦ C H 1.2m W 1.2m (4 x 4ft) Zone 6

'Old Blush' ('Parson's Pink', Monthly rose, 'Pallida', Common Monthly)
Introduced Parson, China 1789
Parentage Not recorded
An important parent to many roses. Loosely formed, fragrant flowers open from globular buds to semi-double, deep blush-pink with lilac undertones. Borne in clusters on a reasonably vigorous, moderately thorny plant. Mid-green foliage. There is also a more vigorous climbing form reaching 5 x 3m (15 x 10ft).
◑ ♦♦ C H 1.8m W 1.2m (6 x 4ft) Zone 6

'Papillon'
Introduced Dubourg, France 1900
Parentage Not recorded
Semi-double, salmon and pink flowers with a faint yellow base, reminiscent of butterflies when fully open. Light fragrance. Growth vigorous and bushy with ample, semi-glossy, greyish green foliage.
☼ ♦ C H 1.2m W 90cm (4 x 3ft) Zone 7

'Parks' Yellow' (Tea-scented China, *R.* x *odorata* 'Ochroleuca')
Introduced Parks, UK 1824
Parentage Not recorded
Large, semi-double, soft sulphur-yellow flowers suffused with orange as they age. Fragrant. Growth vigorous. Foliage bronzy green. A good first flush, but only occasionally repeating in autumn. (In my book *Classic Roses* I listed this as a Tea rose. I now feel it is better placed here in the Chinas.)
☼ ♦♦ R H 1.8m W 1.2m (6 x 4ft) Zone 7

'Perle d'Or' ('Yellow Cécile Brünner')
Introduced Rambaux, France 1883
Parentage Possibly *R. multiflora* seedling x 'Mme Falcot'
A delightful China. Fully double flowers of golden bronzy yellow, produced in clusters on an upright, bushy plant. Mild fragrance. Foliage bronze-green. Excellent in pots, also good for group planting.
☼ ♦ C H 1.2m W 90cm (4 x 3ft) Zone 6

'Pompon de Paris' Climbing
Introduced c.1839
Parentage Not recorded
A most useful climbing China. A vigorous plant with many small, fully double, bright rose-pink flowers. Lots of small, dark green leaves. A good first flush; autumn flowers intermittent. Best grown on walls.
◑ ♦ R H 4m W 1.8m (12 x 6ft) Zone 6

'Sanguinea' (Miss Lowe's rose)
Introduced Pre-1824
Parentage Seedling of 'Slater's Crimson'
Small clusters of single, bright red flowers with pronounced stamens. No fragrance. Growth angular, sparse, bushy. Mid-green foliage also sparse. A temperamental but historically important rose.
☼ C H 90cm W 60cm (3 x 2ft) Zone 7

'Slater's Crimson' (Old crimson China, 'Semperflorens')
Introduced Slater, UK 1792
Parentage Not recorded
Crimson-red flowers in small clusters; some petals have an occasional white streak. Unscented. Growth branching and bushy. Dark green foliage a little sparse. Enjoys growing close to walls when it will get taller than stated height. Good in pots.
☼ C H 90cm W 90cm (3 x 3ft) Zone 6

'Sophie's Perpetual'
Introduced UK, pre-1928
Rediscovered Brooke, UK 1960
Parentage Not recorded
Clusters of fully double flowers in a mix of cherry-red and silvery pink. Slightly fragrant. Growth very vigorous, with abundant, glossy, mid-green foliage. Makes a lax bush, but perhaps better on walls as a shorter climber.
☼ ♦ C H 1.8–3m W 1.2m (6–10 x 4ft) Zone 7

'Viridiflora' (Green rose, *R. viridiflora*)
Origin Unknown **First noted** c.1833
Parentage Not recorded
Flowers made up of green and brown bracts. Bushy, dense growth; healthy, mid-green foliage. Good in pots. Easy to grow, but more a novelty than of great garden value.
◑ C H 90cm W 90cm (3 x 3ft) Zone 5

The Portlands

'Arthur de Sansal'
Introduced Cochet, France 1855
Parentage Not recorded
Large, double, rosette-like flowers of crimson-purple. Scented. Repeat flowering. A compact plant, densely covered with dark green foliage. Slightly prone to mildew and rust later in the season.
◯ ◆◆ R ⊙ **H** 90cm **W** 60cm (3 x 2ft) Zone 5

'Comte de Chambord'
Introduced Moreau-Robert, France 1863
Parentage 'Baronne Prévost' x 'Duchess of Portland'
An excellent rose with many attributes. Substantial, fully double, rich warm pink flowers with a strong, "expensive" perfume. Foliage is abundant, large, and grey-green. Well suited to mass planting.
☼ ◆◆◆ C **H** 60cm **W** 60cm (2 x 2ft) Zone 5

'De Rescht' ('Rose de Rescht')
Discovered Lindsay 1930s
Parentage Not recorded
Pompon-like blooms are fuchsia-red to magenta and somewhat smaller than other Portlands. Produced in small, erect, short-stemmed clusters. Copious, dark green foliage on a neat and tidy plant. Very fragrant and free flowering, with excellent autumn repeats.
☼ ◆◆◆ C **H** 90cm **W** 60cm (3 x 2ft) Zone 5

'Duchess of Portland' (Portland rose, 'Paestana')
Origin Italy **First noted** c.1790
Parentage Possibly 'Quatre Saisons' x 'Slater's Crimson'
The first of the Portland line. Semi-double, scented, cerise-red blooms produced freely and repetitively. Dark green foliage. A tidy rose best used in groups but also attractive as a pot plant.
◯ ◆◆ C **H** 60cm **W** 60cm (2 x 2ft) Zone 5

'Indigo'
Introduced Laffay, France c.1830
Parentage Not recorded
Fully double, scented, deep purple blooms with the occasional thin, white stripe on some petals. Upright growth with abundant rich green leaves. Should be more widely grown. Excellent in pots.
☼ ◆◆ C **H** 90cm **W** 60cm (3 x 2ft) Zone 5

'Jacques Cartier' (USA 'Marchesa Boccella')
Introduced Moreau-Robert, France 1868
Parentage Not recorded
A superb rose with large, fully double, flat, slightly ragged and quartered flowers of deep pink, fading to softer pink at petal edges. Highly perfumed. Foliage leathery, dark green. An accommodating rose useful for mass planting, low hedges, or pots.
☼ ◆◆◆ C **H** 90cm **W** 60cm (3 x 2ft) Zone 5

'Marbrée'
Introduced Moreau-Robert, France 1858
Parentage Not recorded
Fully double flowers, pink mottled purple, with slightly fewer petals than most other Portlands, opening flat. Sadly, little or no scent. Growth upright with darkish green foliage. Rather tall for a Portland.
☼ C **H** 1.2m **W** 90cm (4 x 3ft) Zone 6

'Pergolèse'
Introduced Moreau, France 1860
Parentage Not recorded
Clusters of fully double flowers of crimson-purple, paling to lilac. Well scented. Foliage dark green. Growth tidy, bushy.
☼ ◆◆ C **H** 90cm **W** 90cm (3 x 3ft) Zone 6

The Bourbons

'Adam Messerich'
Introduced Lambert, Germany 1920
Parentage 'Frau Oberhofgärtner Singer' x ('Louise Odier' seedling x 'Louis Philippe')
Loosely double, blowsy blooms are bright rosy-pink to red, fading slightly in strong sun, in medium-sized clusters. Pleasingly perfumed. Mid-green foliage with a slight sheen. A shrub of large proportions, which can also be used as a small climber.
☼ ◆◆ C **H** 1.5m **W** 1.2m (5 x 4ft) Zone 5

'Blairii No. 2'
Introduced Blair, UK 1867
Parentage Not recorded
A climbing rose with full, flat flowers of many petals, deep pink paling to blush around the edges. Highly scented. Foliage dark green and matt-textured. Tends to suffer from mildew, but only after flowers are spent in midsummer.
☼ ◆◆◆ S ⊙ **H** 4m **W** 1.8m (12 x 6ft) Zone 6

'Boule de Neige'
Origin France **First noted** 1867
Parentage 'Blanche Lafitte' x 'Sappho'
A lovely rose whose buds usually have red to purple markings on the outer petals. When open, blooms are pure white with densely packed, slightly reflexed petals. Highly scented. A stiff, upright shrub of neat proportions with few thorns; well clothed with leathery, mid- to dark green foliage.
☼ ◆◆◆ C **H** 1.2m **W** 90cm (4 x 3ft) Zone 6

'Bourbon Queen' ('Queen of Bourbons', 'Reine des Îles Bourbon', 'Souvenir de la Princesse de Lamballe')
Introduced Mauget, France 1934
Parentage Not recorded
Slightly cupped, semi-double flowers of rose-pink appear en masse in midsummer but, unlike the majority of Bourbons, seldom repeat later on. Delightful perfume. A strong-growing shrub or small climber, amply clothed with grey-green foliage.
☼ ◆◆ S **H** 1.8m **W** 1.2m (6 x 4ft) Zone 5

'Commandant Beaurepaire'
Introduced Moreau-Robert, France 1874
Parentage Not recorded
Sizeable, almost fully double, scented flowers are crimson, streaked purple, and marbled with white; a pleasing combination. Intermittent flowers in autumn. Dense, mid-green foliage. A good shrub that will tolerate shade and poor soil. Ideal for a hedge or a mixed border.
◯ ◆◆ R **H** 1.2m **W** 1.2m (4 x 4ft) Zone 5

'Coupe d'Hébé'
Introduced Laffay, France 1840
Parentage Bourbon hybrid x China hybrid
Initially cupped blooms open almost double, with textured, soft pink petals. They are scented and very prolific, more so in the first flush. A tall shrub with ample, glossy, light green foliage. Can be susceptible to mildew later in the season.
☼ ◆◆◆ R ⊙ **H** 2.2m **W** 1.5m (7 x 5ft) Zone 5

'Fulgens' ('Malton')
Introduced Guérin, France 1830
Parentage Not recorded
A lesser-known Bourbon, thought to be one of the parents of the early Hybrid Perpetuals. Semi-double, lightly scented flowers are bright crimson often marbled deeper red. Dark green foliage on a somewhat lax plant. Repeat flowering.
☼ ◆ R **H** 1.5m **W** 1.2m (5 x 4ft) Zone 6

'De Rescht'

'Indigo'

'Bourbon Queen'

'Coupe d'Hébé'

'Gipsy Boy'

'Gipsy Boy' ('Zigeunerknabe')
Introduced Lambert, Germany 1909
Parentage Seedling of 'Russelliana'
Very well known. Medium-sized, double, fragrant flowers of crimson to purple, displaying golden stamens when fully open. Once flowering, but in great abundance. Coarse, dark green foliage. Growth is vigorous. Useful as a shrub or small climber.
○ ◆◆ S H 1.8m W 1.2m (6 x 4ft) Zone 4

'Honorine de Brabant'
Origin & parentage Unknown
Large, blowsy, cupped blooms, off-white heavily striped lilac and pinkish purple. Mild fragrance. Grey-green leaves, large and pointed, are copious on stems armed with few thorns. Can be grown as a shrub or a small climber.
○ ◆ C H 1.8m W 1.5m (6 x 5ft) Zone 6

'Kathleen Harrop'
Introduced Dickson, UK 1919
Parentage Sport of 'Zéphirine Drouhin'
Semi-double, shell- to blush-pink blooms are delightfully perfumed. Greyish dark green foliage. Stems completely thornless. Rather prone to disease.
☼ ◆◆◆ C ☉ H 3m W 1.8m (10 x 6ft) Zone 5

'La Reine Victoria'
Introduced Schwartz, France 1872
Parentage Not recorded
Truly cupped, double blooms are rich lilac-pink with a silky texture and delightfully scented. Foliage grey green with a slight sheen. A plant of accommodating size. Requires the best husbandry, but the results can be extremely rewarding.
☼ ◆◆◆ C H 1.2m W 90cm (4 x 3ft) Zone 6

'Louise Odier'
Introduced Margottin, France 1851
Parentage Not recorded
One of the best-known Bourbons. Compact, double, bright rose-pink blooms, almost camellia-like. Richly perfumed and produced in clusters. Healthy, mid-green foliage on a sometimes lax but vigorous plant. Probably best in a mixed border.
☼ ◆◆◆ C H 1.5m W 1.2m (5 x 4ft) Zone 5

'Mme Ernst Calvat'
Introduced Schwartz, France 1888
Parentage Sport of 'Mme Isaac Pereire'
Large, double, blowsy blooms are soft rose-pink, and strongly perfumed. Excellent dark green foliage on a somewhat arching shrub.
○ ◆◆◆ C H 1.5m W 1.2m (5 x 4ft) Zone 6

'Mme Isaac Pereire'
Introduced Garçon, France 1881
Parentage Not recorded
A most lovely rose. Shaggy, fully double flowers are large, weighty. and seductive, purple to magenta in colour, with strong fragrance. A vigorous plant, well clothed in mid- to dark green foliage. May also be grown as a small wall climber. Suffers from black spot without due care and attention.
○ ◆◆◆ C ☉ H 2.2m W 1.5m (7 x 5ft) Zone 6

'Mme Lauriol de Barny'
Introduced Trouillard, France 1868
Parentage Not recorded
Flat, semi-double blooms are deep silvery pink and exude a strong, rather unusual fruity scent. Has a good first flush, but flowers intermittently later on. Vigorous and healthy, adapting well to most types of soil. Foliage dark green. A useful addition to any mixed border.
○ ◆◆ R H 1.5m W 1.2m (5 x 4ft) Zone 5

'Mme Pierre Oger'

'Mme Pierre Oger'
Introduced Verdier, France 1878
Parentage Sport of 'La Reine Victoria'
Double, cupped blooms with translucent petals in mother of pearl pink and ivory; in appearance, one of the most delicate and fragile of roses. Richly perfumed. Ample grey-green foliage has a slight sheen. Tends to be a little prone to black spot later in the season.
☼ ◆◆◆ C ☉ H 1.2m W 1.2m (4 x 4ft) Zone 6

'Mrs Yamada'
Introduced Beales, UK 2004
Parentage Sport of 'Variegata di Bologna'
Plum-red, fragrant blooms are initially cupped, opening fully double and flat. Foliage dark green. Useful for a mixed border.
☼ ◆◆◆ C H 1.5m W 1.2m (5 x 4ft) Zone 5

'Prince Charles'
Introduced Pre-1918
Parentage Not recorded
Fully double flowers of considerable size, crimson, heavily veined maroon, with golden anthers, fading slightly with maturity. Foliage dark green. A lax shrub but very garden worthy even though flowers are present for only a short time.
○ ◆◆◆ S H 1.5m W 1.2m (5 x 4ft) Zone 5

'Queen of Bedders'
Introduced Noble, UK 1871
Parentage Seedling of 'Sir Joseph Paxton'
A shorter-growing Bourbon. Flowers are shapely, semi-double, deep carmine, changing to deep pink with age. Takes a short break between flushes. Dark green foliage. Useful at the front of shrubberies and in mixed borders; also good in pots.
○ ◆◆ R H 90cm W 60cm (3 x 2ft) Zone 5

'Rose Édouard' ('Rose Edward')
Introduced Bréon, Île de Réunion (France) c.1818
Parentage Probably 'Old Blush' x early form of 'Quatre Saisons'
Fully double, highly perfumed, deep reddish pink flowers with high centres, opening flat and muddled. Repeat flowering. Growth short and bushy. Foliage rough to touch, plentiful, and grey-green.
○ ◆◆◆ R H 90cm W 60cm (3 x 2ft) Zone 5

'Souvenir de la Malmaison' ('Queen of Beauty and Fragrance')
Introduced Beluze, France 1843
Parentage 'Mme Desprez' x Tea rose
Soft blush-pink to ivory blooms consist of very many petals in a flat and quartered arrangement. Strong, sweet fragrance. Greyish mid-green foliage. One of the most beautiful of all roses when at its best. Sadly flowers sometimes marred by heavy rain; this rose hates wet weather, nor will it thrive in too much hot sun. There is also a popular climbing form.
☼ ◆◆◆ C H 90cm W 90cm (3 x 3ft) Zone 6

'Souvenir de St Anne's'
Introduced Hilling, UK 1950
Parentage Sport of 'Souvenir de la Malmaison'
Flowers are almost cupped, semi-double, and soft blush-pink. Greyish mid-green foliage. Easily placed in the garden; also ideal for containers. Free flowering, usually with an excellent autumn flush.
☼ ◆◆◆ C H 1.5m W 1.2m (5 x 4ft) Zone 6

'Souvenir de la Malmaison'

'Zéphirine Drouhin'

'Variegata di Bologna'
Introduced Bonfiglioli, Italy 1909
Parentage Not recorded
An unusual rose, cup-shaped in bud opening to fully double, milky white blooms with purple stripes and mottling. Fragrant and free flowering. Darkish green foliage a little coarse; growth a little sprawling.
☼ ♦♦♦ C H 1.5m W 1.2m (5 x 4ft) Zone 5

'Zéphirine Drouhin'
Introduced Bizot, France 1868
Parentage Not recorded
An extremely popular rose, blooming profusely all summer and completely lacking in thorns. Semi-double, heavily scented flowers in an attractive shade of cerise-pink. Leathery, dark green foliage. Sadly, a martyr to black spot, but still has many uses as either shrub or climber.
☼ ♦♦♦ C ⊙ H 3m W 1.8m (10 x 6ft) Zone 5

The Hybrid Perpetuals

'Baroness Rothschild' ('Baronne Adolphe de Rothschild')
Introduced Pernet Père, France 1868
Parentage Sport of 'Souvenir de la Reine d'Angleterre'
Very large, almost cupped, fully double flowers with thick, clear soft pink petals, with a somewhat porcelain quality. Held on strong stems well covered with grey-green foliage. Good in pots, in groups of three or more, and for mass bedding. I believe this rose to be fragrant; others disagree.
☼ ♦ R H 90cm W 90cm (3 x 3ft) Zone 5

'Baron Girod de l'Ain'
Introduced Reverchon, France 1897
Parentage Sport of 'Eugène Fürst'
Very double flowers of deep crimson with crinkled petal edges outlined with white. Not just a novelty; very worthy of garden space. Highly scented. Sturdy in growth, with dense, leathery, mid-green foliage. Inclined to mildew a little.
☼ ♦♦♦ R ⊙ H 1.2m W 90cm (4 x 3ft) Zone 5

'Baronne Prévost'
Introduced Desprez, France 1842
Parentage Not recorded
Large, very double, deep rose-pink blooms opening flat from globular buds. Fragrant. Very free flowering in its first flush but rather spasmodic later. Foliage dark green and a little coarse. Growth relaxed. A slight tendency to mildew later in the season. Good in mixed borders; also a superb specimen shrub.
☼ ♦♦ R ⊙ H 1.5m W 1.2m (5 x 4ft) Zone 5

'Dupuy Jamain'
Introduced Jamain, France 1868
Parentage Not recorded
One of my favourite Hybrid Perpetuals. Large, full flowers, strongly scented, cerise-red, borne erect on strong, moderately thorny stems. Plentiful healthy, grey-green foliage. Superb in pots or mixed borders.
☼ ♦♦♦ R H 1.2m W 90cm (4 x 3ft) Zone 5

'Éclair'
Introduced Lacharme, France 1833
Parentage 'Général Jacqueminot' x seedling
An upright plant with very dark red flowers, almost black a times, globular at first, opening flat and rosette-like. Delightfully perfumed. Leathery, dark green foliage. Slightly disease prone and requiring a little extra attention, but repays this with near-perfect blooms. Lends itself well to mixed planting.
☼ ♦♦♦ R ⊙ H 1.2m W 90cm (4 x 3ft) Zone 5

'Empereur du Maroc' ('Emperor of Morocco')
Introduced Guinoisseau, France 1858
Parentage Seedling of 'Géant des Batailles'
Sumptuous blooms of medium size in rich dark red with tinges of maroon. Flowers held in clusters but, sadly, with weak necks, partly due to the weight of blooms they carry. Foliage dark green. Tends to be a little prone to rust, but responds well to extra care. Best with support.
☼ ♦♦♦ R ⊙ H 1.2m W 90cm (4 x 3ft) Zone 5

'Enfant de France'
Introduced Lartay, France 1860
Parentage Not recorded
Sizeable, quartered, fully double flowers of mid- to soft pink with a silky texture. Delightfully perfumed. Growth upright and tidy, with ample greyish dark green foliage. Good in smaller gardens, perhaps together with Portlands. Authenticity has been challenged by some experts, but what else can it be?
☼ ♦♦♦ R H 90cm W 60cm (3 x 2ft) Zone 5

'Eugène Fürst'
Introduced Soupert & Notting, Luxembourg 1875
Parentage 'Baron de Bonstetten' x unknown
Large, cupped, double, crimson-purple flowers with crinkled petal edges. Very fragrant. Growth upright with flowers held on strong necks. Foliage dark green. A little prone to mildew.
☼ ♦♦♦ R H 1.2m W 90cm (4 x 3ft) Zone 5

'Ferdinand Pichard'
Introduced Tanne, France 1921
Parentage Not recorded
Good-sized, almost fully double, carmine-red flowers overlaid greyish white and soft pink; irregularly streaked and splashed rather than uniformly striped. Sweetly perfumed. Large, greyish green leaves on a vigorous, healthy, and thorny shrub.
☼ ♦♦ R H 1.2m W 1.2m (4 x 4ft) Zone 5

'Frau Karl Druschki' ('Snow Queen', 'Reine des Neiges', 'White American Beauty')
Introduced Lambert, Germany 1901
Parentage 'Merveille de Lyon' x 'Mme Caroline Testout'
High-centred buds open to large, sumptuous, fully double, pure white flowers. Scentless. Growth vigorous, thorny, and strong, with ample grey- to mid-green foliage. Blooms unfortunately hate wet weather. There is also an excellent climbing form.
☼ R H 1.2m W 90cm (4 x 3ft) Zone 5

'Général Jacqueminot' (General Jack, Jack's rose)
Introduced Roussel, France 1853
Parentage Seedling of 'Gloire des Rosomanes'
Well-formed, double, fragrant, clear red flowers emerge from pointed buds on long stems. Flowers more continuously than most Hybrid Perpetuals. Mid-green foliage on a vigorous shrub. A little prone to rust and mildew later on. Needs extra attention and hard pruning each spring to thrive.
☼ ♦♦ C ⊙ H 1.2m W 1.2m (4 x 4ft) Zone 5

'Gloire Lyonnaise'
Introduced Guillot Fils, France 1885
Parentage 'Baroness Rothschild' x 'Mme Falcot'
Semi-double, creamy white flowers opening flat to show off golden stamens. Free flowering and scented. Strong, stout, upright stems with good, healthy, dark green foliage. Mixes well with herbaceous perennials.
☼ ♦♦ R H 1.2m W 60cm (4 x 2ft) Zone 7

'Baroness Rothschild'

'Baron Girod de l'Ain'

'Eugène Fürst'

'Frau Karl Druschki'

'Hugh Dickson'

'Paul's Early Blush'

'Anne of Geierstein'

'Lord Penzance'

'Hugh Dickson'
Introduced Dickson, UK 1905
Parentage 'Lord Bacon' x 'Grüss an Teplitz'
Double flowers are rich dark red and highly scented.
Foliage dark green tinted maroon. A shrub of
vigorous, lanky growth, probably best used as
a pillar rose or grown against a fence or wall.
☼ ♦♦♦ R H 2.5m W 1.5m (8 x 5ft) Zone 5

'Mrs John Laing'
Introduced Bennett, UK 1887
Parentage Seedling of 'François Michelon'
Large, shapely, double flowers are soft to mid-pink
and highly scented. Borne abundantly on an upright
shrub with large, healthy, mid greyish green leaves.
A superior Hybrid Perpetual, flowering more
continuously than most, but sometimes marred
by a little mildew. Good for mass planting.
☼ ♦♦♦ C ☉ H 90cm W 90cm (3 x 3ft) Zone 5

'Paul Neyron'
Introduced Levet, France 1869
Parentage R. wichurana x 'Monsieur Tillier'
Very large, fully double, bright warm pink flowers,
with darker and lighter highlights. Blooms
disproportionate to size of plant. Petals sometimes
appear in disarray, but attractively so. Very highly
perfumed. Large, dark greyish green foliage.
☼ ♦♦♦ R H 90cm W 60cm (3 x 2ft) Zone 5

'Paul's Early Blush' ('Mrs Harkness')
Introduced Paul, UK 1893
Parentage Sport of 'Heinreich Schultheis'
Beautiful, blush-pink flowers appearing just a little
earlier than most. They are fairly large, fully double,
and scented. Strong, thorny growth with dark greyish
green foliage. An accommodating rose, easy to grow.
☼ ♦♦♦ R H 90cm W 90cm (3 x 3ft) Zone 5

'Prince Camille de Rohan' ('La Rossière')
Introduced Verdier, France 1861
Parentage 'Général Jacqueminot' x 'Géant des
Batailles'
Huge, fully double, perfumed, deep red blooms with
a darker sheen. Quite beautiful. Sadly the weight of
the flowers is often too much for the flexible stems.
Foliage dark green. Growth rather sprawling, and
best with support. Rather prone to mildew.
☼ ♦♦♦ R ☉ H 1.2m W 90cm (4 x 3ft) Zone 6

'Reine des Violettes'
Introduced Millet-Mallet, France 1860
Parentage Seedling of 'Pius IX'
Large, flat, and delightfully quartered flowers of soft
velvety violet. Scented. Held erect on strong stems,
sometimes nestling into abundant grey-green foliage.
Upright and tidy in growth. A good all-rounder and
one of my favourite roses. Continuous flowering.
☼ ♦♦♦ C H 1.5m W 90cm (5 x 3ft) Zone 5

'Souvenir du Docteur Jamain'
Introduced Lacharme, France 1865
Parentage Seedling of 'Charles Lefèbvre'
Cup-shaped, rich deep ruby-red flowers open almost
fully double to show off golden stamens. Best kept
away from direct sun to avoid petal scorch. Fragrant.
Growth moderately vigorous with few thorns. Dark
green foliage. An excellent small climbing rose,
especially attractive with white clematis.
○ ♦♦♦ R H 4m W 2.2m (12 x 7ft) Zone 6

The Sweet Briars

'Amy Robsart'
Introduced Penzance, UK 1894
Parentage Not recorded
Large, almost single, deep pink flowers with soft
yellow stamens. Slightly apple scented. Growth very
vigorous, thorny. Foliage plentiful, aromatic, dark
green. Orange hips plump, oval. Good for hedging.
○ ♦ S H 3m W 2.5m (10 x 8ft) Zone 5

'Anne of Geierstein'
Introduced Penzance, UK 1894
Parentage Not recorded
Single, fragrant, bright crimson flowers with golden
stamens. Growth very vigorous, thorny. Foliage dark
green, smelling of apples. Medium-sized, orange
hips. A first-class hedging rose.
○ ♦♦ S H 3m W 2.5m (10 x 8ft) Zone 5

'Flora McIvor'
Introduced Penzance, UK 1894
Parentage Not recorded
Flowers single, fragrant, and white with deep pink
edges and yellow stamens. Thorny stems. Foliage
dark green, apple scented. A good crop of medium-
sized, dark red hips. Useful in shrubberies.
○ ♦♦ S H 2.5m W 1.8m (8 x 6ft) Zone 5

'Greenmantle'
Introduced Penzance, UK 1894
Parentage Not recorded
Single, fragrant, rosy red flowers with golden
stamens, in profusion, followed by dark red hips.
Growth upright, thorny. Foliage dark green and
apple scented. Makes an excellent upright hedge.
○ ♦♦ S H 2.5m W 1.5m (8 x 5ft) Zone 5

'Janet's Pride' ('Clementine')
Introduced Paul, UK 1892
Parentage Not recorded
Almost single, fragrant flowers, creamy white with
bright pink markings on the edges of petals. Growth
twiggy. Foliage leathery, scented, and mid-green.
Small, orange hips. Useful in groups in shrubberies.
○ ♦♦ S H 1.5m W 1.2m (5 x 4ft) Zone 5

'La Belle Distinguée' ('La Petite Duchesse', Scarlet sweet briar)
Origin & parentage Unknown
Fully double, scarlet flowers in small clusters. Growth
bushy, compact, with few thorns. Light fragrance.
Copious, slightly aromatic foliage, rather coarse to
touch, dark green edged purple.
○ ♦ S H 90cm W 90cm (3 x 3ft) Zone 6

'Lady Penzance'
Introduced Penzance, UK c.1894
Parentage R. rubiginosa x R. foetida 'Bicolor'
An excellent Sweet Briar, the most strongly apple
scented of all. Flowers single, salmon-pink, with
touches of yellow and lovely stamens. Foliage soft
green. Growth angular, thorny. A smattering of
orange hips in autumn. Good in open woodland.
Slightly prone to black spot.
○ ♦♦♦ S ☉ H 2.2m W 1.8m (7 x 6ft) Zone 4

'Lord Penzance'
Introduced Penzance, UK c.1890
Parentage R. rubiginosa x 'Harison's Yellow'
Single, fragrant flowers of buff-yellow tinted pink,
followed by a few orange hips. Growth angular,
bushy. Foliage soft green and very aromatic.
Most attractive in groups in open woodland.
A little susceptible to black spot.
○ ♦♦♦ S ☉ H 2.2m W 1.8m (7 x 6ft) Zone 5

'Magnifica'

Introduced Hesse, Germany 1916
Parentage Seedling of 'Lucy Ashton'
Semi-double, purplish pink blooms with white centres and a good array of stamens. Only slightly scented. Growth vigorous, bushy. Lush, dark green foliage is mildly aromatic.
○ ● S H 1.2m W 1.5m (4 x 5ft) Zone 5

'Manning's Blush'

Origin Unknown **First noted** *c.*1800
Parentage Not recorded
A very good, unusual shrub with coarse, almost fern-like, apple-scented, dark green foliage. Stout, bushy, thorny growth. Blooms fully double and white flushed pink, repeated regularly throughout summer. Excellent for mixed shrubberies.
○ ●● R H 1.5m W 1.2m (5 x 4ft) Zone 5

'Meg Merrilies'

Introduced Penzance, UK 1894
Parentage Not recorded
Almost single, fragrant, crimson flowers in great profusion followed by abundant oval, orange-red hips. Thorny and wide growing. Plentiful dark green foliage, a little coarse in texture and smelling slightly of apples.
○ ●● S H 2.5m W 2.2m (8 x 7ft) Zone 5

The Rugosas

'Belle Poitevine'

Introduced Bruant, France 1894
Parentage Not recorded
Large, almost fully double, very fragrant flowers of magenta-pink, opening from long, pointed buds. Has a long flowering season. A tall shrub with typically thorny stems and abundant lightish green foliage. Good hips. Excellent for hedging.
○ ●●● C H 1.8m W 1.5m (6 x 5ft) Zone 5

'Blanc Double de Coubert'

Introduced Cochet-Cochet, France 1892
Parentage *R. rugosa* x 'Sombreuil'
One of the classic Rugosa hybrids. Fully double, highly scented, pure white blooms profusely borne throughout summer. Growth bushy and tidy. Foliage mid-green, crinkled. Sets hips only intermittently.
○ ●●● C H 1.5m W 1.2m (5 x 4ft) Zone 4

'Dr Eckener'

Introduced Berger, Germany 1930
Parentage 'Golden Emblem' x *R. rugosa* hybrid
Large, semi-double blooms of soft yellow to bronzy yellow, changing to pink. A good repeat flowerer. Lightly fragrant. Very spiky thorns on long stems forming an open plant. Foliage dark green. Needs support or very hard pruning to give of its best.
○ ● R H 3m W 2.5m (10 x 8ft) Zone 5

'Fimbriata' ('Phoebe's Frilled Pink', 'Dianthiflora')

Introduced Morlet, France 1891
Parentage *R. rugosa* x 'Mme Alfred Carrière'
A rather untypical Rugosa. Upright branches with dense, soft to touch, light green foliage. Semi-double flowers in small clusters, blush-pink to blush-white, crinkled, rather resembling dianthus. Fragrant. Repeat flowering. Makes a good hedge and mixes well.
○ ●● R H 90cm W 90cm (3 x 3ft) Zone 4

'F.J. Grootendorst'

Introduced De Goey, Holland 1918
Parentage *R. rugosa* 'Rubra' x 'Nobert Levavasseur'
Very double, frilly petalled, deep red flowers in sizeable, upright clusters. A rugged, thorny plant with coarse, dark green foliage. Constantly in flower and fragrant. Pink, white, and crimson sports have also occurred; all frequently revert back to the original.
○ ●● C H 1.2m W 90cm (4 x 3ft) Zone 4

'Fru Dagmar Hastrup' ('Fru Dagmar Hartopp', 'Frau Dagmar Hartopp')

Introduced Hastrup, Denmark 1914
Parentage Not recorded
Large, single, silvery pink flowers with a strong scent, borne profusely and continuously. Tidy and wide growing with healthy, dark green foliage. Large, tomato-like hips. Excellent for ground cover.
○ ●● C H 90cm W 90cm (3 x 3ft) Zone 4

'Hansa'

Introduced Schaum & Van Tol, Holland 1905
Parentage Not recorded
Large, fully double, fragrant, crimson-purple flowers produced continuously throughout summer and autumn. Foliage crisp and dark green. Huge, elliptical, dark red hips. An outstanding all-round shrub or hedging rose and especially good in pots.
○ ●● C H 1.2m W 90cm (4 x 3ft) Zone 4

'Max Graf'

Introduced Bowditch, USA 1919
Parentage *R. rugosa* x *R. wichurana*
Single, fragrant, deep silvery pink flowers in early summer, with an occasional repeat. Foliage dark green. Seldom sets fruit. A trailing rose, excellent for ground cover on banks or as a climber.
○ ●● R H 60cm W 2.5m (2 x 8ft) Zone 5

'Mrs Anthony Waterer'

Introduced Waterer, UK 1898
Parentage *R. rugosa* x 'Général Jacqueminot'
Semi-double, highly fragrant, deep crimson flowers borne all summer. A bushy, thorny plant, rather wide growing, with lots of very dark green foliage. A useful dense hedging rose. Rather prone to mildew.
○ ●●● C ☉ H 1.2m W 1.2m (4 x 4ft) Zone 5

'Roseraie de l'Haÿ'

Introduced Cochet-Cochet, France 1901
Parentage Sport of an unknown Rugosa hybrid
Large, almost double flowers of crimson-purple, opening ruffled, produced freely all summer. Clove-like fragrance. Growth dense, thorny. Foliage dark green. Rarely sets hips. A superb Rugosa, and one of the best hedging roses ever.
○ ●●● C H 1.8m W 1.5m (6 x 5ft) Zone 4

'Scabrosa'

Introduced Harkness, UK 1950
Parentage Foundling
Large, single, fragrant, magenta-cerise flowers, with prominent stamens, freely borne all summer. Foliage robust and mid-green on a bushy, vigorous plant. Superb hips, like small tomatoes. Good for hedging.
○ ●●● C H 1.8m W 1.2m (6 x 4ft) Zone 4

'Schneezwerg' ('Snow Dwarf')

Introduced Lambert, Germany 1912
Parentage *R. rugosa* x Polyantha
Abundant, semi-double, fragrant, pure white flowers with golden stamens, borne continuously. Greyish mid-green foliage. An upright-growing, thorny shrub. Has a good crop of round, red hips. Attractive in groups in shrubberies.
○ ●● C H 1.2m W 1.2m (4 x 4ft) Zone 4

'Belle Poitevine'

'Hansa'

'Max Graf'

'Scabrosa'

'Eva'

'Pax'

'Penelope'

'Vanity'

The Hybrid Musks

'Ballerina'

Introduced Bentall, UK 1937
Parentage Not recorded
A superb rose. Very large sprays of single, slightly fragrant, pink flowers like apple blossom, on a tidy-growing shrub. Foliage slightly glossy, dark green. Excellent as a hedge or in groups.
❍ ♦ C **H** 90cm **W** 90cm (3 x 3ft) Zone 6

'Belinda'

Introduced Bentall, UK 1936
Parentage Not recorded
A vigorous and strong Hybrid Musk bearing large trusses of semi-double, slightly fragrant, mid- to deep pink flowers. Foliage dark green, semi-glossy. A good hedging rose.
❍ ♦ C **H** 1.5m **W** 1.2m (5 x 4ft) Zone 6

'Buff Beauty'

Introduced Bentall, UK 1939
Parentage 'William Allen Richardson' x unknown
One of the best Hybrid Musks. Large clusters of double, buff-yellow flowers. Fragrant. Foliage dark green, bronzy. Growth shrubby, broad, and arching.
❍ ♦♦ C **H** 1.2m **W** 1.2m (4 x 4ft) Zone 6

'Cornelia'

Introduced Pemberton, UK 1925
Parentage Not recorded
Very large clusters of semi-double, shrimp-pink flowers on arching, relatively thornless stems. Mild fragrance. Foliage bronzy dark green. A useful rose for an informal hedge.
❍ ♦ C **H** 1.5m **W** 1.5m (5 x 5ft) Zone 6

'Danaë'

Introduced Pemberton, UK 1913
Parentage 'Trier' x 'Gloire de Chédane-Guinoisseau'
Many clusters of semi-double, lightly fragrant flowers, mustard-yellow paling to cream. Tidy in habit. Foliage mid-green. Will double its size as a wall climber.
❍ ♦ C **H** 1.2m **W** 1.2m (4 x 4ft) Zone 6

'Daybreak'

Introduced Pemberton, UK 1918
Parentage 'Trier' x 'Liberty'
A shorter-growing Hybrid Musk with darkish green wood and foliage. Sizeable clusters of mildly fragrant flowers, deep yellow in bud opening to soft yellow. Good for hedging. A little prone to mildew.
❍ ♦ C ⊙ **H** 90cm **W** 90cm (3 x 3ft) Zone 6

'Eva'

Introduced Kordes, Germany 1933
Parentage 'Robin Hood' x 'J.C. Thornton'
A taller Hybrid Musk for a mixed shrubbery. Clusters of almost single, bright red flowers, paling towards their centres. Light fragrance. Foliage plentiful, dark green. Best pruned regularly when established.
❍ ♦ C **H** 1.5m **W** 1.2m (5 x 4ft) Zone 6

'Felicia'

Introduced Pemberton, UK 1928
Parentage 'Trier' x 'Ophelia'
Very lovely, fragrant flowers in large clusters. Shapely in bud opening fully double to salmon-pink, paling to soft pink at the edges. Growth is upright, bushy, and compact. Foliage is bluish green.
❍ ♦♦ C **H** 1.2m **W** 1.2m (4 x 4ft) Zone 6

'Francesca'

Introduced Pemberton, UK 1922
Parentage 'Danaë' x 'Sunburst'
Large, long sprays of semi-double flowers borne on a wide bush. Slightly scented blooms are deep yellowish apricot to begin with, paling to soft yellow. Purplish green stems and glossy, dark green foliage.
❍ ♦ C **H** 1.2m **W** 1.2m (4 x 4ft) Zone 6

'Moonlight'

Introduced Pemberton, UK 1913
Parentage 'Trier' x 'Sulphurea'
A vigorous rose with sizeable clusters of lightly scented, lemon-white flowers, a little more than single. Stems dark green and rather arching in habit. Foliage also dark green. Good for hedging.
❍ ♦ C **H** 1.5m **W** 1.2m (5 x 4ft) Zone 7

'Mozart'

Introduced Lambert, Germany 1937
Parentage `Robin Hood' x `Rote Pharisäer'
Huge clusters of small, single, carmine flowers with white centres. Mildly scented. Growth dense and bushy. Copious mid-green foliage.
❍ ♦ C **H** 1.2m **W** 90cm (4 x 3ft) Zone 6

'Nur Mahal'

Introduced Pemberton, UK 1923
Parentage 'Château de Clos Vougeot' x Hybrid Musk seedling
A tallish rose with sturdy, upright stems. Sizeable clusters of slightly more than single, perfumed, bright crimson flowers. Healthy, mid- to dark green foliage.
❍ ♦♦ C **H** 1.5m **W** 1.2m (5 x 4ft) Zone 6

'Pax'

Introduced Pemberton, UK 1918
Parentage 'Trier' x 'Sunburst'
Large, semi-double, creamy white flowers with golden stamens, in small clusters. Fragrant. Stems almost thornless, dark green. Foliage also dark green.
❍ ♦♦ C **H** 1.8m **W** 1.5m (6 x 5ft) Zone 6

'Penelope'

Introduced Pemberton, UK 1924
Parentage 'Ophelia' x seedling or, possibly, 'William Allen Richardson' or 'Trier'
Semi-double, soft pink to cream flowers in clusters. Mildly fragrant. Fairly thornless stems. Foliage darkish green touched purple. Inclined to mildew.
❍ ♦ C ⊙ **H** 1.5m **W** 1.2m (5 x 4ft) Zone 7

'Prosperity'

Introduced Pemberton, UK 1919
Partentage 'Marie-Jeanne' x 'Perle des Jardins'
A superb Hybrid Musk with clusters of fully double, fragrant, creamy white flowers with just a hint of pink. Growth relatively thornless. Dark green foliage.
❍ ♦♦ C **H** 1.5m **W** 1.2m (5 x 4ft) Zone 6

'Robin Hood'

Introduced Pemberton, UK 1927
Parentage Seedling x 'Miss Edith Cavell'
Densely packed clusters of small, semi-double, lightly scented, pinkish scarlet flowers. A tidy-growing shrub with lots of good, mid-green foliage.
☼ ♦ C **H** 90cm **W** 90cm (3 x 3ft) Zone 6

'Vanity'

Introduced Pemberton, UK 1920
Parentage 'Château de Clos Vougeot' x seedling
Large sprays of sizeable, almost single, fragrant, shocking pink flowers, with yellow stamens. Angular growth with light green foliage. Flowers erratically after first flush. Perhaps best as a wall plant.
❍ ♦♦ R **H** 1.8m **W** 1.5m (6 x 5ft) Zone 6

The Teas

'Alexander Hill Gray' ('Yellow Maman Cochet', 'Yellow Cochet')
Introduced Dickson, UK 1911
Parentage Not recorded
Fully double blooms are large and bright yellow, deepening as they mature. Fragrant. Mid-green, slightly polished foliage. Growth is angular, although bushy and vigorous.
☼ ◖◖ C H 1.2m W 90cm (4 x 3ft) Zone 7

'Archiduc Joseph'
Introduced Nabonnand, France 1872
Parentage Seedling of 'Mme Lombard'
One of the best Tea roses. Many petalled blooms, flat and cushion-like when fully open, in pink, purple, and orange with hints of yellow and gold. Fragrant. Lots of dark greyish green leaves, and relatively thorn-free. Will also grow as a small wall climber.
☼ ◖◖ C H 1.5m W 90cm (5 x 3ft) Zone 7

'Belle Lyonnaise'
Introduced Levet, France 1870
Parentage Not recorded
Large, fully double flowers, appearing freely, open flat and quartered; soft yellow fading to creamy white with maturity. Perfumed. Dark green foliage. Needs a sheltered site.
☼ ◖◖◖ C H 3m W 1.8m (10 x 6ft) Zone 7

'Catherine Mermet'
Introduced Guillot Fils, France 1869
Parentage Not recorded
Well-formed, semi-double, lilac-pink flowers emerging from pointed buds on lengthy stems. Fragrant. Well endowed with healthy, copper-tinted, mid-green leaves. Happy if given a favourable place in the garden. Excellent under glass.
☼ ◖◖ C H 1.2m W 90cm (4 x 3ft) Zone 7

'Clementina Carbonieri'
Introduced Bonfiglioli, Italy 1913
Parentage Not recorded
A very colourful, fully double, fragrant rose, in orange, salmon-pink, and yellow. Very free flowering. Growth bushy and averagely thorny. Foliage darkish green with a light gloss. A superb pot rose.
☼ ◖◖ C H 90cm W 60cm (3 x 2ft) Zone 7

'Dr Grill'
Introduced Bonnaire, France 1886
Parentage 'Ophirie' x 'Souvenir de Victor Hugo'
Flowers beautiful, clear pink overlaid soft copper. Initially high centred opening to little more than semi-double. Scented. Large darkish green leaves. Growth rather angular. Excellent under glass.
☼ ◖◖ C H 90cm W 60cm (3 x 2ft) Zone 7

'Duchesse de Brabant' ('Comtesse de Labanthe', 'Comtesse Ouwaroff')
Introduced Bernède, France 1857
Parentage Not recorded
Double, cupped, clear soft shell-pink flowers freely produced. Perfumed. Wide growing with good glossy, darkish grey-green foliage. One of the nicest Teas.
☼ ◖◖ C H 90cm W 90cm (3 x 3ft) Zone 7

'Général Schablikine'
Introduced Nabonnand, France 1878
Parentage Not recorded
Semi-double flowers combining pink, cherry-red, and copper. Mild perfume. A compact but tallish plant with semi-glossy, leathery, dark green foliage. Very attractive in groups.
☼ ◖ C H 90cm W 60cm (3 x 2ft) Zone 7

'Homère'
Introduced Moreau-Robert, France 1858
Parentage Not recorded
Shapely, cupped, fully double flowers of creamy white with a slight blush and rose-red petal margins. Fragrant. Growth upright, bushy, and twiggy. Foliage dark green, semi-glossy. Hardier than most Teas.
☼ ◖◖ C H 90cm W 60cm (3 x 2ft) Zone 7

'Lady Hillingdon'
Introduced Lowe & Shawyer, UK 1910
Parentage 'Papa Gontier' x 'Mme Hoste'
High-centred buds open to blowsy, almost double flowers of rich yellow. Highly scented. Growth moderately thorny, plum coloured, and twiggy. Foliage plentiful, dark green overlaid plum.
☼ ◖◖◖ C H 90cm W 60cm (3 x 2ft) Zone 8

'Maman Cochet'
Introduced Cochet, France 1893
Parentage 'Marie Van Houtte' x 'Mme Lombard'
High-centred blooms, pale pink flushed deeper pink, become blowsy when fully open, showing lemon centres. Highly perfumed. Growth vigorous with relatively few thorns. Foliage leathery, slightly glossy, darkish green. A white form is also in cultivation.
☼ ◖◖◖ C H 90cm W 60cm (3 x 2ft) Zone 7

'Monsieur Tillier'
Introduced Bernaix, France 1891
Parentage Not recorded
Shapely buds open to rather blowsy, semi-double to double flowers of deep red smudged violet. Scented. Freely produced on a twiggy, vigorous, rather lax plant. Foliage dark green, glossy.
☼ ◖◖ C H 1.2m W 90cm (4 x 3ft) Zone 7

'Papa Gontier'
Introduced Nabonnand, France 1883
Parentage Not recorded
Semi-double, deep rich pink flowers, bordering on red, with the occasional white streak on some petals. Fragrant. Growth rather twiggy and not over generously endowed with dark green foliage.
☼ ◖◖ C H 90cm W 60cm (3 x 2ft) Zone 7

'Rosette Delizy'
Introduced Nabonnand, France 1922
Parentage 'Général Gallieni' x 'Comtesse Bardi'
Almost fully double flowers, multicoloured but predominantly a striking combination of deep pink, apricot, and buff-yellow, with darker colouring on the outside of the petals. Growth branching and twiggy. Very healthy, leathery, glossy, mid- to bluish green foliage. Ideal for pots.
☼ ◖◖ C H 1.1m W 60cm (3½ x 2ft) Zone 7

'Safrano'
Introduced Beauregard, France 1839
Parentage Not recorded
Very freely produced, rich golden yellow flowers varying from fully double to less than semi-double. Fragrant. Growth bushy with semi-glossy, darkish green foliage. Good in groups and in pots.
☼ ◖◖◖ C H 90cm W 60cm (3 x 2ft) Zone 8

'Tipsy Imperial Concubine'
Discovered Le Rougetel, China 1982
Introduced Beales, UK 1989
Parentage Not recorded
Large, fully double, cup-shaped, pink flowers subtly overlaid with various soft shades of lemon and deeper pink. Growth twiggy, bushy, and short. Foliage plentiful, dark green. Does well in pots and under glass.
☼ ◖◖ C H 60cm W 60cm (2 x 2ft) Zone 8

'Archiduc Joseph'

'Clementina Carbonieri'

'Dr Grill'

'Maman Cochet'

Alexander

'Dame Edith Helen'

'Lady Sylvia'

'Mrs Oakley Fisher'

The Hybrid Teas

Alec's Red ('Cored')
Introduced Cocker, UK 1973
Parentage Fragrant Cloud x 'Dame de Coeur'
Large, well-formed, very fragrant, deep velvety red flowers on strong, stout, thorny stems. Foliage dark green, moderately glossy. Growth medium bushy.
☼ ♦♦♦ C H 60cm W 60cm (2 x 2ft) Zone 5

Alexander ('Harex') Alexandra
Introduced Harkness, UK 1972
Parentage Super Star x ('Ann Elizabeth' x 'Allgold')
Long, pointed buds open to semi-double, blowsy, bright vermilion blooms. Light scent. Foliage mid- to dark green, copious, healthy. Growth tall and upright.
☼ ♦ C H 1.2m W 60cm (4 x 2ft) Zone 6

'Crimson Glory'
Introduced Kordes, Germany 1935
Parentage 'Catherine Kordes' seedling x 'W.E. Chaplin'
Globular, high-centred, deep velvety red blooms, on rather weak stalks. Superb fragrance. Foliage dark green. Thorny, bushy growth. An excellent old HT.
☼ ♦♦♦ C H 60cm W 60cm (2 x 2ft) Zone 5

'Dainty Bess'
Introduced Archer, UK 1925
Parentage 'Ophelia' x 'K of K'
Small clusters of beautiful, single flowers, soft silvery pink with delightful golden stamens. Large, matt, darkish green leaves. Growth moderately bushy.
☼ ♦♦ C H 60cm W 60cm (2 x 2ft) Zone 5

'Dame Edith Helen'
Introduced Dickson, UK 1926
Parentage Not recorded
Very large, fully double, bright glowing pink flowers, opening flat and cushion-like. Fragrant. Growth rather thorny and bushy. Foliage dark green, leathery.
☼ ♦♦ C H 60cm W 60cm (2 x 2ft) Zone 6

Double Delight ('Andeli')
Introduced Armstrong, USA 1977
Parentage Granada x Garden Party
Freely produced, shapely, fully double, fragrant flowers, cream heavily suffused pinkish red. Foliage mid-green, semi-glossy. Growth medium bushy.
☼ ♦♦ C H 90cm W 60cm (3 x 2ft) Zone 5

Elina ('Dicjana') Peaudouce
Introduced Dickson, UK 1983
Parentage 'Nana Mouskouri' x Lolita
An outstanding rose. Large, shapely blooms of many petals, soft yellow to cream. Very freely produced. Fragrant. Widely bushy with lots of dark green leaves.
☼ ♦♦ C H 90cm W 60cm (3 x 2ft) Zone 5

Golden Melody ('Irene Churruca')
Introduced La Florida, USA 1934
Parentage 'Mme Butterfly' x ('Lady Hillingdon' x 'Souvenir de Claudius Pernet')
Superb, shapely, high-centred flowers, golden fading to cream, on strong necks. Good fragrance. Leathery, dark green foliage. Growth upright, bushy, thorny.
☼ ♦♦♦ C H 75cm W 60cm (2½ x 2ft) Zone 6

'Grandpa Dickson' (USA 'Irish Gold')
Introduced Dickson, UK 1966
Parentage (Perfecta x Governador Braga da Cruz) x Piccadilly
Freely produced, large, shapely, fragrant, soft yellow flowers on an upright, thorny plant. Foliage leathery, glossy, mid-green. Excellent for bedding.
☼ ♦♦ C H 75cm W 60cm (2½ x 2ft) Zone 6

'Just Joey'
Introduced Cant, UK 1972
Parentage Fragrant Cloud x 'Dr A.J. Verhage'
Very large, shapely, coppery orange flowers veined soft red. Strong scent. Foliage plentiful, dark green, and leathery. Growth broadly upright and thorny.
☼ ♦♦♦ C H 60cm W 60cm (2 x 2ft) Zone 6

'Lady Mary Fitzwilliam'
Introduced Bennett, UK 1882
Rediscovered Money, UK 1975
Parentage 'Devoniensis' x 'Victor Verdier'
Shapely, high-centred, soft pink flowers flushed deeper pink. Fragrant. Growth bushy, thorny. Foliage copious, dark green.
☼ ♦♦ C H 75cm W 75cm (2½ x 2½ft) Zone 6

'Lady Sylvia'
Introduced Stevens, UK 1926
Parentage Sport of 'Mme Butterfly'
Shapely buds open to full flowers of soft flesh-pink with deeper shadings, on strong necks. Foliage dark green. Growth bushy. Good under glass.
☼ ♦♦♦ C H 60cm W 60cm (2 x 2ft) Zone 6

'La France'
Introduced Guillot, France 1867
Parentage Tea x Hybrid Perpetual
The first Hybrid Tea. Plump, silvery pink blooms open blowsy and full. Fragrant. Growth bushy, with grey-green leaves. Repeat flowering. Prone to mildew.
☼ ♦♦ R ⊙ H 60cm W 60cm (2 x 2ft) Zone 6

'Mme Butterfly'
Introduced Hill, USA 1918
Parentage Sport of 'Ophelia'
Similar to its parent 'Ophelia' except deeper pink in colour. Good under glass as a cutting rose.
☼ ♦♦♦ C H 60cm W 60cm (2 x 2ft) Zone 6

'Mrs Oakley Fisher'
Introduced Cant, UK 1921
Parentage Not recorded
A real delight. Single, golden yellow flowers with distinctive golden brown stamens. Fragrant. Bushy, upright growth. Foliage very dark green, semi-glossy.
☼ ♦♦ C H 45cm W 45cm (1½ x 1½ft) Zone 6

'Ophelia'
Introduced Paul, UK 1912
Parentage Chance seedling of 'Antoine Rivoire'
Shapely, high-centred buds open to cupped, soft blush-pink blooms with hints of lemon deep down. Intensely fragrant. Growth bushy, foliage dark green. Good under glass.
☼ ♦♦♦ C H 60cm W 60cm (2 x 2ft) Zone 6

Pascali ('Lenip') Blanche Pasca
Introduced Lens, Belgium 1963
Parentage Queen Elizabeth x 'White Butterfly'
Tight, globular buds open to large, shapely flowers of soft creamy white. Held on very strong stems with few thorns and lots of dark green foliage.
☼ ♦♦ C H 90cm W 60cm (3 x 2ft) Zone 6

Peace ('Mme A. Meilland') Gloria Dei
Introduced Meilland, France 1945
Parentage [(('George Dickson' x 'Souvenir de Claudius Pernet') x ('Joanna Hill' x 'Charles P. Kilham')) x 'Margaret McGredy']
Perhaps the most famous rose of all time. Globular buds open to large, cabbage-like blooms, soft yellow with orange-red markings. Sweetly scented. Foliage large, leathery, and glossy, dark green. Growth strong, bushy. Excellent in a mixed border.
☼ ♦♦ C H 1.2m W 60cm (4 x 2ft) Zone 6

Piccadilly ('Macar')
Introduced McGredy, New Zealand 1960
Parentage 'McGredy's Yellow' x 'Karl Herbst'
Tight clusters of high-centred buds, opening to full, bright yellow and red flowers. Fragrant. Freely borne. Very thorny growth. Foliage glossy, brownish green.
☼ ◖◖ C H 75cm W 60cm (2½ x 2ft) Zone 5

'Pinta'
Introduced Beales, UK 1973
Parentage 'Ena Harkness' x Pascali
Semi-double, creamy white flowers, not large but shapely and freely produced. Sweet Briar fragrance. Growth bushy, thorny. Foliage leathery, dark green.
☼ ◖◖ C H 60cm W 60cm (2 x 2ft) Zone 5

Polar Star ('Tanlarpost') Polarstern
Introduced Tantau, Germany 1985
Parentage Not recorded
Shapely, fully double, soft cream to white flowers emerge from large, globular buds, held on strong stems. Fragrant. Foliage plentiful, leathery, dark green. Growth vigorous, upright. Good for cutting.
☼ ◖◖ C H 90cm W 60cm (3 x 2ft) Zone 5

Remember Me ('Cocdestin')
Introduced Cocker, UK 1984
Parentage 'Anne Letts' x ('Dainty Maid' x 'Pink Favourite')
Pointed buds open to cupped, full flowers of yellow blended with copper and gold. Fragrant. Foliage dark green, glossy. Growth upright. Excellent for bedding.
☼ ◖ C H 75cm W 60cm (2½ x 2ft) Zone 6

Royal William ('Korzaun') Duftzauber '84
Introduced Kordes, Germany 1984
Parentage 'Feuerzauber' x unnamed seedling
An outstanding, well-formed, deep velvety red rose with a strong fragrance. Growth upright, very thorny. Foliage plum coloured, leathery, semi-glossy.
☼ ◖◖◖ C H 90cm W 60cm (3 x 2ft) Zone 6

Savoy Hotel ('Harvintage')
Introduced Harkness, UK 1987
Parentage 'Silver Jubilee' x Amber Queen
Very large, cabbage-like, soft pink flowers, freely borne. Perfumed. Bushy, with dark green foliage.
☼ ◖◖ C H 90cm W 60cm (3 x 2ft) Zone 6

'Silver Jubilee'
Introduced Cocker, UK 1978
Parentage [(('Highlight' x Colour Wonder) x ('Parkdirektor Riggers' x Piccadilly)) x Mischief]
A perfect modern HT. Many-petalled, silvery pink to apricot blooms, high centred just before opening fully. Very fragrant. Glossy, mid-green leaves. Growth thorny, bushy. Superb for mass planting.
☼ ◖◖◖ C H 75cm W 60cm (2½ x 2ft) Zone 6

'Soleil d'Or'
Introduced Pernet-Ducher, France 1900
Parentage 'Antoine Ducher' seedling x *R. foetida* 'Persiana'
Tight, round buds open to flat, rich yellow flowers with muddled centres. Growth upright, thorny. Foliage rich green. Rather prone to black spot.
☼ ◖◖ C ⊙ H 90cm W 60cm (3 x 2ft) Zone 6

Summer Fragrance ('Tanfudermos') Sommerduft
Introduced Tantau, Germany 1985
Parentage Not recorded
Shapely, high-centred, double flowers on strong necks. Very deep red and very free flowering. Good fragrance. Growth upright. Foliage dark green, glossy.
☼ ◖◖◖ C H 75cm W 60cm (2½ x 2ft) Zone 6

The Floribundas

Amanda ('Beesian')
Introduced Bees, UK 1979
Parentage 'Arthur Bell' x Zambra
Clusters of globular buds open to full flowers of rich yellow with hints of orange and red. Fragrant. Foliage glossy, mid-green. Growth medium bushy.
☼ ◖◖ C H 90cm W 75cm (3 x 2½ft) Zone 6

Amber Queen ('Harroony')
Introduced Harkness, UK 1984
Parentage 'Southampton' x 'Typhoon'
Large clusters of initially cupped, fully double blooms of apricot-gold, opening from plump buds. Spicy scent. Foliage glossy, copper-tinted dark green.
☼ ◖◖ C H 60cm W 60cm (2 x 2ft) Zone 6

Beautiful Britain ('Dicfire')
Introduced Dickson, UK 1983
Parentage 'Red Planet' x 'Eurorose'
Sizeable clusters of semi-double, bright tomato-red flowers with a modest fragrance. Upright growth, fairly thorny. Dark green foliage with a bronze tinge.
☼ ◖ C H 90cm W 60cm (3 x 2ft) Zone 6

'Chinatown'
Introduced Poulsen, Denmark 1963
Parentage 'Columbine' x 'Cläre Grammerstorf'
Tightly packed clusters of slightly weak-necked, fully double blooms of soft yellow, touched orange. Foliage rich lime-green, glossy, and plentiful. Growth upright, vigorous. Slightly prone to mildew.
☼ ◖◖ C ⊙ H 1.2m W 60cm (4 x 2ft) Zone 5

Crazy For You ('Wekroalt') USA Fourth of July
Introduced Weeks, USA 1999
Parentage Rollercoaster x Altissimo
Large clusters of almost single flowers with ruffled petals, randomly striped red, yellow, and orange. Mild scent. Growth tall. Glossy, darkish green foliage.
☼ ◖ C H 1.2m W 90cm (4 x 3ft) Zone 5

'English Miss'
Introduced Cant, UK 1979
Parentage ('Dearest' x 'The Optimist') x 'Sweet Repose'
Sizeable clusters of shapely, full, soft pink flowers. Fragrant. Foliage purplish dark green. Growth short, bushy. A superb bedding rose.
☼ ◖◖ C H 45cm W 45cm (1½ x 1½ft) Zone 6

Escapade ('Harpade')
Introduced Harkness, UK 1967
Parentage 'Pink Parfait' x 'Baby Faurax'
Large clusters of loosely semi-double flowers of magenta-lilac overlaid pink. Modest fragrance. Foliage plentiful, glossy, mid-green. Growth upright, tall.
☼ ◖ C H 1.1m W 60cm (3½ x 2ft) Zone 5

'Grüss an Aachen'
Introduced Geduldig, Germany 1909
Parentage 'Frau Karl Druschki' x 'Franz Deegen'
Fully double, flattish, flesh-pink flowers paling to soft cream, with deeper centres. Fragrant. Growth bushy and short. Foliage rich green, leathery. Superb.
☼ ◖◖ C H 45cm W 45cm (1½ x 1½ft) Zone 6

Iceberg ('Korbin') Schneewittchen, Fée des Neiges
Introduced Kordes, Germany 1958
Parentage 'Robin Hood' x 'Virgo'
Loose clusters of semi-double, pure white flowers. Fragrant. Foliage glossy, light green. Outstanding.
◑ ◖◖ C H 90cm W 60cm (3 x 2ft) Zone 5

Polar Star

Savoy Hotel

Amber Queen

Escapade

Lilli Marlene

Queen Elizabeth

Autumn Fire

'Autumn Sunset'

'Korresia' ('Sunsprite', 'Friesia')
Introduced Kordes, Germany 1977
Parentage 'Friedrich Wörlein' x 'Spanish Sun'
Very freely produced, almost fully double, deep yellow flowers in large clusters. Fragrant. Growth tidy, upright, with dark green foliage. Especially good in groups and for mass planting.
☼ ♠♠ **C H** 90cm **W** 60cm (3 x 2ft) Zone 5

'Lilac Charm'
Introduced LeGrice, UK 1962
Parentage 'Lavender Pinocchio' x unknown
Large clusters of single, fragrant flowers, pastel lilac-mauve with honey-coloured stamens. Foliage grey-green. Growth bushy, upright. Lovely with perennials.
☼ ♠♠ **C H** 45cm **W** 45cm (1½ x 1½ft) Zone 6

Lilli Marlene ('Korlima') Lilli Marleen
Introduced Kordes, Germany 1959
Parentage ('Our Princess' x 'Rudolph Timm') x 'Ama'
Fully double, dark red blooms in very large clusters. Light fragrance. Foliage plentiful, dark green. Growth bushy, stems very thorny. An excellent bedding rose.
○ ♠ **C H** 75cm **W** 60cm (2½ x 2ft) Zone 5

Margaret Merril ('Harkuly')
Introduced Harkness, UK 1977
Parentage ('Rudolph Timm' x 'Dedication') x Pascali
Large clusters of semi-double, soft blush to white flowers, opening to show off golden stamens. Very fragrant. Foliage dark green. Thorny, upright growth.
☼ ♠♠♠ **C H** 90cm **W** 60cm (3 x 2ft) Zone 6

'Norwich Castle'
Introduced Beales, UK 1976
Parentage Whisky Mac x 'Arthur Bell'
Sizeable clusters of semi-double to double, ginger-orange flowers. Fragrant. Growth upright, bushy, and thorny, with dark green foliage. Useful in groups and for mass planting.
☼ ♠♠ **C H** 1.1m **W** 75cm (3½ x 2½ft) Zone 6

'Pink Grüss an Aachen'
Introduced Kluis & Koning, Holland 1929
Parentage Sport of 'Grüss an Aachen'
An old Floribunda, equally as good as its parent. Smallish clusters of fully double, fragrant flowers in salmon and pink. Foliage rich green, leathery. Growth short, bushy.
☼ ♠♠ **C H** 45cm **W** 45cm (1½ x 1½ft) Zone 6

'Pink Parfait'
Introduced Swim, USA 1960
Parentage 'First Love' x Pinocchio
Sizeable clusters of almost fully double flowers in a blend of many shades of pink. Good fragrance. Dark green leaves. Growth fairly thorn free, upright, bushy.
☼ ♠♠ **C H** 90cm **W** 60cm (3 x 2ft) Zone 5

Queen Elizabeth ('The Queen Elizabeth')
Introduced Lammerts, USA 1954
Parentage 'Charlotte Armstrong' x 'Floradora'
Clusters of double, silvery pink flowers held upright on a tall plant. Plenty of large, grey-green leaves. Superb as a tall hedging rose. Virtually scentless.
○ ♠ **C H** 1.5m **W** 90cm (5 x 3ft) Zone 6

Sexy Rexy ('Macrexy') Heckenzauber
Introduced McGredy, New Zealand 1984
Parentage Seaspray x Dreaming
Very double, flattish, salmon to soft pink flowers in large clusters. Slightly fragrant. Foliage light green. Growth thorny, bushy.
♠ **C H** 45cm **W** 45cm (1½ x 1½ft) Zone 6

The Modern Shrub Roses

'Agnes'
Introduced Saunders Central Experimental Farm, Canada 1922
Parentage R. rugosa x R. foetida 'Persiana'
Sizeable, fully double, rather muddled, soft primrose-yellow blooms produced a little sparingly but successively. Very fragrant. Tall, thorny growth, with wrinkled, dark green foliage. A very good Rugosa-type Modern Shrub rose.
○ ♠♠♠ **C H** 1.8m **W** 1.5m (6 x 5ft) Zone 4

'Anna Pavlova'
Introduced Beales, UK 1981
Parentage Not recorded
Fully double, delicate soft pink blooms, almost flat when fully open, emerge from tight, pointed buds. Superbly fragrant. Sometimes a little shy in flowering in poor soil. Foliage large, leathery, and dark green.
☼ ♠♠♠ **C H** 1.2m **W** 90cm (4 x 3ft) Zone 6

Autumn Fire ('Herbstfeuer')
Introduced Kordes, Germany 1961
Parentage R. rubiginosa hybrid
Large, semi-double, fragrant, dark red flowers in large clusters in early and midsummer. Sometimes repeated in autumn. Growth vigorous and bushy with dark green foliage. Very large, narrowly pear-shaped, bright red fruit.
○ ♠♠ **R H** 1.5m **W** 1.2m (5 x 4ft) Zone 6

'Autumn Sunset'
Introduced Lowe, USA 1987
Parentage Sport of Westerland
An eye-catching rose with large clusters of semi-double blooms opening a little unkempt, bright yellow with touches of amber. Slight scent. Growth strong and upright. Foliage leathery and mid-green.
○ ♠ **C H** 1.2m **W** 1.2m (4 x 4ft) Zone 5

Bonica '82 ('Meidomonac')
Introduced Meilland, France 1982
Parentage Not recorded
An outstanding rose of modern times. Large clusters of semi-double, bright pink flowers from early summer to late autumn. Fragrant. Growth wide and bushy. Foliage mid-green, copper tinted. Excellent for mass planting or pot culture.
○ ♠♠ **C H** 1.2m **W** 1.2m (4 x 4ft) Zone 5

'Canary Bird'
Origin China **First noted** c.1908
Parentage Probably R. xanthina hugonis x R. xanthina
Large, single, bright yellow flowers borne on plum-coloured stems. Light fragrance. Soft, fern-like, dark green foliage. One of the first to bloom each year; also occasionally produces the odd bloom in midsummer and autumn. A good shrub, also often grown as a standard ("tree rose").
○ ♠ **Sp H** 2.5m **W** 1.8m (8 x 6ft) Zone 5

'Cantabrigiensis' (Cambridge rose, R. x cantabrigiensis)
Introduced Cambridge Botanic Gardens, UK 1931
Parentage R. xanthina hugonis x R. sericea
A lovely, single, slightly fragrant, bright primrose-yellow rose, flowering in mid-spring. Thorny, fawn-to brown-coloured wood and lots of fern-like, darkish green foliage. Growth gracefully arching and tall. Good for a mixed shrubbery.
○ ♠ **Sp H** 3m **W** 1.5m (10 x 5ft) Zone 5

'Cerise Bouquet'

Introduced Kordes, Germany 1958
Parentage *R. multibracteata* x 'Crimson Glory'
Flowers are fully double, cerise, and produced in small clusters in midsummer. Light fragrance. Grey-green foliage. Arching habit, quite thorny. A real spectacle when full grown.
◯ ♦ **S H** 4m **W** 4m (12 x 12ft) Zone 5

'City of Oelde'

Introduced Beales, UK 2002
Parentage Seedling of Bonica '82
Mid candy-pink flowers are semi-double when fully open, borne in clusters. Mildly scented. Healthy, glossy, mid-green foliage. A compact, upright, free-flowering shrub.
◯ ♦ **C H** 1.2m **W** 90cm (4 x 3ft) Zone 5

Countess of Wessex ('Beacream')

Introduced Beales, UK 2004
Parentage City of York x 'Maigold'
Clusters of almost fully double, creamy white flowers with a very good fragrance. Free flowering. Growth upright and tidy. Foliage copious, light green. Very healthy. A lovely rose.
◯ ♦♦♦ **C H** 1.2m **W** 90cm (4 x 3ft) Zone 5

'Dortmund'

Introduced Kordes, Germany 1955
Parentage Seedling x *R. kordesii*
Long, pointed buds open to large, single, red flowers with a creamy white eye, produced in clusters. Fragrant. Foliage is dark green and glossy. A very vigorous shrub or climber that can tolerate shade and poorer soil. Repeat flowering.
◯ ♦♦ **R H** 2.5m **W** 1.8m (8 x 6ft) Zone 5

'Evelyn May'

Introduced Beales, UK 2000
Parentage Elizabeth of Glamis x 'Arthur Bell'
Double flowers in a pleasing blend of orange, salmon, and yellow, with a strong perfume. Upright growth with dark green foliage. An effective specimen shrub and good for hedging.
☼ ♦♦♦ **C H** 1.2m **W** 60cm (4 x 2ft) Zone 6

'Fountain' ('Fontaine', 'Red Prince')

Introduced Tantau, Germany 1972
Parentage 'Olala' x Duftwolke
Large, cupped, semi-double blooms of blood-red to crimson. Fragrant and freely produced. Shrubby in habit and well endowed with disease-resistant, dark green foliage. An excellent rose worthy of a good position in any garden.
☼ ♦♦ **C H** 2.2m **W** 1.2m (7 x 4ft) Zone 6

'Frühlingsgold'

Introduced Kordes, Germany 1937
Parentage 'Joanna Hill' x *R. pimpinellifolia* hybrid
Large, blowsy, near single, clear yellow blooms, with pronounced stamens, fading with age to creamy yellow. Flowers very early, in late spring. Fragrant. Stems somewhat thorny, with dark green foliage on an upright plant. Absolutely stunning in full flush.
◯ ♦♦ **Sp H** 2.5m **W** 1.5m (8 x 5ft) Zone 5

'Frühlingsmorgen'

Introduced Kordes, Germany 1942
Parentage ('E.G. Hill' x 'Catherine Kordes') x *R. pimpinellifolia* 'Grandiflora'
Medium-sized, saucer-like, single, cherry-pink blooms with yellow-splashed centres, followed by maroon hips. Scented. Dark green leaves. A handsome rose, spectacular en masse in late spring, with occasional, less flamboyant repeats.
◯ ♦♦ **Sp H** 2.5m **W** 1.5m (8 x 5ft) Zone 5

'Goldbusch'

Introduced Kordes, Germany 1954
Parentage 'Golden Glow' x *R. rubiginosa* hybrid
Large, semi-double flowers in clusters are buff to yellow and highly fragrant. Slightly glossy, dark green foliage with the faintest scent of apple. A tall, relaxed shrub best with support; can be grown as a climber.
◯ ♦♦♦ **C H** 2.5m **W** 1.5m (8 x 5ft) Zone 6

'Golden Chersonese'

Introduced Allen, UK 1963
Parentage *R. ecae* x 'Canary Bird'
An upright-growing rose with brownish, thorny stems and lots of medium-sized, single, deep golden yellow flowers in late spring. Foliage fern-like, soft to touch, and mid- to dark green.
◯ **Sp H** 1.8m **W** 1.2m (6 x 4ft) Zone 6

'Golden Wings'

Introduced Shepherd, USA 1956
Parentage ('Soeur Thérèse' x *R. pimpinellifolia* 'Grandiflora') x 'Ormiston Roy'
Beautiful, single, saucer-like flowers, soft golden yellow with golden stamens. Sweetly scented. An easy-going shrub with large, leathery, lightish green leaves. Good hips in autumn if spent flowers are not removed.
◯ ♦♦ **C H** 1.5m **W** 1.2m (5 x 4ft) Zone 5

'Hazel Le Rougetel' ('Corylus')

Raised Hazel Le Rougetel
Introduced Beales, UK 1988
Parentage *R. rugosa* x *R. nitida*
Mid rose-pink flowers are large, single, and set off by a lovely coronet of stamens. Lightly scented and repeated through the summer. Feathery, light green leaves, taking on shades of russet, yellow, and flame in autumn. Oval, bright orange to red hips. Free suckering if on own roots.
◯ ♦ **R H** 90cm **W** 90cm (3 x 3ft) Zone 4

'Helen Knight'

Introduced Knight, UK 1963
Parentage *R. ecae* x *R. pimpinellifolia* 'Grandiflora'
Single, deep golden yellow flowers in abundance along thorny, arching, mahogany-coloured stems. Light fragrance. Delicate fern-like, darkish green leaves. A handsome shrub flowering in late spring to early summer. Tolerant of poor soil.
◯ ♦ **Sp H** 1.5m **W** 1.2m (5 x 4ft) Zone 5

'Hidcote Gold'

Introduced Hilling, UK 1948
Parentage Seedling of *R. sericea*
A strong, robust shrub with single, lightly scented, bright yellow flowers borne in small clusters early each season. Many small, fern-like, dark green leaves on stems liberally armed with wedge-shaped thorns. A beautiful rose to enhance any shrubbery.
◯ ♦ **Sp H** 2.5m **W** 1.8m (8 x 6ft) Zone 6

Jacqueline du Pré ('Harwanna')

Introduced Harkness, UK 1989
Parentage Radox Bouquet x 'Maigold'
Graceful, semi-double, pink-tinged white flowers, like water-lilies in shape, with a centre of golden red stamens. Fragrant and freely produced. Healthy, lime-green foliage. Well suited to growing in pots but equally at home in a mixed border.
☼ ♦♦ **C H** 1.2m **W** 1.5m (4 x 5ft) Zone 6

Countess of Wessex

'Evelyn May'

'Fountain'

'Goldbusch'

'Marguerite Hilling'

'Raymond Carver'

St Ethelburga

'Henry Kelsey'

'James Mason'
Introduced Beales, UK 1982
Parentage 'Scharlachglut' x 'Tuscany Superb'
Large blooms are almost single, of rich, non-fading dark velvety red, with beautiful golden stamens. Fragrant. Foliage healthy, dense, and dark green. A good summer-flowering specimen plant.
○ ♦♦ **S H** 1.5m **W** 1.2m (5 x 4ft) Zone 4

Louise Clements ('Clelou')
Introduced Clements, USA 1998
Parentage Not recorded
Old-fashioned, fully double, coppery orange flowers, opening flat and cushion-like. Strong perfume. Upright growth with bronze-green foliage.
☼ ♦♦♦ **C H** 1.2m **W** 90cm (4 x 3ft) Zone 5

Macmillan Nurse ('Beamac')
Introduced Beales, UK 1998
Parentage Bonica '82 x 'Maigold'
An excellent smaller Shrub rose. Very double, rosette-like, almost quartered, white flowers, often flushed peach, especially near their centres. Borne in large clusters, well into autumn. Mild scent. Healthy, glossy, dark green foliage. Attractive in groups.
○ ♦ **C H** 90cm **W** 90cm (3 x 3ft) Zone 5

'Marguerite Hilling'
Introduced Hilling, UK 1959
Parentage Sport of 'Nevada'
Almost single, blowsy, soft pink blooms with large, wing-like petals. Light fragrance. A very showy rose, sensational in early summer; blooms intermittently through to autumn. Wide, slightly sprawling growth. Probably best in a shrubbery or mixed border.
○ ♦ **R H** 2.5m **W** 2.2m (8 x 7ft) Zone 4

'Nevada'
Introduced Dot, Spain 1927
Parentage Possibly a *R. moyesii* hybrid
Large, semi-double flowers of ivory-white finished off with a crown of golden stamens. Mildly scented. Stunning in early summer, with an occasional later bloom. Leaves fresh green and rounded. Branches brown and angular. Good for mixed borders.
○ ♦ **R H** 2.5m **W** 2.2m (8 x 7ft) Zone 4

Peter Beales ('Cleexpert')
Introduced Clements, USA 2000
Parentage Not recorded
Clusters of single, bright crimson blooms, splashed at their centres with yellow. Mildly fragrant. Upright stems well clothed in dark green leaves. A good, continuous-flowering rose.
○ ♦ **C H** 1.2m **W** 90cm (4 x 3ft) Zone 5

'Raymond Carver'
Raised Horner, UK
Introduced Beales, UK 1999
Parentage Lichtkönigin Lucia x Summer Wine
Large, fully double, coppery yellow flowers, old-fashioned in style. Good fragrance. Growth is upright and strong with healthy, coppery green foliage. An excellent Shrub rose, one of the best of its colour.
☼ ♦♦ **C H** 1.2m **W** 90cm (4 x 3ft) Zone 5

Rhapsody in Blue ('Frantasia')
Introduced Cowlishaw, UK 2003
Parentage [((Summer Wine x 'Montezuma') x ('Violacea' x 'Seefield')) x (Blue Moon x 'Seefield')) x (International Herald Tribune x Summer Wine)]
One of the more blue of the so-called blue roses. Shapely, semi-double flowers of purplish mauve in good-sized clusters. Subtly fragrant. Growth upright, bushy. Foliage dark green and plentiful.
○ ♦ **C H** 1.2m **W** 90cm (4 x 3ft) Zone 6

'Sadler's Wells'
Introduced Beales, UK 1983
Parentage 'Penelope' x Rose Gaujard
Large clusters of semi-double blooms, silvery pink overlaid with cherry-red, especially on the outer edges. Light scent. Never troubled by damp weather. Growth is upright, with large, dark green leaves. Blooms well into autumn. Long-lasting as cut flowers.
○ ♦ **C H** 1.2m **W** 90cm (4 x 3ft) Zone 6

'Scharlachglut' (Scarlet Fire)
Introduced Kordes, Germany 1952
Parentage 'Poinsettia' x 'Alika'
Large, single, mildly fragrant flowers, bright velvety red with golden stamens, in early summer. Pear-shaped, orange-red hips. Leaves dark green tinted soft purple. Thorny stems. A tough rose, good as a wall plant or specimen shrub; will also climb trees.
○ ♦ **S H** 3m **W** 1.8m (10 x 6ft) Zone 4

St Ethelburga ('Beabimbo')
Introduced Beales, UK 2003
Parentage 'Comte de Chambord' x 'Aloha'
A beautiful, classic pink rose sharing the best attributes of its famous parents. Flowers are fully double, soft icing-sugar pink. Very heavily perfumed. Foliage is healthy, dark green, and abundant.
☼ ♦♦♦ **C H** 1.2m **W** 90cm (4 x 3ft) Zone 5

Westerland ('Korwest')
Introduced Kordes, Germany 1969
Parentage 'Friedrich Wörlein' x 'Circus'
Semi-double flowers of extremely bright orange-apricot, deeper in colour towards the outer edges, borne in clusters. Mild scent. Bright, soft green foliage on strong, upright growth. Free flowering.
○ ♦ **C H** 1.2m **W** 90cm (4 x 3ft) Zone 5

The Explorer Series

'Cuthbert Grant'
Introduced Dept of Agriculture, Canada 1967
Parentage ('Crimson Glory' x 'Assiniboine') x 'Assiniboine'
Large, semi-double, crimson-red, velvety textured flowers. Fragrant. Prolific first flush followed by a good autumn display. Growth bushy, dense, and disease resistant. Foliage dark green.
○ ♦♦ **R H** 1.2m **W** 90cm (4 x 3ft) Zone 4

'George Vancouver'
Introduced Dept of Agriculture, Canada 1994
Parentage Seedling of *R. kordesii*
Large clusters of semi-double flowers open very bright red and shapely, changing to blowsy, softer red. Growth spreading and bushy. Foliage dark green.
○ **C H** 90cm **W** 90cm (3 x 3ft) Zone 4

'Henry Kelsey'
Introduced Dept of Agriculture, Canada 1984
Parentage *R. kordesii* x unnamed seedling
A real delight. Clusters of semi-double, mid- to bright red flowers open to show off straw-coloured stamens. Modest fragrance. Growth vigorous, bushy. Foliage dark green, glossy.
○ ♦ **C H** 1.5m **W** 1.5m (5 x 5ft) Zone 4

'Jens Munk'
Introduced Dept of Agriculture, Canada 1974
Parentage 'Schneezwerg' x 'Fru Dagmar Hastrup'
Semi-double to double, lilac to mauve-pink flowers opening to show good yellow stamens. Fragrant. Very free flowering. Growth dense, bushy, and upright. Foliage greyish mid-green.
○ ♦♦ **C H** 1.2m **W** 1.2m (4 x 4ft) Zone 4

'John Cabot'
Introduced Dept of Agriculture, Canada 1978
Parentage *R. kordesii* x unnamed seedling
Sizeable, semi-double flowers of soft red to cerise, opening to display golden stamens. Slightly fragrant. Produced freely in early summer, spasmodically later. Foliage greyish green. Growth vigorous and of climbing proportions.
○ ● R H 2.5m W 2.2m (8 x 7ft) Zone 4

'Martin Frobisher'
Introduced Dept of Agriculture, Canada 1968
Parentage Seedling of 'Schneezwerg'
Fully double, almost blush-pink flowers with a good fragrance, freely produced. Growth bushy and upright. Foliage grey-green, perhaps a little sparse.
○ ●● C H 1.5m W 1.2m (5 x 4ft) Zone 4

'William Baffin'
Introduced Dept of Agriculture, Canada 1983
Parentage Seedling of *R. kordesii*
Large, semi-double, soft pinkish red flowers show off pronounced golden stamens when fully open. Freely produced. Lightly scented. Foliage greyish green. Growth very vigorous, and can also climb.
○ ● C H 2.5m W 2.2m (8 x 7ft) Zone 3

The New English Roses

Abraham Darby ('Auscot')
Introduced Austin, UK 1985
Parentage 'Aloha' x 'Yellow Cushion'
Very large, full, apricot and yellow flowers in the old-fashioned style, with a rich, fruity fragrance. Growth bushy but arching. Foliage plentiful, leathery, and dark green.
☼ ●● C H 1.5m W 1.2m (5 x 4ft) Zone 6

Chianti ('Auswine')
Introduced Austin, UK 1967
Parentage *R. x macrantha* x 'Vanity'
Loose clusters of large, semi-double, deep purple flowers opening to display golden stamens. Fragrant and once flowering. Foliage matt, dark green. Growth medium and wide.
○ ●● S H 1.5m W 1.2m (5 x 4ft) Zone 6

Constance Spry ('Austance')
Introduced Austin, UK 1960
Parentage 'Belle Isis' x 'Dainty Maid'
Large, loosely cupped, fully double, bright pink flowers, borne in summer. Myrrh-like scent. Vigorous and thorny, with coarse, grey-green foliage. A large shrub needing support; can be grown as a climber.
○ ●●● S H 5m W 3m (15 x 10ft) Zone 6

Geoff Hamilton ('Ausham')
Introduced Austin, UK 1987
Parentage Heritage x seedling
Cupped, double flowers are soft pink, with paler edges, borne in clusters. Fragrant with a hint of apple. Glossy, darkish green foliage.
☼ ●● C H 1.5m W 1.2m (5 x 4ft) Zone 6

Gertrude Jekyll ('Ausbord')
Introduced Austin, UK 1986
Parentage Wife of Bath x 'Comte de Chambord'
One of the most beautiful of its group. Magnificent flowers in the old-fashioned style, fully double, highly scented, and deep pink. Greyish green foliage on an upright, bushy plant.
☼ ●●● C H 1.2m W 90cm (4 x 3ft) Zone 5

Glamis Castle ('Auslevel')
Introduced Austin, UK 1992
Parentage Graham Thomas x Mary Rose
Large, cupped, semi-double, almost peony-like blooms are pure white with a myrhh-like fragrance. Growth upright and dense. Foliage glossy and mid-green. Good for mass planting or growing in tubs.
☼ ●● C H 90cm W 60cm (3 x 2ft) Zone 6

Graham Thomas ('Ausmas')
Introduced Austin, UK 1983
Parentage Seedling x (Charles Austin x Iceberg seedling)
An excellent rose. Cupped, fully double blooms, old-fashioned in form, are rich golden yellow, borne in good-sized clusters. Myrrh-like scent. Healthy, mid- to bright green foliage and bushy growth. Also makes a useful short climber.
☼ ●●● C H 1.2m W 90cm (4 x 3ft) Zone 6

Heritage ('Ausblush')
Introduced Austin, UK 1984
Parentage Seedling x (Iceberg x Wife of Bath)
Very double, cupped, almost globular flowers, soft silky pink with slightly deeper centres. Very fragrant. Glossy, mid-green foliage and bushy growth. Good for mass planting and pots.
☼ ●●● C H 1.2m W 90cm (4 x 3ft) Zone 6

Jayne Austin ('Ausbreak')
Introduced Austin, UK 1990
Parentage Graham Thomas x Tamora
Blooms cupped at first, opening to large, flat rosettes of soft yellow with shades of apricot. Lovely fragrance. Foliage soft grey-green. Growth bushy, upright, with the occasional longer shoot.
☼ ●● C H 1.1m W 90cm (3½ x 3ft) Zone 6

L.D. Braithwaite ('Auscrim')
Introduced Austin, UK 1988
Parentage The Squire x Mary Rose
Double, unfading bright crimson-red flowers, less cupped than others in this group. Abundantly produced. Fragrant. A broad, bushy plant with leathery, dark green foliage and many thorns.
☼ ●● C H 1.1m W 90cm (3½ x 3ft) Zone 6

Mary Rose ('Ausmary')
Introduced Austin, UK 1983
Parentage Seedling x 'The Friar'
Not quite fully double, blowsy blooms, mid rose-pink and modestly scented. Foliage glossy, mid-green on a tidy, upright, bushy plant. Free flowering.
☼ ● C H 1.2m W 90cm (4 x 3ft) Zone 6

Molineux ('Ausmol')
Introduced Austin, UK 1994
Parentage 'Golden Showers' seedling x seedling
More compact in growth than most of its kind. Flowers double and cupped, rich eggy yellow in colour. Good fragrance. Foliage dark green and glossy. Ideal as a bedding rose or in pots.
☼ ●● C H 90cm W 90cm (3 x 3ft) Zone 6

William Shakespeare ('Ausroyal')
Introduced Austin, UK 1987
Parentage The Squire x Mary Rose
Clusters of rich crimson to purple flowers made up of many petals, opening flat and cushion-like. Very fragrant. Semi-glossy, dark green foliage on a bushy, thorny plant. Good in groups. Sadly, tends to be prone to disease.
☼ ●●● C ⊙ H 1.1m W 90cm (3½ x 3ft) Zone 6

'Jens Munk'

Abraham Darby

Glamis Castle

Heritage

Climbers

'Blush Noisette'

'Lady Hillingdon'

'Clarence House'

Della Balfour

The Noisettes

'Aimée Vibert' ('Bouquet de la Mariée', 'Nivea')
Introduced Vibert, France 1828
Parentage 'Champneys' Pink Cluster' x *R. sempervirens* hybrid
Small, drooping clusters of double, scented, pure white flowers. Abundant light green foliage on stems almost without thorns. Very vigorous. Comes into bloom late in summer, and goes on into winter.
○ ◆◆ **C** **H** 4m **W** 3m (12 x 10ft) Zone 6

'Alister Stella Gray' ('Golden Rambler')
Introduced Gray, UK 1894
Parentage Not recorded
Large, cascading clusters of muddled-petalled, yellow flowers with deeper yellow centres, all summer. Perfumed. Growth a little slender, but dense, and almost thornless. Foliage dark green, plentiful.
○ ◆◆ **C** **H** 5m **W** 3m (15 x 10ft) Zone 7

'Blush Noisette' ('Noisette Carnée')
Introduced Noisette, France c.1814
Parentage Seedling of 'Champneys' Pink Cluster'
Continually produces clusters of initially cupped, semi-double flowers of lilac-pink all summer through. Fragrant. Growth tidy, dense, virtually thornless. Foliage soft, grey-green, abundant. Excellent on a wall or trellis, or as a free-standing shrub.
○ ◆◆ **C** **H** 2.5m **W** 1.2m (8 x 4ft) Zone 7

'Céline Forestier'
Introduced Trouillard, France 1842
Parentage Not recorded
Tight, round buds open to large, flat, and quartered flowers of bright lemon, sometimes faintly touched orange. Fragrant. Flowers all summer. Light green leaves. Growth bushy, with few thorns. Best on walls.
☼ ◆◆ **C** **H** 2.5m **W** 1.2m (8 x 4ft) Zone 5

'Crépuscule'
Introduced Dubreuil, France 1904
Parentage Not recorded
Semi-double, rather muddled-petalled flowers, rich apricot-yellow, borne in profusion all summer. Fragrant. Medium growth, with almost thornless, dark wood and rich green foliage. Lovely on an arbour.
☼ ◆◆ **C** **H** 3m **W** 2.2m (10 x 7ft) Zone 7

'Mme Alfred Carrière'
Introduced Schwartz, France 1879
Parentage Not recorded
A superb Noisette. Shapely buds open to rather loosely formed, blush-white to pinkish white flowers with a superb perfume. Growth wide and dense, with few thorns. Foliage semi-glossy, greyish green. Good on a north wall, or any wall for that matter.
○ ◆◆◆ **C** **H** 5m **W** 3m (15 x 10ft) Zone 7

The Climbing Teas

'Gloire de Dijon'
Introduced Jacotot, France 1853
Parentage Unknown Tea rose x 'Souvenir de la Malmaison'
The best-known Tea rose. Tight, rounded buds open to large, flat, cushion-like blooms with many petals of buff-apricot to soft orange. A good first flush, with a few flowers in autumn. Very fragrant. Growth vigorous, with dark green foliage.
○ ◆◆◆ **R** **H** 4m **W** 2.5m (12 x 8ft) Zone 7

'Lady Hillingdon' (Climbing sport)
Introduced Hicks, UK 1917
Parentage (Bush form) 'Papa Gontier' x 'Mme Hoste'
Tight, pointed buds open to loosely informal flowers of unfading rich yellow. Fragrant. Repeats in autumn. Growth quite vigorous, with plum-coloured wood and foliage. Virtually thornless. Best on walls.
☼ ◆◆ **R** **H** 5m **W** 2.5m (15 x 8ft) Zone 6

'Sombreuil'
Introduced Robert, France 1850
Parentage Not recorded
Shapely buds open to fully double, flat, cushion-like blooms of creamy white with peachy undertones. Very fragrant. Constantly in flower. Growth thorny, vigorous, spreading. Foliage very dark green, plentiful. Best on walls.
☼ ◆◆◆ **C** **H** 2.5m **W** 1.5m (8 x 5ft) Zone 5

'Souvenir de Mme Léonie Viennot'
Introduced Bernaix, France 1897
Parentage Not recorded
Double, many petalled flowers, opening rather blowsily, in a blend of primrose and yellow, with copper and honey overtones. Two good flushes of flowers. Vigorous growth and dark green foliage. Perhaps just a fraction tender in northern Europe.
☼ ◆◆ **R** **H** 4m **W** 2.5m (12 x 8ft) Zone 7

The Modern Climbers

'Aloha'
Introduced Boener, USA 1949
Parentage 'Mercedes Gallart' x 'New Dawn'
Large, fully double blooms, a mix of rose-pink and magenta, with the occasional peachy tinge. Very fragrant. Continuously produced. Growth upright, bushy, vigorous. Foliage leathery and glossy, dark green. Also makes a good free-standing shrub.
☼ ◆◆◆ **C** **H** 3m **W** 1.8m (10 x 6ft) Zone 5

Breath of Life ('Harquanne')
Introduced Harkness, UK 1981
Parentage 'Red Dandy' x Alexander
High-centred, fragrant, apricot flowers in profusion throughout summer. Broad, dense growth. Foliage leathery, dark green. Good on walls and pillars.
☼ ◆◆ **C** **H** 3m **W** 1.8m (10 x 6ft) Zone 6

'Bright Ideas'
Raised Horner, UK
Introduced Beales, UK 2003
Parentage [(('Lichterloh' x 'New Penny') x ('White Pet' x 'Stars 'n' Stripes') x ('Southampton' x Tall Story)) x 'Lichterloh']
Flowers semi-double, deep cerise, striped and mottled greyish white. Fragrant. Flowers all summer. Growth upright but bushy. Foliage dark green and copious. Also makes a free-standing shrub.
○ ◆◆ **C** **H** 2.5m **W** 2.5m (8 x 8ft) Zone 6

'Clarence House'
Introduced Beales, UK 2000
Parentage City of York x 'Aloha'
Clusters of fully double, creamy white blooms opening flat and cushion-like throughout summer. Very fragrant. Growth vigorous and wide. Foliage glossy, dark green and leathery.
☼ ◆◆◆ **C** **H** 4m **W** 3m (12 x 10ft) Zone 6

Della Balfour ('Harblend') Desert Glo, Renown's Desert Glo, Royal Pageant
Introduced Harkness, UK 1994
Parentage Rosemary Harkness x Elina
Shapely, high-centred, fully double flowers, deep yellow tinted pinkish orange, borne in clusters all summer. Fragrant. Growth dense and wide. Foliage glossy, dark green, and plentiful.
☼ ◐◐ C H 2.5m W 1.8m (8 x 6ft) Zone 6

Dublin Bay ('Macdub')
Introduced McGredy, New Zealand 1976
Parentage 'Bantry Bay' x Altissimo
High-centred buds open to full, deep velvety red blooms. Light fragrance. Flowers all summer. Growth upright with ample leathery, slightly glossy, dark green foliage. Excellent for pillars and obelisks.
☼ ◐ C H 2.5m W 1.5m (8 x 5ft) Zone 5

Eden Rose '88 ('Meiviolin') Pierre de Ronsard
Introduced Meilland, France 1987
Parentage (Danse des Sylphes x Handel) x Pink Wonder
Large, fully double flowers, initially globular, opening cabbage shaped, creamy white heavily touched pinkish red. Fragrant. Continuous flowering. Growth vigorous. Foliage leathery and glossy, dark green.
☼ ◐◐ C H 4m W 1.8m (12 x 6ft) Zone 6

'Golden Showers'
Introduced Lammerts, USA 1956
Parentage 'Charlotte Armstrong' x 'Captain Thomas'
Rather ragged, semi-double, lightly scented, golden yellow flowers, fading to soft primrose. Very freely produced all summer. Growth upright, with relatively few thorns. Foliage leathery, and glossy, dark green.
◐ ◐ C H 3m W 1.8m (10 x 6ft) Zone 7

Handel ('Macha')
Introduced McGredy, UK 1965
Parentage 'Columbine' x Heidelberg
A pretty rose, shapely in all stages of development. Mildly scented, silvery white blooms with red and pink brushmarks, borne all summer. Growth upright, dense. Foliage dark green. Good on pillars.
◐ ◐ C H 4m W 2.5m (12 x 8ft) Zone 7

'Karlsruhe'
Introduced Kordes, Germany 1957
Parentage R. kordesii seedling
Large, full clusters of very double, flat blooms of deep glowing rosy pink. Fragrant. Flowers throughout summer. Growth vigorous, thorny, and wide. Foliage leathery and glossy, mid- to dark green. Does well on arches and trellis.
◐ ◐◐ C H 2.5m W 2.5m (8 x 8ft) Zone 5

'Leverkusen'
Introduced Kordes, Germany 1954
Parentage R. kordesii x 'Golden Glow'
Semi-double to double, lightly scented flowers open from shapely, soft yellow buds, paling to lemon. In flower all summer. Growth vigorous, dense, wide. Foliage lightish green, well serrated, and plentiful.
◐ ◐ C H 3m W 2.5m (10 x 8ft) Zone 4

'Maigold'
Introduced Kordes, Germany 1953
Parentage 'Poulsen's Pink' x 'Frühlingstag'
One of the earliest roses to come into flower, and often has a good second flush. Initially pointed buds open to informal, semi-double flowers of yellowish burnt-orange. Fragrant. Growth very thorny. Foliage well serrated, glossy, light green, and plentiful.
◐ ◐◐ R H 4m W 2.5m (12 x 8ft) Zone 5

'Meg'
Introduced Gosset, UK 1954
Parentage Probably 'Paul's Lemon Pillar' x 'Mme Butterfly'
Large, almost single flowers of great beauty, buff-yellow flushed apricot and peach. Borne all summer. Growth upright and branching. Foliage copious and dark green. Good perfume.
☼ ◐◐ C H 4m W 2.5m (12 x 8ft) Zone 6

'Parkdirektor Riggers'
Introduced Kordes, Germany 1957
Parentage R. kordesii x 'Our Princess'
Very large clusters of almost single, deep crimson to velvety red flowers. Blooms all summer. Growth vigorous and wide. Foliage glossy, very dark green.
◐ C H 5m W 4m (15 x 12ft) Zone 5

Penny Lane ('Hardwell')
Introduced Harkness, UK 1998
Parentage Seedling of 'New Dawn'
Large flowers, initially cupped, opening flat and fully double, blush-pink quickly changing to soft peach. Highly perfumed. Continuous flowering. Growth upright, expanded. Foliage glossy, dark green.
☼ ◐◐◐ C H 4m W 2.5m (12 x 8ft) Zone 5

'Phyllis Bide'
Introduced Bide, UK 1923
Parentage 'Perle d'Or' x 'Gloire de Dijon'
Large clusters of semi-double, slightly ragged flowers of soft yellow, cream, and pink, deepening with age. Mildly fragrant. Continuous flowering. Growth slender but dense. Light green foliage, scant but adequate.
◐ ◐ C H 4m W 1.8m (12 x 6ft) Zone 6

'White Cockade'
Introduced Cocker, UK 1969
Parentage 'New Dawn' x 'Circus'
Shapely, fully double, lightly scented flowers of pure white, borne all summer. Glossy, mid-green foliage. Wide, dense growth with thorny stems. Best on walls; will tolerate a cold position in partial shade.
◐ ◐ C H 2.5m W 1.8m (8 x 6ft) Zone 6

The Climbing Hybrid Teas

'Crimson Glory' (Climbing sport)
Introduced Jackson & Perkins, USA 1946
Parentage (Bush form) 'Catherine Kordes' seedling x 'W.E. Chaplin'
Shapely, velvety, smoky dark red blooms hanging gracefully from rather weak stems. Once flowering. Growth strong, thorny, and stiff. Foliage dark green.
☼ ◐◐◐ S H 5m W 2.5m (15 x 8ft) Zone 6

'Cupid'
Introduced Cant, UK 1915
Parentage Not recorded
Delightful, single flowers of peachy pink with discreet lemon centres, produced in two flushes. Moderately fragrant. Stems thick, thorny, and unyielding. Foliage large, plentiful, greyish green. Good on walls. Occasionally just a little shy at flowering.
☼ ◐◐ R H 3m W 1.8m (10 x 6ft) Zone 6

'Ena Harkness' (Climbing sport)
Introduced Murrell, UK 1954
Parentage (Bush form) 'Crimson Glory' x 'Southport'
High-centred, strongly scented, bright velvety red blooms hang from weak stems, allowing them to be seen from below. Once flowering. Growth thorny, stiff. Foliage dark green but lacking a little lustre.
☼ ◐◐◐ S H 5m W 2.5m (15 x 8ft) Zone 6

Handel

'Maigold'

'Meg'

'Cupid'

'Lady Sylvia'

'Albertine'

'American Pillar'

Awakening

'Guinée'
Introduced Mallerin, France 1938
Parentage 'Souvenir de Claudius Denoyel' x 'Ami Quinard'
Fully double, high-centred, velvety dark red blooms, opening flat and informal. Very fragrant. A good first flush, with a few blooms in autumn. Angular growth. Dark green foliage. Slightly prone to black spot.
☼ ♦♦♦ R ⊙ H 4m W 2.5m (12 x 8ft) Zone 6

'Lady Sylvia' (Climbing sport)
Introduced Stevens, UK 1926
Parentage (Bush form) Sport of 'Mme Butterfly'
Shapely, high-centred flowers, informal when fully open, bright pink with deeper shadings and discreet yellow centres. Very fragrant. Repeat flowering. Growth stiff and thorny. Mid- to dark green foliage.
☼ ♦♦♦ R H 5m W 3m (15 x 10ft) Zone 6

'Mme Grégoire Staechelin' ('Spanish Beauty')
Introduced Dot, Spain 1927
Parentage 'Frau Karl Druschki' x 'Château de Clos Vougeot'
Blowsy, very fragrant flowers, heavily veined bright pink with softer pink edges, open from cupped buds early in summer. Vigorous, sturdy. Foliage dark grey-green. Turnip-shaped hips. Can be temperamental.
☼ ♦♦♦ S H 5m W 3m (15 x 10ft) Zone 7

'Paul's Lemon Pillar'
Introduced Paul, UK 1915
Parentage 'Frau Karl Druschki' x 'Maréchal Niel'
Sizeable, high-centred, fragrant, creamy white blooms. A good first flush, just a few blooms later. Sturdy, stiff growth. Foliage large, fairly dark green.
☼ ♦♦ R H 5m W 3m (15 x 10ft) Zone 7

'Shot Silk' (Climbing sport)
Introduced Knight, Australia 1931
Parentage (Bush form) 'Hugh Dickson' seedling x 'Sunstar'
Fully double, silky blooms, initially cupped, mainly soft cerise and pink with golden yellow deep down in the centre. Very fragrant. Repeat flowering. Growth vigorous, with large, semi-glossy, mid-green leaves.
☼ ♦♦♦ R H 5.5m W 3m (18 x 10ft) Zone 7

Climbing Floribundas

'Allgold' (Climbing sport)
Introduced Gandy, UK 1961
Parentage (Bush form) 'Goldilocks' x 'Ellinor LeGrice'
Initially shapely blooms, opening semi-double, of unfading, bright yellow. Slightly fragrant. Repeat flowering. Thorny growth, with plentiful, glossy, dark green foliage. Outstanding.
☼ ♦ R H 4m W 3m (12 x 10ft) Zone 5

Iceberg ('Korbin') Schneewittchen, Fée des Neiges (Climbing sport)
Introduced Cant, UK 1968
Parentage (Bush form) 'Robin Hood' x 'Virgo'
Semi-double, pure white flowers borne very freely in early to midsummer, only a very few later. Fragrant. Foliage glossy, light green. Relatively few thorns.
○ ♦♦ R H 5.5m W 3m (18 x 10ft) Zone 5

'Masquerade' (Climbing sport)
Introduced Gregory, UK 1958
Parentage (Bush form) 'Goldilocks' x 'Holiday'
Masses of loose, semi-double blooms, yellow in bud, changing to deep red. Once flowering. Light scent. Growth thorny. Foliage semi-glossy, darkish green.
☼ ♦ S H 3m W 3m (10 x 10ft) Zone 6

The Wichurana Ramblers

'Albéric Barbier'
Introduced Barbier, France 1900
Parentage R. wichurana x 'Shirley Hibbard'
Shapely flowers, scrolled in bud, opening double, creamy white flushed lemon, turning to pure white with age. Slight fragrance. Glossy, dark green foliage. Vigorous, sparsely thorny. Flowers have a slight tendency to shatter in wind.
○ ♦ S H 6m W 3m (20 x 10ft) Zone 7

'Albertine'
Introduced Barbier, France 1921
Parentage R. wichurana x 'Mrs Arthur Robert Waddell'
A famous Rambler. Attractive, many petalled, lobster-pink flowers, golden at the base. Fragrant. Plentiful foliage brushed coppery red. Rather inclined to mildew after flowering, but still a lovely rose.
○ ♦♦ S ⊙ H 5m W 3m (15 x 10ft) Zone 7

'Alexandre Girault'
Introduced Barbier, France 1909
Parentage R. wichurana x 'Papa Gontier'
Almost double, deep rose-pink and cerise flowers touched yellow. Fruity scent. Foliage glossy, dark green. Pliable growth. Excellent on arches and trellis.
○ ♦ S H 4m W 4m (12 x 12ft) Zone 6

'American Pillar'
Introduced Van Fleet, USA 1902
Parentage (R. wichurana x R. setigera) x 'Red Letter Day'
Large clusters of single, lightly perfumed flowers, bright pink with creamy white centres, paling to clear pink. Strong-growing, thorny, with abundant, dark green foliage. Inclined to mildew after flowering in poorer soils.
○ ♦ S ⊙ H 5.5m W 4m (18 x 12ft) Zone 5

'Auguste Gervais'
Introduced Barbier, France 1918
Parentage R. wichurana x 'Le Progrès'
Sizeable, fully double, salmon-suffused coppery yellow flowers, paling to creamy buff. Slight scent. Shiny, dark green leaves. Useful as ground cover.
○ ♦ S H 4m W 2.5m (12 x 8ft) Zone 7

Awakening ('Probuzini')
Introduced Blatna Nurseries, former Czechoslovakia 1935
Reintroduced Beales, UK 1988
Parentage Sport of 'New Dawn'
Outstanding, fully double flowers of warm, glowing pink, produced even into winter. Lovely fragrance. Not over keen on prolonged wet weather. Small, dark green leaves. Especially good on walls.
○ ♦♦ C H 3m W 2.5m (10 x 8ft) Zone 5

'Breeze Hill'
Introduced Van Fleet, USA 1926
Parentage R. wichurana x 'Beauté de Lyon'
Cupped, fully double, clear pink flowers flushed soft peachy buff, produced in clusters. Lightly fragrant. Vigorous with glossy, dark green foliage. Does well scrambling up into trees.
○ ♦ S H 5.5m W 4m (18 x 12ft) Zone 5

'Debutante'
Introduced Walsh, USA 1902
Parentage R. wichurana x 'Baroness Rothschild'
Drooping clusters of small, fully double, fragrant, soft lilac-pink flowers. Abundant glossy, dark green foliage. Needs training to achieve best effect.
○ ♦♦ S H 4m W 3m (12 x 10ft) Zone 5

'Dorothy Perkins'
Introduced Jackson & Perkins, USA 1901
Parentage *R. wichurana* x 'Gabrielle Luizet'
Cascades of small, almost double, clear pink flowers. Slight fragrance. Pliable growth with ample mid-green foliage. Very prone to mildew after flowering.
○ ● S ☉ H 5m W 2.5m (15 x 8ft) Zone 5

'Dr W. Van Fleet'
Introduced Van Fleet, USA 1910
Parentage *R. wichurana* x 'Safrano'
Semi-double, sweetly perfumed, blush-pink flowers in large clusters. Very vigorous. Masses of dark green foliage on thorny stems. Good into trees.
○ ●● S H 6m W 3m (20 x 10ft) Zone 6

'Easlea's Golden Rambler'
Introduced Easlea, UK 1932
Parentage Not recorded
Very large, rich golden yellow flowers, almost Hybrid Tea shaped, on strong, thorny stems. Light scent. Leaves large, glossy, rich dark green, and abundant. Can easily outgrow its supports unless well secured.
○ ● S H 6m W 5m (20 x 15ft) Zone 6

'Emily Gray'
Introduced Williams, UK 1918
Parentage 'Jersey Beauty' x 'Comtesse du Cayla'
Semi-double, golden yellow flowers, paling to lemon. Fragrant. Very freely produced in midsummer, with a few later. Vigorous, pliable growth with well-polished, dark green foliage. Few thorns. Superb on arches.
○ ●● R H 5m W 3m (15 x 10ft) Zone 7

'Ethel'
Introduced Turner, UK 1912
Parentage Seedling of 'Dorothy Perkins'
Large trusses of cupped, semi-double, soft blush-pink flowers. Light scent. Growth strong, robust, very vigorous and thorny. Foliage dark green, profuse. Synonymous with 'Belvedere' in my opinion.
○ ● S H 6m W 5m (20 x 15ft) Zone 6

'Evangeline'
Introduced Walsh, USA 1906
Parentage *R. wichurana* x 'Crimson Rambler'
Small, almost single, pinkish white flowers in midsummer, slightly later than other Wichuranas. Vigorous. Foliage leathery, and glossy, dark green.
○ ● S H 5m W 4m (15 x 12ft) Zone 6

'Excelsa' ('Red Dorothy Perkins')
Introduced Walsh, USA 1909
Parentage Sport of 'Dorothy Perkins'
Large, cascading clusters of small, double, slightly fragrant, crimson flowers. Semi-glossy, lightish green foliage. Prone to mildew but only after flowering.
○ ● S ☉ H 5m W 4m (15 x 12ft) Zone 5

'François Juranville'
Introduced Barbier, France 1906
Parentage *R. wichurana* x 'Mme Laurette Messimy'
An exceptionally free-flowering rose. Sizeable, fully double blooms of lobster-pink with deeper highlights. Slightly fragrant. Foliage dark green, burnished bronze. Pliable shoots with few thorns.
○ ● S H 5m W 3m (15 x 10ft) Zone 6

'Gardenia'
Introduced Manda, USA 1899
Parentage *R. wichurana* x 'Perle des Jardins'
Beautiful, large, double, soft creamy yellow flowers reminiscent of gardenias. Occasionally repeats, with a very few blooms in autumn. Distinct apple scent. Dense, pliable growth, with bronzy green foliage.
○ ●● R H 6m W 5m (20 x 15ft) Zone 6

'Léontine Gervais'
Introduced Barbier, France 1903
Parentage *R. wichurana* x 'Souvenir de Claudius Denoyel'
Clusters of semi-double, flattish, slightly fragrant flowers of deep salmon, heavily brushed yellow, orange, and pink. Semi-vigorous, pliable growth with abundant glossy, dark green foliage. Tends to hide its flowers among the leaves just a little.
○ ● S H 4m W 3m (12 x 10ft) Zone 7

'Minnehaha'
Introduced Walsh, USA 1905
Parentage *R. wichurana* x 'Paul Neyron'
Large, cascading clusters of double, slightly fragrant, deep pink flowers, paling with age. Ample glossy, dark green foliage. Growth vigorous, pliable.
○ ● S H 3m W 2.5m (10 x 8ft) Zone 5

'New Dawn'
Introduced Somerset Rose Co, USA 1930
Parentage Sport of 'Dr W. Van Fleet'
Semi-double, blush-pink flowers with a lovely fragrance. Continuous flowering. Foliage grey-green and glossy. A truly outstanding sport.
○ ●● C H 3m W 2.5m (10 x 8ft) Zone 6

'Paul Transon'
Introduced Barbier, France 1900
Parentage *R. wichurana* x 'L'Idéal'
Flattish, fully double, peachy buff flowers with a coppery salmon base. Good fragrance. Occasionally repeats in the autumn. Very dark green foliage.
○ ●● R H 5m W 2.5m (15 x 8ft) Zone 6

'Sanders' White Rambler'
Introduced Sanders, UK 1912
Parentage Not recorded
One of the best of the white Ramblers. Double, rosette-shaped flowers in cascading clusters. Slight fragrance. Pliable growth; plentiful, glossy, mid-green foliage. Blooms not often tarnished by wet weather.
○ ● S H 4m W 2.5m (12 x 8ft) Zone 5

The Multiflora Ramblers

'Astra Desmond'
Discovered Neame, UK
Introduced Hilliers, UK, early 20th century
Parentage Sport of 'Mrs F.W. Flight'
Flowers semi-double, fragrant, and greenish white, in huge clusters. Vigorous, moderately thorny, and capable of reaching great heights. Fresh, light green foliage. Synonymous with 'White Flight'.
○ ●● S H 6m W 3m (20 x 10ft) Zone 6

'Bleu Magenta'
Introduced Probably *c*.1900
Parentage Not recorded
Small, fully double, rich purple flowers with bold yellow stamens when fully open, in medium-size clusters. Slight fragrance. Moderately vigorous and relatively thorn free. Foliage dark green. A little prone to mildew after flowering.
○ ● S ☉ H 4m W 3m (12 x 10ft) Zone 6

'Blush Rambler'
Introduced Cant, UK 1903
Parentage 'Crimson Rambler' x 'The Garland'
Slightly more than single blooms of blush-pink with deeper pink markings, borne in heavy trusses. Sadly, little scent. Vigorous and relatively thorn free. Foliage abundant, and light green. A popular cottage garden rose in Edwardian times.
○ ● S H 5m W 3m (15 x 10ft) Zone 6

'Easlea's Golden Rambler'

'Excelsa'

'François Juranville'

'Gardenia'

'Francis E. Lester'

'Ghislaine de Féligonde'

'Rose-Marie Viaud'

'Anemone Rose'

'Bobbie James'
Introduced Sunningdale Nurseries, UK 1961
Parentage Foundling
Sizeable, white flowers, slightly more than single, in large, drooping trusses. Sweetly perfumed. Vigorous, thorny. Foliage large, shiny, slightly coppery green.
◐ ♦♦ S H 10m W 6m (30 x 20ft) Zone 5

'Francis E. Lester'
Introduced Lester Rose Gardens, USA 1946
Parentage 'Kathleen' x unnamed seedling
Beautiful single, pink-splashed, blush-white flowers, in large clusters. Light fragrance. Small, red hips. Fairly thorn free. Foliage dark green tinged maroon.
◐ ♦ S H 5m W 3m (15 x 10ft) Zone 5

'Ghislaine de Féligonde'
Introduced Turbat, France 1916
Parentage 'Goldfinch' x unknown
Small clusters of fully double, soft apricot flowers, paling to cream. Light fragrance. Flowers freely all summer. Glossy, light green leaves. Vigorous, dense, fairly thorn free. A little prone to downy mildew.
◐ ♦ C ⊙ H 2.5m W 2.5m (8 x 8ft) Zone 6

'Goldfinch'
Introduced Paul, UK 1907
Parentage 'Hélène' x unknown
Large clusters of nearly semi-double, bright yellow flowers fading to cream, with rich yellow stamens. Light scent. Very free flowering. Semi-glossy, mid-green foliage on almost thornless, brownish wood.
◐ ♦ S H 2.5m W 1.5m (8 x 5ft) Zone 6

'Lauré Davoust' ('Marjorie W. Lester')
Introduced Laffay, France 1843
Parentage Not recorded
Small, fully double, cupped blooms, rosette-like when open, soft lilac to lavender-pink, fading with age. Fragrant. Mid-green foliage. Almost thornless.
◐ ♦♦ S H 3m W 2.5m (10 x 8ft) Zone 6

'Mannington Mauve Rambler'
Discovered Walpole, UK
Introduced Beales, UK 2001
Parentage Sport or seedling of 'The Garland'
Large clusters of dainty, semi-double, pinky mauve flowers, fading slightly with age. Light scent. Strong, vigorous, fairly thorny growth. Dark green foliage.
◐ ♦♦ S H 5m W 3m (15 x 10ft) Zone 6

R. multiflora **'Carnea' ('Carnea')**
Origin China **First noted** 1804
Large, cascading clusters of semi-double, scented, blush-white flowers flushed lilac-mauve. Repeated in autumn. Vigorous, flexible, relatively thornless growth. Foliage copious, semi-glossy, darkish green.
◐ ♦♦ R H 6m W 4m (20 x 12ft) Zone 5

R. multiflora **'Platyphylla' (*R. multiflora* 'Grevillei', Seven sisters rose)**
Origin China **First noted** 1816
Clusters of double, rather muddled-petalled flowers of about seven shades of pink, magenta, and lilac. Light scent. Not too vigorous, and moderately thorny. Foliage coarse and dark green.
◐ ♦ S H 4m W 1.8m (12 x 6ft) Zone 6

'Rambling Rector'
Introduced 1913, but certainly much older
Parentage Not recorded
Large trusses of semi-double, creamy white flowers opening to display golden stamens. Delightful, musky perfume. Very vigorous, thorny growth with soft, grey-green leaves. A good display of hips in autumn.
◐ ♦♦♦ S H 10m W 5m (30 x 15ft) Zone 7

'Rose-Marie Viaud'
Introduced Igoult, France 1924
Parentage Seedling of 'Veilchenblau'
Large, drooping clusters of smallish, fully double, rich purple flowers fading to greyish mauve. Slightly fragrant. Foliage light green. Vigorous and relatively thornless. Slightly prone to mildew after flowering.
◐ ♦ S ⊙ H 5m W 1.8m (15 x 6ft) Zone 6

'Seagull'
Introduced Pritchard, UK 1907
Parentage *R. multiflora* x 'Général Jacqueminot'
Large clusters of single, pure white flowers with pronounced golden stamens. Scented. Very vigorous, fairly thorny growth, with grey-green foliage. Happily finds its way through hedges and trees.
◐ ♦♦ S H 8m W 5m (25 x 15ft) Zone 6

'The Garland'
Introduced Wills, UK 1835
Parentage *R. multiflora* x *R. moschata*
Large clusters of semi-double, ragged, fragrant, white flowers, sometimes lightly touched pink, with yellow stamens. Very vigorous with abundant, mid- to dark green foliage. Stems armed with hooked thorns.
◐ ♦♦ S H 6m W 3m (20 x 10ft) Zone 6

'Veilchenblau'
Introduced Schmidt, Germany 1909
Parentage 'Crimson Rambler' x unknown seedling
Clusters of small, semi-double, purple-violet flowers, paling to lavender-grey, with white brushmarks. Scented. Vigorous, almost thornless growth with mid- to light green leaves.
◐ ♦♦ S H 5m W 4m (15 x 12ft) Zone 6

'Violette'
Introduced Turbat, France 1921
Parentage Not recorded
Clusters of semi-double, rosette-shaped, rich violet-purple flowers, flecked white and yellow at the base, with bright golden stamens. Light fragrance. Dark green foliage. Relatively thornless.
◐ ♦ S H 4m W 3m (12 x 10ft) Zone 6

Miscellaneous Ramblers

'Adélaïde d'Orléans'
Introduced Jacques, France 1826
Parentage *R. sempervirens* hybrid
Cascading clusters of small, semi-double, white to soft pink flowers, like ruffled rosettes. Fragrant. Growth rather spindly and sprawling, almost thornless. Purple-tinged, dark green foliage. Excellent for arches and gazebos.
◐ ♦♦ S H 5m W 3m (15 x 10ft) Zone 5

'Anemone Rose' (*R. anemonoides*, 'Anemone')
Introduced Schmidt, Germany 1895
Parentage *R. laevigata* x unknown Tea
Very large, single, papery textured, soft pink flowers heavily veined deeper pink, with a boss of yellow stamens. Slightly fragrant. Growth angular and very thorny. Foliage crisp, glossy, dark green.
☼ ♦ S H 3m W 2.5m (10 x 8ft) Zone 7

'Baltimore Belle'
Introduced Feast, USA 1843
Parentage. *R. setigera* x Gallica hybrid
Smallish, drooping clusters of fully double, lightly scented, silky clear pink flowers. A slightly reticent plant, with pliable stems and few thorns. Leathery, dark green foliage. Needs a little extra care to thrive.
☼ ♦ S H 5m W 2.5m (15 x 8ft) Zone 7

'Chevy Chase'
Introduced Hansen, USA 1939
Parentage *R. soulieana* x 'Eblouissant'
Many cascading clusters of fully double, pompon-like, bright red flowers. Growth flexible, almost thornless. Vigorous. Foliage copious and mid-green. Good on arches and in trees.
○ **S H** 6m **W** 3m (20 x 10ft) Zone 6

'Cooper's Burmese' (*R. cooperi, R. laevigata cooperi*)
Introduced Cooper, UK 1927
Parentage Assumed *R. laevigata* x *R. gigantea*
A most beautiful, large, single, pure white rose with golden stamens. Scented. Growth thorny with dark stems and plentiful, leathery, dark green foliage. A superb, vigorous Rambler to cover eyesores.
☼ ♦♦ **S H** 5m **W** 5m (15 x 15ft) Zone 7

'Dundee Rambler'
Introduced Martin, UK *c.*1850
Parentage *R. arvensis* x unknown Noisette
Clusters of smallish, fully double, pure white flowers with a slight fragrance. Growth dense, vigorous, and slightly thorny. Foliage dark green and plentiful. Flowers only once each summer, but prolifically.
○ ♦ **S H** 6m **W** 3m (20 x 10ft) Zone 5

'Félicité Perpétue'
Introduced Jacques, France 1827
Parentage *R. sempervirens* x unknown Noisette
A delightful rose with cascading clusters of well-shaped, rosette-like, fully double flowers, soft creamy white with hints of pink. Growth vigorous, with numerous bluish tinted, dark green leaves. Evergreen. Ideal for arches.
○ ♦♦ **S H** 5.5m **W** 3m (18 x 10ft) Zone 5

'Kew Rambler'
Introduced Kew Gardens, UK 1912
Parentage *R. soulieana* x 'Hiawatha'
Small clusters of single, lightly scented, mid-pink flowers, paling to creamy white in the centre. Freely produced. Foliage durable, mid-green. Very vigorous and thorny, capable of scrambling into trees. Bright red hips in autumn.
○ ♦ **S H** 5m **W** 2.5m (15 x 8ft) Zone 5

R. x *l'heritierana*
Origin Probably Europe **First noted** Pre-1820
Parentage *R. pendulina* hybrid
Semi-double, deep pink flowers fairly early in summer, occasionally repeating later. Foliage plum-tinted dark green. Upright, thornless shrub with reddish brown stems.
☼ **R H** 2.5m **W** 1.2m (8 x 4ft) Zone 6

'Long John Silver'
Introduced Horvath, USA 1934
Parentage *R. setigera* seedling x 'Sunburst'
Large, old-fashioned style, fully double, pure white flowers in tightly packed clusters in early summer, perhaps with a few blooms later. Growth firm, light green, only slightly thorny. Foliage light green, heavily veined. Good on trellis.
○ **R H** 5m **W** 3m (15 x 10ft) Zone 4

'Mermaid'
Introduced Paul, UK 1918
Parentage *R. bracteata* x double, yellow Tea rose
Large, single flowers, soft yellow with honey-coloured stamens, borne throughout summer. Lovely perfume. Growth vigorous with brownish bark and many hooked thorns. Foliage plentiful and shiny, mid-green. Superb, especially on walls.
○ ♦♦ **C H** 10m **W** 6m (30 x 20ft) Zone 6

'Mme de Sancy de Parabère'
Introduced Bonnet, France *c.*1874
Parentage Not recorded
A shapely, very double rose, flat and cushion-like when open, rich bright pink, with softer pink edges. Mildly scented. Growth vigorous, with thornless, purple stems. Foliage darkish green. Best on a wall.
○ ♦ **S H** 5m **W** 3m (15 x 10ft) Zone 5

'Paul's Himalayan Musk'
Introduced Paul, UK, probably late 19th century
Parentage Foundling
Small, semi-double, fragrant flowers, soft blush to lilac-pink. Very pretty. Slender, glossy, mid-green leaves on pliable stems, fairly thorn free.
○ ♦♦ **S H** 12m **W** 4m (40 x 12ft) Zone 7

'Princesse Louise'
Introduced Jacques, France 1829
Parentage *R. sempervirens* hybrid
Sizeable, full-petalled, cup-shaped, creamy white flowers, opening flat, in cascading clusters. Fragrant. Very healthy growth, pliable, robust, and slightly thorny. Foliage dark green and copious. Evergreen.
○ ♦♦ **S H** 5m **W** 3m (15 x 10ft) Zone 7

'Princesse Marie'
Introduced Jacques, France 1829
Parentage *R. sempervirens* hybrid
Flowers very similar in form to 'Princesse Louise' but pinkish lilac in colour. Fragrant. Growth pliable, slightly thorny. Foliage dark green. Almost evergreen.
○ ♦♦ **S H** 4m **W** 3m (12 x 10ft) Zone 7

'Ramona' ('Red Cherokee')
Introduced Dietrich & Turner, USA 1913
Parentage Sport of 'Anemone Rose'
Similar in all respects to 'Anemone Rose', except darker in colour. Single, slightly fragrant, pinkish red blooms and dark green foliage. Growth very thorny.
☼ ♦ **S H** 3m **W** 2.5m (10 x 8ft) Zone 7

'Sir Cedric Morris'
Discovered Morris, UK
Introduced Beales, UK 1979
Parentage *R. glauca* seedling x possibly *R. mulliganii*
Huge trusses of small, single, fragrant, white flowers with golden stamens. Very vigorous. Stems bluish green with many thorns. Foliage glaucous, grey-green. Many orange-red hips in autumn.
○ ♦♦ **S H** 10m **W** 6m (30 x 20ft) Zone 7

'Venusta Pendula' (Ayrshire rose)
Reintroduced Kordes, Germany 1928
Parentage Not recorded
Shapely, fully double, soft white flowers, heavily flushed pink. Foliage dull, dark green. Growth plum-red and quite thorny. A little prone to mildew.
○ **S** ◉ **H** 5m **W** 3m (15 x 10ft) Zone 6

'Wedding Day'
Discovered Stern, UK 1950
Parentage *R. sinowilsonii* x unknown
Clusters of many small, single flowers of soft yellow paling to white, with prominent stamens. Sweet fragrance. Very vigorous, flexible, moderately thorny growth. Foliage glossy, dark green.
○ ♦♦ **S H** 10m **W** 3m (30 x 10ft) Zone 6

'Wickwar'
Introduced Steadman, UK 1960
Parentage Seedling of *R. soulieana*
Masses of large, single, pure white flowers with golden stamens. Light fragrance. Stems rigid, very thorny. Foliage greyish green. Good hips in autumn.
○ ♦ **S H** 4m **W** 2.2m (12 x 7ft) Zone 6

'Chevy Chase'

'Mermaid'

'Mme de Sancy de Parabère'

'Sir Cedric Morris'

Procumbent and Compact Roses

The Procumbent Roses

Avon ('Poulmulti') Niagara, Sunnyside, Fairy Lights
Introduced Poulsen, Denmark 1992
Parentage Not recorded
Semi-double, slightly fragrant, pearly white flowers with a hint of pink, in sizeable clusters. Blooms throughout summer if regularly deadheaded. Spreading, dense growth with dark green foliage.
○ ◐ **C H** 30cm **W** 90cm (1 x 3ft) Zone 5

'Barakura'
Introduced Beales, UK 1998
Parentage Bonica '82 x 'Rambling Rector'
Large clusters of rosette-like, mildly fragrant flowers of soft pink to blush-white. Foliage copious and light green. Growth bushy and spreading. Needs deadheading to ensure continuity of bloom.
✲ ◐ **C H** 60cm **W** 1.2m (2 x 4ft) Zone 5

Berkshire ('Korpinka') Sommermärchen, Summer Fairytale, Xenia, Pink Sensation
Introduced Kordes, Germany 1991
Parentage Not recorded
Very large clusters of semi-double, bright pinkish red flowers, showing off stamens when fully open. Light scent. Flowers very freely, all summer if deadheaded. Growth wide, bushy. Foliage dark green, healthy.
○ ◐ **C H** 60cm **W** 1.2m (2 x 4ft) Zone 5

Cambridgeshire ('Korhaugen') Carpet of Colour
Introduced Kordes, Germany 1994
Parentage Not recorded
Cupped, semi-double flowers in a mixture of orange, bright pink, and yellow, borne in medium-sized clusters all through summer. Growth dense, spreading, and tough. Foliage glossy, mid-green. Superb when cascading from tall pots.
○ ◐ **C H** 90cm **W** 1.2m (3 x 4ft) Zone 6

Cardinal Hume ('Harregale')
Introduced Harkness, UK 1984
Parentage [((Seedling x ('Orange Sensation' x 'Allgold') x R. californica)) x 'Frank Naylor']
A very good if unusual rose. Beetroot-red to purple flowers, rather more than semi-double, in large clusters. Fragrant. In bloom all summer if regularly deadheaded. Foliage very dark green, coarse to touch. Growth dense, thorny.
○ ◐◐ **C H** 90cm **W** 1.2m (3 x 4ft) Zone 6

'Dunwich Rose'
Introduced UK 1950s
Parentage Sport of R. pimpinellifolia
Many single, faintly scented flowers of soft creamy white in late spring. Growth wide and very prickly. Foliage copious, fern-like, and mid- to bright green. Mahogany hips in autumn. Ideal for group planting.
○ ◐ **Sp H** 90cm **W** 1.8m (3 x 6ft) Zone 5

Ferdy ('Keitoli')
Introduced Suzuki, Japan 1984
Parentage Unnamed seedling x Petite Folie seedling)
Very large, arching clusters of semi-double, salmon-pink flowers, borne in great profusion in early summer, occasionally with a few later on. Lightly scented. Mid-green foliage plentiful but small. Growth wide spreading and very thorny. Also makes a useful small climber
✲ ◐ **S H** 90cm **W** 1.8m (3 x 6ft) Zone 6

Fiona ('Meibeluxen')
Introduced Meilland, France 1982
Parentage 'Sea Foam' x Picasso
A broader than tall shrub. Shapely buds open to rather more then semi-double, bright red flowers, produced in generously sized clusters all through summer. Modestly fragrant. Red hips in autumn if not deadheaded. Foliage dark green. Growth bushy, thorny, and wide. Good in groups.
○ ◐ **C H** 90cm **W** 1.2m (3 x 4ft) Zone 5

Grouse ('Korimro') Immensee, Lacrose
Introduced Kordes, Germany 1982
Parentage 'The Fairy' x R. wichurana seedling
Masses of small, single, lightly scented, blush to white flowers in early to midsummer, with occasional blooms later on. Followed by many small hips. Foliage abundant, light green. Extremely vigorous, healthy growth, very wide and spreading. An outstanding ground-covering rose. Also makes a good scrambler.
○ ◐ **R H** 60cm **W** 3m (2 x 10ft) Zone 5

'Harry Maasz'
Introduced Kordes, Germany 1939
Parentage 'Barcelona' x 'Daisy Hill'
Rather less than semi-double blooms of soft cerise-pink, with prominent yellow stamens. Fragrant. Flowers only once in summer, but very freely. Very vigorous. Foliage matt, dark greyish green.
○ ◐◐ **S H** 1.2m **W** 2.5m (4 x 8ft) Zone 5

Magic Carpet ('Jaclover') Tapis Magique
Introduced Jackson & Perkins, USA 1994
Parentage Grouse x Class Act
Clusters of semi-double, pink flowers suffused lavender, borne continuously. Spicy perfume. Foliage glossy, very dark green, and extremely healthy. Growth dense, bushy, and spreading. The perfect ground cover.
○ ◐◐ **C H** 60cm **W** 1.2m (2 x 4ft) Zone 6

Norfolk ('Poulfolk')
Introduced Poulsen, Denmark 1989
Parentage Not recorded
One of the few Procumbent roses with yellow flowers. Clusters of fully double, rosette-like, bright yellow blooms, borne very freely all through summer. Mild fragrance. Growth dense and widely bushy. Copious small, dark green leaves. Good in pots.
○ ◐ **C H** 60cm **W** 90cm (2 x 3ft) Zone 5

'Nozomi' ('Heideröslein Nozomi')
Introduced Onodera, Japan 1968
Parentage 'Fairy Princess' x 'Sweet Fairy'
Small, single, star-like, soft pink flowers, lightly scented. Borne in great profusion in early summer, but seldom produces any more later. Growth cascading, wide, and dense. Foliage plentiful and dark green. Best over banks, tree stumps, etc.
○ ◐ **S H** 90cm **W** 1.8m (3 x 6ft) Zone 6

Pearl Drift ('Leggab')
Introduced LeGrice, UK 1980
Parentage 'Mermaid' x 'New Dawn'
More a wide-growing shrub than a truly prostrate rose. Large clusters of semi-double, fragrant, milky white flowers throughout summer. Stout, relatively thornless branches with copious, semi-glossy, dark green foliage. Good in groups of three.
○ ◐◐ **C H** 90cm **W** 1.2m (3 x 4ft) Zone 6

'Barakura'

Cardinal Hume

Magic Carpet

Pearl Drift

Pheasant ('Kordapt') Heidekönigin, Palissade
Introduced Kordes, Germany 1985
Parentage Zwergkönig '78 x *R. wichurana* seedling
Flowers semi-double, lightly fragrant, rich clear pink, in large clusters. Repeat flowering. Growth rather thorny. Foliage dark green and dense. A wide-spreading, vigorous plant; may also be grown as a small climber.
○ ◗ R H 90cm W 3m (3 x 10ft) Zone 6

Pink Bells ('Poulbells')
Introduced Poulsen, Denmark 1983
Parentage 'Mini-Poul' x 'Temple Bells'
Densely packed clusters of small, double, rosette-like, clear pink flowers in early summer, with a few more, very occasionally, later on. Light scent. Foliage also dense, and dark green. Growth bushy and wide. Excellent in groups of three or more.
○ ◗ R H 60cm W 1.2m (2 x 4ft) Zone 6

Queen Mother ('Korquemu')
Introduced Kordes, Germany 1991
Parentage Not recorded
Semi-double, slightly fragrant, bright pink flowers in large clusters, initially in great profusion followed by a good second crop. Foliage glossy, dark green. Growth wide and dense.
○ ◗ R H 30cm W 60cm (1 x 2ft) Zone 5

'Raubritter' ('Macrantha Raubritter')
Introduced Kordes, Germany 1936
Parentage 'Daisy Hill' x 'Solarium'
A shrub with considerable charm. Densely produced, almost double, cupped flowers of clear silvery pink, in great profusion in early summer. Richly scented. Wide, dense growth with dark greyish green foliage. Rather prone to mildew after flowering.
☼ ◗◗◗ S ◉ H 90cm W 2.5m (3 x 8ft) Zone 5

Red Bells ('Poulred')
Introduced Poulsen, Denmark 1983
Parentage 'Mini-Poul' x 'Temple Bells'
As Pink Bells except for colour, which is deep red, and slightly less double flowers; also slightly taller.
○ ◗ R H 75cm W 1.2m (2½ x 4ft) Zone 6

Red Blanket ('Intercell')
Introduced Ilsink, Netherlands 1979
Parentage 'Yesterday' x unnamed seedling
A sprawling, shrubby plant capable of climbing. Produces sizeable clusters of rather more than single, red flowers with paler centres and good yellow stamens. Lightly scented. Repeat flowering. Foliage very dark green and lush.
○ ◗ R H 90cm W 1.8m (3 x 6ft) Zone 6

Red Max Graf ('Kormax') Rote Max Graf
Introduced Kordes, Germany 1980
Parentage *R. kordesii* x seedling
Large clusters of sizeable, single, bright red flowers in great profusion in early summer, intermittently thereafter. Slightly fragrant. Has a good crop of red hips if not deadheaded. Leaves plentiful, glossy, and dark green. Vigorous, wide growing, and thorny.
○ ◗ R H 90cm W 3m (3 x 10ft) Zone 5

'Summer Sunrise'
Introduced Beales, UK 1994
Parentage Bonica '82 x 'New Dawn'
Masses of delightful, rather more than single, candy-pink flowers throughout summer if regularly deadheaded. Mildly scented. Foliage glossy, dark green, and plentiful. Good red hips if spent flowers not removed. Also makes a good small climber.
○ ◗ C H 45cm W 1.2m (1½ x 4ft) Zone 5

'Summer Sunset'
Introduced Beales, UK 1994
Parentage Bonica '82 x Robin Redbreast
Very similar to 'Summer Sunrise' but with slightly smaller flowers, in larger clusters. Some petals streaked white. Also a good small climber.
○ ◗ C H 45cm W 1.2m (1½ x 4ft) Zone 5

Sussex ('Poulave')
Introduced Poulsen, Denmark 1991
Parentage Not recorded
Clusters of semi-double, fairly ragged, bright apricot-orange flowers, changing to bright pinkish buff, borne in great profusion all summer. Foliage glossy, dark green. Growth spreading and bushy.
○ C H 60cm W 90cm (2 x 3ft) Zone 6

Tall Story ('Dickooky')
Introduced Dickson, UK 1984
Parentage 'Korresia' x 'Yesterday'
Clusters of semi-double, fragrant, creamy white flowers, deep yellow in bud. Blooms throughout the season. Good, almost glossy, dark green foliage. Growth bushy but wide.
○ ◗◗ C H 90cm W 1.2m (3 x 4ft) Zone 6

'The Fairy' ('Féerie')
Introduced Bentall, UK 1932
Parentage 'Paul Crampel' x 'Lady Gay'
Really a spreading Polyantha rose. Large clusters of small, semi-double, soft pink flowers all summer through. Foliage dark green. Growth dense and wide. Good in groups of three or more.
○ C H 45cm W 75cm (1½ x 2½ft) Zone 6

White Bells ('Poulwhite')
Introduced Poulsen, Denmark 1983
Parentage 'Mini-Poul' x 'Temple Bells'
As Pink Bells in all respects except colour, which is soft yellow paling to white.
○ ◗ R H 60cm W 1.2m (2 x 4ft) Zone 6

Wiltshire ('Kormuse')
Introduced Kordes, Germany 1993
Parentage Not recorded
Large clusters of sizeable flowers, bright reddish pink in colour, initially cupped, opening semi-double to double. Slightly fragrant. Flowers freely all summer. Growth wide and dense, with rather crisp and crinkly, dark green foliage.
○ ◗ C H 60cm W 1.2m (2 x 4ft) Zone 6

The Compact Floribundas and Miniature Roses

'Baby Albéric' (Compact Floribunda)
Introduced Chaplin, UK 1932
Parentage Not recorded
A lovely miniature version of the Rambler 'Albéric Barbier', although flowers are not much smaller than on the Rambler. Yellow buds open to double, lightly scented, creamy white flowers. Foliage very glossy, dark green. Growth compact, tidy.
○ ◗ C H 45cm W 45cm (1½ x 1½ft) Zone 7

'Dresden Doll' (Miniature)
Introduced Moore, USA 1975
Parentage 'Fairy Moss' x Moss seedling
A delightful, Miniature Moss rose, with lots of moss around its buds and stems. Clusters of lightly fragrant, soft pinkish buff flowers, initially cup shaped, opening semi-double. Growth upright, compact. Foliage greyish green. Superb in pots.
☼ ◗ C H 30cm W 30cm (1 x 1ft) Zone 6

Queen Mother

Red Blanket

Tall Story

'Dresden Doll'

Regensberg

'Rouletii'

Sweet Dream

Twenty-fifth

Gentle Touch ('Diclulu') (Compact Floribunda)
Introduced Dickson, UK 1986
Parentage ('Liverpol Echo' x 'Woman's Own') x Memento
Semi-double flowers of soft lilac-pink in large clusters on a compact plant. Light fragrance. Foliage greyish green. Attractive in groups in a border, as a pot plant, or even a low hedge.
☼ ◖ **C H** 30cm **W** 30cm (1 x 1ft) Zone 6

'Happenstance' (Compact Floribunda)
Introduced Buss, USA 1950
Parentage Not recorded
An unusual rose, rather like a miniature 'Mermaid', with sizeable, mildly scented, soft yellow flowers with golden stamens. Two good flushes. Growth very thorny and wide. Foliage shiny, mid-green.
◐ ◖ **R H** 45cm **W** 60cm (1½ x 2ft) Zone 6

'Maude Elizabeth' (Compact Floribunda)
Introduced Beales, UK 2000
Parentage Robin Redbreast x Bonica '82
Masses of small, single, clear dark red blooms with golden stamens. Growth compact and bushy, with copious, dark green foliage. Excellent in pots or as a bedding rose.
☼ **C H** 38cm **W** 38cm (1¼ x 1¼ft) Zone 6

'Mr Bluebird' (Miniature)
Introduced Moore, USA 1960
Parentage 'Old Blush' x 'Old Blush'
An unusual Miniature rose. Clusters of almost single, lavender-mauve flowers with white centres. Tidy, upright growth with grey-green foliage. Good in pots.
☼ **C H** 30cm **W** 30cm (1 x 1ft) Zone 6

Orange Sunblaze ('Meijikatar') Sunblaze, Orange Meillandina (Compact Floribunda)
Introduced Meilland, France 1980
Parentage Parador x (Baby Bettina x 'Permanent Wave')
Very bright, cupped flowers of orange-red, opening semi-double, borne in clusters. Upright, bushy growth with plentiful semi-glossy, dark green foliage.
☼ **C H** 45cm **W** 30cm (1½ x 1ft) Zone 6

'Perla de Montserrat' (Miniature)
Introduced Dot, Spain 1945
Parentage 'Cécile Brünner' x 'Rouletii'
Upright sprays of shapely, fully double flowers resembling baby HTs. Soft blush-pink with deeper centres. Light fragrance. Growth bushy, upright. Foliage matt, dark green. Best in pots.
☼ ◖ **C H** 23cm **W** 23cm (9 x 9in) Zone 6

Red Ace ('Amruda') Amanda (Miniature)
Introduced de Ruiter, Holland 1979
Parentage Scarletta x seedling
Small clusters of shapely, fully double, deep red flowers. Lightly scented. Growth compact, bushy. Foliage semi-glossy, mid-green. Lovely in pots.
☼ ◖ **C H** 30cm **W** 60cm (1 x 2ft) Zone 6

Regensberg ('Macyoumis') Young Mistress, Buffalo Bill (Compact Floribunda)
Introduced McGredy, New Zealand 1979
Parentage 'Geoff Boycott' x Old Master
Large, shapely, fully double flowers, cherry-pink with silvery white markings. Mild fragrance. Borne in profusion on a compact, bushy plant, with glossy, mid-green foliage. Superb in pots or groups.
☼ ◖ **C H** 45cm **W** 45cm (1½ x 1½ft) Zone 6

Robin Redbreast ('Interrob') (Compact Floribunda)
Introduced Interplant, Holland 1984
Parentage Unnamed seedling x Eye Paint
Single, bright red blooms, with discreet, creamy yellow centres, produced in small clusters. Slight fragrance. Growth upright. Foliage glossy, mid-green. Good in groups.
☼ ◖ **C H** 45cm **W** 30cm (1½ x 1ft) Zone 6

'Rouletii' (*R. rouletii, R. chinensis minima*) (Miniature)
Parentage Not recorded
Introduced Correvon, Switzerland 1922
The original Miniature. Small clusters of small, semi-double, deep rose-pink flowers. Bushy growth with lots of matt, dark green foliage. Best in pots or window boxes.
☼ **C H** 30cm **W** 23cm (12 x 9in) Zone 6

Snowball ('Macangel') Angelita (Miniature)
Introduced McGredy, New Zealand 1982
Parentage 'Moana' x Snow Carpet
Many fully double, globular, pure white flowers. Compact growth, with copious tiny, light green leaves. A delightful little rose, ideal as a pot plant.
☼ **C H** 23cm **W** 30cm (9 x 12in) Zone 6

Sweet Dream ('Fryminicot') (Compact Floribunda)
Introduced Fryer, UK 1988
Parentage Unnamed seedling x unnamed seedling
Masses of fully double, cupped flowers in clusters, peachy apricot in colour. Light fragrance. Growth bushy, compact. Foliage mid-green and plentiful. Makes a good short hedge; also does well in pots and as bedding.
☼ ◖ **C H** 45cm **W** 30cm (1½ x 1ft) Zone 6

Sweet Magic ('Dicmagic') (Compact Floribunda)
Introduced Dickson, UK 1986
Parentage Peek-a-boo x Bright Smile
Clusters of semi-double, slightly fragrant, rich golden yellow flowers, freely produced. Upright plant with lots of dark green foliage. Good for bedding.
☼ ◖ **C H** 45cm **W** 30cm (1½ x 1ft) Zone 6

'Tom Thumb' ('Peon') (Miniature)
Introduced de Vink, Holland 1936
Parentage 'Rouletii' x 'Gloria Mundi'
Small clusters of semi-double, deep red flowers with white centres. Slightly fragrant. Growth compact, upright. Foliage matt, dark green.
☼ ◖ **C H** 23cm **W** 23cm (9 x 9in) Zone 6

Twenty-fifth ('Beatwe') (Compact Floribunda)
Introduced Beales, UK 1996
Parentage Robin Redbreast x 'Horstmann's Rosenresli'
Large clusters of semi-double, rich ruby-red flowers with golden yellow stamens. Slight fragrance. Growth compact, broad, and thorny. Foliage abundant and dark green. Excellent for low bedding.
☼ ◖ **C H** 45cm **W** 30cm (1½ x 1ft) Zone 6

'White Pet' (Compact Floribunda)
Introduced Henderson, UK 1879
Parentage Sport of 'Félicité Perpetue'
A superb old Compact Floribunda with masses of small, fully double, pompon-like, white flowers opening from pink buds in large clusters. Fragrant. Growth compact bushy. Foliage dark green. Charming in pots and in groups.
◐ ◖◖ **C H** 45cm **W** 45cm (1½ x 1½ft) Zone 5

Hardiness Zones

Roses are woody plants and, unlike herbaceous perennials, whose top growth naturally dies down in winter, they protect themselves from the worst effects of frost by losing their leaves each autumn and becoming dormant, slowing their life processes to a minimum. Because of their ancestry and wide-ranging geographical origins, roses vary greatly in the amount of cold they can tolerate. In the USA, to help gardeners determine where a particular plant will survive the winter unharmed, the Department of Agriculture has developed a map of hardiness zones based on average minimum temperatures in winter across the country. The zones are listed in the chart below, along with the minimum temperature range

for each. For the rest of the world, simply look on the chart for the minimum temperature in the region in question to find the corresponding zone rating. In the Directory section of this book, every rose described has been given a zone number, reflecting the lowest temperature it is likely to endure when grown in the open without protection. However, this should be taken only as a rough guide, since a number of other factors also influence winter hardiness, such as the wind-chill factor, the amount of sunshine in the preceding summer, and the ripeness of woody growth.

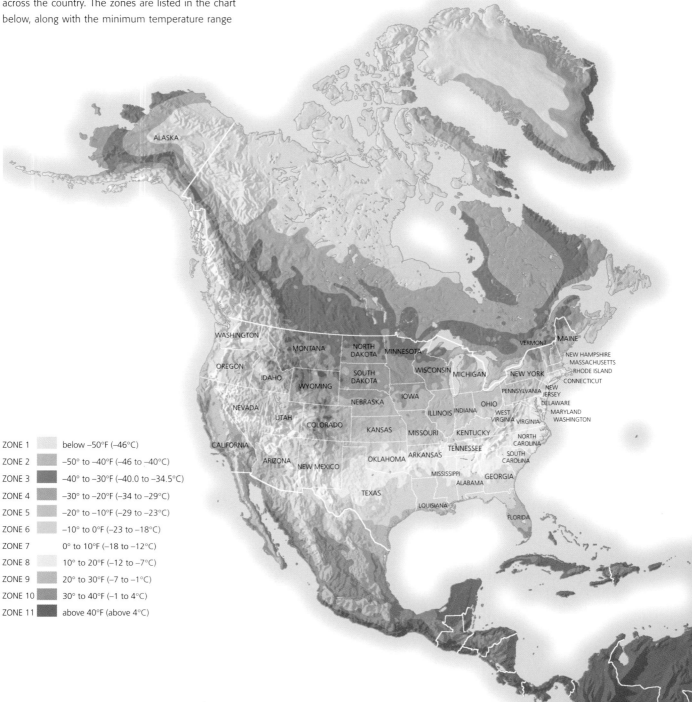

ZONE 1   below −50°F (−46°C)

ZONE 2   −50° to −40°F (−46 to −40°C)

ZONE 3   −40° to −30°F (−40.0 to −34.5°C)

ZONE 4   −30° to −20°F (−34 to −29°C)

ZONE 5   −20° to −10°F (−29 to −23°C)

ZONE 6   −10° to 0°F (−23 to −18°C)

ZONE 7   0° to 10°F (−18 to −12°C)

ZONE 8   10° to 20°F (−12 to −7°C)

ZONE 9   20° to 30°F (−7 to −1°C)

ZONE 10 30° to 40°F (−1 to 4°C)

ZONE 11 above 40°F (above 4°C)

Index

Page numbers in *italic* refer to illustrations

A

Abraham Darby 146, 241, *241*
'Adam Messerich' 87, 229
'Adélaïde d'Orléans' 196–7, *196*, 246
'Agatha' 57, 223, *223*
'Agnes' 140, 238
'Agrippina' *see* 'Cramoisi Supérieur'
Aimée Vibert' 156, *156*, 242
'Alain Blanchard' 59, *59*, 223
'Alba Maxima' *see* 'Maxima'
'Alba Semi-Plena' *see* 'Semi-Plena'
'Albéric Barbier' *174*, 175, *197*, 244
'Albertine' 41, 175–6, *175*, 244, *244*
Alec's Red 123, 236
Alexander *118*, 122, 236, *236*
'Alexander Hill Gray' 235
Alexandra *see* Alexander
'Alexandre Girault' 176, *180*, 244
'Alfred de Dalmas' 66–7, 225, *225*
'Alister Stella Gray' *154*, 155, 242
'Allgold' Climbing 169, 244
'Aloha' *158*, 159, 242
Alpine rose *see* Rosa pendulina
Amanda 130, 237; *see also* Red Ace
Amber Queen 129, 237, *237*
'American Pillar' *16*, 176, *177*, 244, *244*
'Amruda' *see* Red Ace
'Amy Robsart' 96–7, *97*, 232
'Anais Ségales' 223
'Andeli' *see* Double Delight
'Anemone' *see* 'Anemone Rose'
'Anemone Rose' 194, 196, 246, *246*
Angelita *see* Snowball
'Anna Pavlova' 12, 140, *140*, 238
'Anne of Geierstein' 97, 232, *232*
Apothecary's rose *see* Rosa gallica
  officinalis
Apple rose *see* Rosa villosa
'Archiduc Joseph' *112*, 114, 235, *235*
'Arethusa' 77, 227, *227*
'Armosa' *see* 'Hermosa'
'Arthur de Sansal' 82, *83*, 229
'Astra Desmond' 184–5, *185*, 245
'Auguste Gervais' 176, 244
'Ausblush' *see* Heritage
'Ausbord' *see* Gertrude Jekyll
'Ausbreak' *see* Jayne Austin
'Auscot' *see* Abraham Darby
'Auscrim' *see* L.D. Braithwaite
'Ausham' *see* Geoff Hamilton
'Auslevel' *see* Glamis Castle
'Ausmary' *see* Mary Rose
'Ausmas' *see* Graham Thomas
'Ausmol' *see* Molineux
'Ausroyal' *see* William Shakespeare
'Austance' *see* Constance Spry
Austrian briar *see* Rosa foetida
Austrian copper *see* Rosa foetida
  'Bicolor'
'Auswine' *see* Chianti
Autumn Damask *see* 'Quatre Saisons'
Autumn Fire 139, 238, *238*
'Autumn Sunset' 138, 238, *238*
Avon 248

B

'Baby Albéric' 210, 249
'Ballerina' *17*, 107, *107*, 109, 234
'Baltimore Belle' 199, *199*, 246
'Barakura' 204, 248, *248*
'Baroness Rothschild' 91, 93, 231, *231*
'Baron Girod de l'Ain' 93, 231, *231*
'Baronne Adolphe de Rothschild' *see*
  'Baroness Rothschild'
'Baronne Prévost' *91*, 93, 231
'Beabimbo' *see* St Ethelburga
'Beacream' *see* Countess of Wessex
'Beamac' *see* Macmillan Nurse
'Beatwe' *see* Twenty-fifth
Beautiful Britain 130, *131*, 237
'Beesian' *see* Amanda
'Belinda' 109, 234
'Belle Amour' 221
'Belle de Crécy' 57–8, 60, 223, *223*
'Belle des Jardins' *see* 'Village Maid'
'Belle Isis' 223
'Belle Lyonnaise' 235
'Belle Poitevine' 101, 233, *233*
Bengal rose *see* Rosa chinensis
  spontanea
'Bennett's Seedling' 38
Berkshire 204–5, *204*, 248
'Bizarre Triomphant' *see* 'Charles de
  Mills'
'Black Jack' *see* 'Tour de Malakoff'
'Blairii No. 2' 87, *88*, 229
'Blanc Double de Coubert' 102, 233
'Blanchefleur' 222
'Blanche Moreau' 67, 225
'Blanche Pasca' *see* Pascali
'Bleu Magenta' 185, *186*, 245
'Bloomfield Abundance' 74–5, 227
'Bloomfield Courage' 13
'Bloomfield Dainty' 13
'Blush Damask' 48, 50, 221
'Blush Noisette' 152, *153*, 242, *242*
'Blush Rambler' 185–6, *186*, 245
'Bobbie James' 186, *187*, 246
Bonica '82 138–9, *141*, 238
Bonnie Prince Charlie's rose *see*
  'Maxima'
'Boule de Neige' 88, 229
'Bouquet de la Mariée' *see* 'Aimée
  Vibert'
'Bourbon Queen' 88, 229, *229*
Breath of Life 160, 242
'Breeze Hill' 176, 244
'Bright Ideas' 160, 163, 242
Buffalo Bill *see* Regensberg
'Buff Beauty' *108*, 109, 234
'Bullata' 53–4, 222
Burgundian rose *see* 'Pompon de
  Bourgogne'
'Burnet Double Pink' *63*, 64, 225
'Burnet Double White' 64, 225
'Burnet Irish Marbled' 64, 225
'Burnet Marbled Pink' 64, 225
Burnet rose *see* Rosa pimpinellifolia
Burr rose *see* Rosa roxburghii normalis

Awakening 176, *176*, 244, *244*
Ayrshire rose *see* 'Venusta Pendula'

C

Cabbage rose *see* Rosa centifolia
'Camaieux' 58–9, 224
Cambridge rose *see* 'Cantabrigiensis'
Cambridgeshire 205, 248
'Canary Bird' 34, 133, *134*, 238
'Cantabrigiensis' 134, 238
'Capitaine John Ingram' 67–8, *67*, 226
'Cardinal de Richelieu' 59, 224
Cardinal Hume 205, 248, *248*
'Carnea' *see* Rosa multiflora 'Carnea'
Carpet of Colour *see* Cambridgeshire
'Catherine Mermet' 235
'Cécile Brünner' 74–5, 227
'Cécile Brünner' Climbing 227
'Cécile Brünner' White 227, *227*
'Celeste' *see* 'Celestial'
'Celestial' 47, *47*, 221
'Céline Forestier' 155, 242
'Celsiana' 48, 50, 222
'Centfeuille des Peintres' *see* 'Rose des
  Peintres'
'Cerise Bouquet' 14, 140, 239
'Chapeau de Napoléon' 68, *68*, 226
'Charles de Mills' *19*, 59, 224, *224*
Cherokee rose *see* Rosa laevigata
Cheshire rose *see* 'Maxima'
Chestnut rose *see* Rosa roxburghii
  normalis
'Chevy Chase' *197*, 200, 247, *247*
Chianti 144, 241
China rose *see* Rosa chinensis
  spontanea
'Chinatown' 130, 237
'Chloris' 46, 221
'City of Oelde' 15, 239
'Clarence House' 159–60, 242, *242*
'Cleexpert' *see* Peter Beales
'Clelou' *see* Louise Clements
'Clementina Carbonieri' *113*, 114, 235,
  235
'Clementine' *see* 'Janet's Pride'
'Cocdestin' *see* Remember Me
'Colonial White' *see* 'Sombreuil'
'Commandant Beaurepaire' 86, 229
Common Monthly *see* 'Old Blush'
'Common Moss' 66, 68–9, 226, *226*
'Communis' *see* 'Common Moss'
'Complicata' 60, *61*, 224
'Comte de Chambord' *79*, 81, 228, 229
'Comtesse de Labanthe' *see* 'Duchesse
  de Brabant'
'Comtesse de Murinais' 69, 226, *226*
'Comtesse du Cayla' 77, 227
'Comtesse Ouwaroff' *see* 'Duchesse de
  Brabant'
'Conditorum' 224
Constance Spry 144, *144*, 241
'Cooper's Burmese' *193*, 196, 247
'Cored' *see* Alec's Red
Cornelia 109, 234
'Corylus' *see* 'Hazel Le Rougetel'
Countess of Wessex 143, 239, *239*
'Coupe d'Hébé' 88, 229, *229*
'Cramoisi Supérieur' 75–6, 227
'Cramoisi Supérieur' Climbing 75-6, 227
Crazy For You 130, 237

'Crépuscule' 155–6, 242
Crested Moss *see* 'Chapeau de
  Napoléon'
'Crimson Glory' 116, 236
'Crimson Glory' Climbing 166, 243
'Cuisse de Nymphe' *see* 'Great Maiden's
  Blush'
'Cuisse de Nymphe Émue' *see* 'Great
  Maiden's Blush'
'Cupid' 166, 243, *243*
'Cuthbert Grant' 240

D

'Dainty Bess' 116, 236
'Dainty Maid' 13, *13*
Damask rose *see* Rosa x damascena
'Dame Edith Helen' 12, 116, 236, *236*
'Danaë' 106, 109, 234
'Daybreak' 109, 234
'Debutante' 15, 178, *178*, 244
'De la Maître d'École' 60, 224, *224*
Della Balfour 160, *242*, 243
'De Meaux' *53*, 54, 222, *222*
'De Rescht' 81, *82*, 229, *229*
Desert Glo *see* Della Balfour
'Deuil de Paul Fontaine' 69, 226
'Dianthiflora' *see* 'Fimbriata'
'Dicfire' *see* Beautiful Britain
'Dicjana' *see* Elina
'Dickooky' *see* Tall Story
'Diclulu' *see* Gentle Touch
'Dicmagic' *see* Sweet Magic
Dog rose *see* Rosa canina
'Dorothy Perkins' 178–9, 245
'Dortmund' 135, *135*, 239
Double Delight 125, *125*, 236
'Dr Eckener' 102, 233
'Dresden Doll' 210, 249, *249*
'Dr Grill' 235, *235*
'Dr W. Van Fleet' *23*, 179, 182, 245
Dublin Bay *161*, 163, 243
'Duc d'Angoulême' *see* 'Duchesse
  d'Angoulême'
'Duc de Rohan' *see* 'Duchesse de
  Rohan'
'Duchesse d'Angoulême' 224, *224*
'Duchesse de Brabant' 235
'Duchesse de Montebello' 60, 224
'Duchesse de Rohan' *222*, 223
'Duchesse de Verneuil' 226
'Duchesse d'Istrie' *see* 'William Lobb'
'Duchess of Portland' 78, *78*, 83, 229
Duftzauber '84 *see* Royal William
'Dundee Rambler' 38, 192, 247
'Dunwich Rose' 205, 248
'Dupontii' *see* Rosa x dupontii
'Dupuy Jamain' 93, 231
'Dusky Maiden' 13

E

'Easlea's Golden Rambler' 179, 181, *181*,
  245, *245*
'Éclair' 93, 231
Eden Rose '88 159, *159*, 243
Eglantine rose *see* Rosa rubiginosa
Elina *121*, 122, 236
'Emily Gray' *172*, 181, *197*, 245

'Empereur du Maroc' 93, 231
'Emperor of Morocco' see 'Empereur du
    Maroc'
'Empress Josephine' 57, 58, 224
'Ena Harkness' Climbing 166–7, 243
'Enfant de France' 93, 231
'English Miss' 126, 237
Escapade 130, 237, 237
'Ethel' 181, 245
'Eugène Fürst' 231, 231
'Eva' 234, 234
'Evangeline' 181, 245
'Evelyn May' 142–3, 239, 239
'Everest Double Fragrance' 10
'Excelsa' 181, 182, 245, 245

F
Fairy Lights see Avon
'Falkland' 64, 225
'Fantin-Latour' 52, 55, 223
Father David's rose see Rosa davidii
Father Hugo's rose see Rosa xanthina
    hugonis
Fée de Neiges see Iceberg
'Féerie' see 'The Fairy'
'Felicia' 109–10, 109, 234
'Félicité Parmentier' 46, 221
'Félicité Perpétue' 195, 197, 199, 247
'Fellemberg' 227, 227
'Ferdinand Pichard' 92, 93, 231
Ferdy 205, 205, 248
Field rose see Rosa arvensis
Fimbriata' 102, 233
Fiona 206, 206, 248
'F.J. Grootendorst' 102, 103, 233
'Flora McIvor' 97, 232
'Fontaine' see 'Fountain'
'Fountain' 239, 239
Fourth of July see Crazy For You
'Francesca' 110, 110, 234
'Francis E. Lester' 186, 188, 246, 246
'François Juranville' 181, 182, 245, 245
'Frantasia' see Rhapsody in Blue
'Frau Dagmar Hartopp' see 'Fru Dagmar
    Hastrup'
'Frau Karl Druschki' 94, 231, 231
French rose see Rosa gallica
'Friesia' see 'Korresia'
'Fru Dagmar Hartopp' see 'Fru Dagmar
    Hastrup'
'Fru Dagmar Hastrup' 100, 102, 104,
    233
'Frühlingsgold' 133, 239
'Frühlingsmorgen' 133, 239
'Fryminicot' see Sweet Dream
'Fulgens' 229

G
'Gardenia' 181, 245, 245
General Jack see 'Général Jacqueminot'
'Général Jacqueminot' 94, 231
'Général Kléber' 69, 226
'Générale Schablikine' 114, 114, 235
Gentle Touch 250
Geoff Hamilton 146, 241
'George Vancouver' 143, 240
Gertrude Jekyll 145, 148, 241

'Ghislaine de Féligonde' 186, 189, 246,
    246
'Gipsy Boy' 87, 230, 230
Glamis Castle 148, 241, 241
'Gloire de Dijon' 156, 242
'Gloire de France' 224
'Gloire des Mousseux' 56, 69, 69, 226
'Gloire Lyonnaise' 231
'Gloria Dei' see Peace
'Glory of Edzell' 65, 225
'Goldbusch' 139, 239, 239
'Golden Chersonese' 134, 239
Golden Melody 236
'Golden Rambler' see 'Alister Stella Gray'
Golden rose of China see Rosa xanthina
    hugonis
'Golden Showers' 164, 165, 243
'Golden Wings' 132, 133, 239
'Goldfinch' 188, 246
Gooseberry rose see Rosa stellata
    mirifica
Graham Thomas 146, 148, 241
'Grandpa Dickson' 122, 236
'Great Double White' see 'Maxima'
'Great Maiden's Blush' 45, 221
Green rose see 'Viridiflora'
'Greenmantle' 232
'Grootendorst Supreme' 102
Grouse 179, 206, 248
'Grüss an Aachen' 128, 237
'Grüss an Teplitz' 76, 76, 227
'Guinée' 167, 169, 244

H
Handel 162, 164, 243, 243
'Hansa' 100, 104, 233, 233
'Happenstance' 211, 250
'Harblend' see Della Balfour
'Hardwell' see Penny Lane
'Harex' see Alexander
'Harison's Yellow' 64
'Harkuly' see Margaret Merril
'Harpade' see Escapade
'Harquanne' see Breath of Life
'Harregale' see Cardinal Hume
'Harroony' see Amber Queen
'Harry Maasz' 214, 248
'Harvintage' see Savoy Hotel
'Harwanna' see Jacqueline du Pré
'Hazel Le Rougetel' 136, 239
'Hebe's Lip' 50, 222
Heckenzauber see Sexy Rexy
Heidekönigin see Pheasant
'Heideröslein Nozomi' see 'Nozomi'
'Helen Knight' 134, 239
'Henri Martin' 69, 226
'Henry Kelsey' 143, 143, 240, 240
'Herbstfeuer' see Autumn Fire
Heritage 148, 241, 241
'Hermosa' 42, 77, 227
'Hidcote Gold' 134, 239
Himalayan musk rose see Rosa brunonii
'Hippolyte' 60, 224
Holy rose see Rosa x richardii
'Homère' 114–15, 235
'Honorine de Brabant' 86, 89, 230
Hudson Bay rose see Rosa blanda

'Hugh Dickson' 94, 232, 232
'Hume's Blush' see 'Odorata'

I
Iceberg 129, 237
Iceberg Climbing 150, 244
Immensee see Grouse
'Impératrice Joséphine' see 'Empress
    Josephine'
'Incarnata' see 'Great Maiden's Blush'
Incense rose see Rosa primula
'Indigo' 82–3, 229, 229
'Intercell' see Red Blanket
'Interrob' see Robin Redbreast
'Irene Churruca' see Golden Melody
'Irène Watts' 77, 128, 227
'Irish Gold' see 'Grandpa Dickson'
'Ispahan' 48, 50, 222, 222

J
Jack's rose see 'Général Jacqueminot'
'Jaclover' see Magic Carpet
Jacobite rose see 'Maxima'
Jacqueline du Pré 136, 138, 139,
    239
'Jacques Cartier' 80, 81, 229
'James Mason' 135–6, 240
'James Mitchell' 226
'Janet's Pride' 97, 232
Jayne Austin 147, 148, 241
'Jeanne d'Arc' 46, 221
'Jeanne de Montfort' 226, 226
'Jens Munk' 143, 240, 241
'John Cabot' 143, 241
'Juno' 54, 223
'Just Joey' 122, 123, 236

K
'Karlsruhe' 164, 164, 243
'Kathleen Harrop' 85–6, 230
'Kazanlik' 49, 50, 222, 222
'Keitoli' see Ferdy
'Kew Rambler' 200, 200, 247
'Königin von Dänemark' 46, 46, 221,
    221
'Korbin' see Iceberg
'Kordapt' see Pheasant
'Korhaugen' see Cambridgeshire
'Korimro' see Grouse
'Korlima' see Lilli Marlene
'Kormax' see Red Max Graf
'Kormuse' see Wiltshire
'Korpinka' see Berkshire
'Korquemu' see Queen Mother
'Korresia' 129, 238
'Korwest' see Westerland
'Korzaun' see Royal William

L
'La Belle Distinguée' 98, 232
'La Belle Marseillaise' see 'Fellemberg'
'La Belle Sultane' 60, 224
Labrador rose see Rosa blanda
Lacrose see Grouse
Lady Banks' rose see Rosa banksiae
    'Lutea'
'Lady Hillingdon' 115, 235

'Lady Hillingdon' Climbing 156, 157,
    242, 242
'Lady Mary Fitzwilliam' 12, 116, 236
'Lady Penzance' 98, 98, 232
'Lady Sylvia' 116, 236, 236
'Lady Sylvia' Climbing 167–8, 244, 244
'La France' 116, 117, 120, 236
'La Petite Duchesse' see 'La Belle
    Distinguée'
'La Reine Victoria' 86, 230
'La Rossière' see 'Prince Camille de
    Rohan'
'La Rubanée' see 'Village Maid'
'La Séduisante' see 'Great Maiden's
    Blush'
'La Ville de Bruxelles' 222
'La Virginale' see 'Great Maiden's Blush'
'Lauré Davoust' 173, 184, 188, 246
L.D. Braithwaite 241
'Leda' 50, 50, 222
'Leggab' see Pearl Drift
'Lenip' see Pascali
'Léontine Gervais' 182, 245
Lettuce-leaf rose see 'Bullata'
'Leverkusen' 163, 163, 243
'Le Vésuve' 227, 227
'Lilac Charm' 128, 128, 238
Lilli Marleen see Lilli Marlene
Lilli Marlene 127, 128, 238, 238
'Long John Silver' 199, 247
'Lord Penzance' 98, 232, 232
'Louis XIV' 76, 228
Louise Clements 142, 142, 240
'Louise Odier' 86, 87, 230
'Louis Philippe' 228, 228

M
'Macangel' see Snowball
'Macar' see Piccadilly
Macartney rose see Rosa bracteata
'Macdub' see Dublin Bay
'Macha' see Handel
Macmillan Nurse 140, 240
'Macrantha Raubritter' see 'Raubritter'
'Macrexy' see Sexy Rexy
'Macyoumis' see Regensberg
Magic Carpet 206, 248, 248
'Magnifica' 98, 99, 233
'Maiden's Blush' 44–5, 45, 221
'Maigold' 160–1, 243, 243
Maltese rose see 'Cécile Brünner'
'Malton' see 'Fulgens'
'Maman Cochet' 235, 235
Manchu rose see Rosa xanthina
'Manning's Blush' 98, 233
'Mannington Mauve Rambler' 170, 188,
    246
'Marbrée' 83, 229
'Marchesa Boccella' see 'Jacques Cartier'
Margaret Merril 129, 129, 238
'Marguerite Hilling' 136, 240, 240
'Marjorie W. Lester' see 'Lauré Davoust'
'Martin Frobisher' 143, 241
'Mary Queen of Scots' 64–5, 225
Mary Rose 148, 149, 241
'Masquerade' Climbing 169, 244
'Maude Elizabeth' 211, 250

'Max Graf' 104, 233, *233*
'Maxima' 44, 45–6, 221
'McCredy's Sunset' 13
'McCredy's Yellow' 13
Meadow rose *see Rosa blanda*
'Meg' 161, 243, *243*
'Meg Merrilies' 98, 233
'Meibeluxen' *see* Fiona
'Meidomonac' *see* Bonica '82
'Meijikatar' *see* Orange Sunblaze
'Meiviolin' *see* Eden Rose '88
'Mélanie Lemaire' *see* 'Hermosa'
'Mermaid' 14, 194, 247, *247*
Mignon rose *see* 'Cécile Brünner'
'Minnehaha' 179, *179*, 245
Miss Lowe's rose *see* 'Sanguinea'
'Mme A. Meilland' *see* Peace
'Mme Alfred Carrière' 155, *155*, 242
'Mme Butterfly' 116, 236
'Mme de Sancy de Parabère' 193–4, 247, *247*
'Mme Ernst Calvat' 85, 86, 230
'Mme Grégoire Staechelin' *167*, 168, 244
'Mme Hardy' 50–1, *51*, 222
'Mme Hébert' *see* 'Président de Sèze'
'Mme Isaac Pereire' 85, 230
'Mme Knorr' 81
'Mme Laurette Messimy' 77, 228
'Mme Lauriol de Barny' 88, 230
'Mme Legras de St Germain' 47, 221, *221*
'Mme Louis Lévêque' 69–70, 226, *226*
'Mme Neumann' *see* 'Hermosa'
'Mme Pierre Oger' 86, 230, *230*
'Mme Plantier' 47, 221, *221*
Molineux 241
'Monsieur Tillier' 115, 235
Monthly rose *see* 'Old Blush'
'Moonlight' 110–11, 234
'Mousseline' *see* 'Alfred de Dalmas'
'Mozart' *214*, 234
'Mr Bluebird' 211, 250
'Mrs Anthony Waterer' *102*, 104, 233
'Mrs Colville' 65, *65*, 225, *225*
'Mrs Harkness' *see* 'Paul's Early Blush'
'Mrs John Laing' 94, 232
'Mrs Oakley Fisher' 116, 236, *236*
'Mrs William Paul' 70, 226
'Mrs Yamada' 18, 230
Musk rose *see Rosa moschata*
'Mutabilis' *73*, 74, 228

N

'Nevada' 136, *136*, 240
'New Dawn' 23, 41, 159, 176, 182, *183*, 245
Niagara *see* Avon
'Nivea' *see* 'Aimée Vibert'
'Noisette Carnée' *see* 'Blush Noisette'
Norfolk 206–7, 248
'Norwich Castle' 10, 130, *130*, 238
'Norwich Union' 10
'Nozomi' 207, 248
'Nuits de Young' 70, 226
'Nur Mahal' 111, 234

O

'Odorata' 72, 77, 112, 228
'Old Black' *see* 'Nuits de Young'
'Old Blush' 72, *74*, 75, 228
Old crimson China *see* 'Slater's Crimson'
Old pink Moss *see* 'Common Moss'
Old velvet Moss *see* 'William Lobb'
Old velvet rose *see* 'Tuscany'
'Old Yellow Scotch' 64, *64*, 225
'Omar Khayyám' 51, 222
'Ophelia' 116, 236
Orange Sunblaze 211–12, 250

P

'Paestana' *see* 'Duchess of Portland'
Painted Damask *see* 'Leda'
Palissade *see* Pheasant
'Pallida' *see* 'Old Blush'
'Papa Gontier' 235
'Papillon' 228, *228*
'Parkdirektor Riggers' 163, 243
'Parks' Yellow' 72, 77, 112, 228
'Parson's Pink' *see* 'Old Blush'
'Parvifolia' *see* 'Pompon de Bourgogne'
Pascali 122, 236
'Paul Neyron' 94, 232
'Paul's Early Blush' 94, 232, *232*
'Paul's Himalayan Musk' *194*, 196, 247
'Paul's Lemon Pillar' 168, *168*, 244
'Paul Transon' 182, 245
'Pax' 111, 234, *234*
Peace *120*, 121, 166, 236
Pearl Drift 207, 248, *248*
Peaudouce *see* Elina
'Penelope' 111, *111*, 234, *234*
'Penelope Plummer' 10
Penny Lane 159, 243
'Peon' *see* 'Tom Thumb'
'Pergolèse' 83, 229
'Perla de Montserrat' 212, 250
'Perle d'Or' 75, *75*, 228
Persian yellow *see Rosa foetida* 'Persiana'
Peter Beales 135, *137*, 240
'Petite de Hollande' *15*, 223
'Petite Junon de Hollande' *see* 'Petite de Hollande'
Pheasant 207, 249
'Phoebe's Frilled Pink' *see* 'Fimbriata'
'Phyllis Bide' 161, 243
Piccadilly 125, 237
Pierre de Ronsard *see* Eden Rose '88
Pink Bells *15*, 207, *207*, 249
'Pink Grootendorst' *101*, 102
'Pink Grüss an Aachen' 128, *138*, 238
'Pink Parfait' 129–30, 238
Pink Sensation *see* Berkshire
'Pinta' 10, 122, *122*, 237
Polar Star 122, 237, *237*
Polarstern *see* Polar Star
'Pompon Blanc Parfait' 221
'Pompon de Bourgogne' 54, 223, *223*
'Pompon de Paris' Climbing 228
'Pompon des Dames' *see* 'Petite de Hollande'
Portland rose *see* 'Duchess of Portland'
'Poulave' *see* Sussex

'Poulbells' *see* Pink Bells
'Poulfolk' *see* Norfolk
'Poulmulti' *see* Avon
'Poulred' *see* Red Bells
'Poulwhite' *see* White Bells
Prairie rose *see Rosa setigera*
'Président de Sèze' 60, *60*, 224
'Prince Camille de Rohan' *94*, 95, 232
'Prince Charles' 88, 230
'Princesse Louise' 199, 247
'Princesse Marie' 199, 247
'Probuzini' *see* Awakening
'Prosperity' 111, 234
Provence rose *see Rosa x centifolia*

Q

'Quatre Saisons' 51, 78, 222
'Quatre Saisons Blanc Mousseux' 226
Queen Elizabeth 130, 238, *238*
Queen Mother 207–8, 249, *249*
'Queen of Beauty and Fragrance' *see* 'Souvenir de la Malmaison'
'Queen of Bedders' 230
'Queen of Bourbons' *see* 'Bourbon Queen'
'Queen of Denmark' *see* 'Königin von Dänemark'

R

'Rambling Rector' *170*, *184*, 189, *207*, 246
'Ramona' *193*, 196, 247
'Raubritter' 208, *209*, 249
'Raymond Carver' 140, 142, 240, *240*
Red Ace 212, 250
Red Bells 207, 249
Red Blanket 208, 249, *249*
'Red Cherokee' *see* 'Ramona'
'Red Dorothy Perkins' *see* 'Excelsa'
Red Max Graf 208, 249
Red Moss *see* 'Henri Martin'
'Red Prince' *see* 'Fountain'
Red rose of Lancaster *see Rosa gallica officinalis*
Regensberg *211*, 212, 250, *250*
'Reine Blanche' *see* 'Hebe's Lip'
'Reine des Îles Bourbon' *see* 'Bourbon Queen'
'Reine des Neiges' *see* 'Frau Karl Druschki'
'Reine des Violettes' *21*, 95, *95*, 232
Remember Me 123, 237
'René d'Anjou' 226
Renown's Desert Glo *see* Della Balfour
Rhapsody in Blue 139, 240
'Robert le Diable' 54, 223
'Robert Léopold' 70, 227
'Robin Hood' 111, 234
Robin Redbreast 212, *212*, 250
Rosa alba 47, 217
Rosa alba 'Nivea' *see* 'Semi-Plena'
Rosa alba 'Suaveolens' *see* 'Semi-Plena'
Rosa alpina see Rosa pendulina
Rosa anemonoides see 'Anemone Rose'
Rosa arvensis 26, 38, 217

Rosa banksiae 'Alba Plena' *see Rosa banksiae banksiae*
Rosa banksiae banksiae 38, 217, *217*
Rosa banksiae 'Lutea' *24*, 38, *38*, 217
Rosa banksiae 'Lutescens' 38, 217
Rosa banksiae normalis 38, *39*, 217
Rosa blanda 28, 217
Rosa bracteata 41, 217
Rosa brunonii 38, 217, *217*
Rosa burgundica see 'Pompon de Bourgogne'
Rosa californica 28, 217
Rosa canina 26, *26*, 27, 44, 47, 217, *217*
Rosa canina 'Andersonii' 33, 217
Rosa x cantabrigiensis see 'Cantabrigiensis'
Rosa x centifolia 27, 53, *55*, 222
Rosa x centifolia 'Cristata' *see* 'Chapeau de Napoléon'
Rosa x centifolia 'Major' *see* 'Rose des Peintres'
Rosa x centifolia 'Variegata' *see* 'Village Maid'
Rosa chinensis minima see 'Rouletii'
Rosa chinensis spontanea 27, 217
Rosa cooperi see 'Cooper's Burmese'
Rosa x damascena 27, 44, 221
Rosa x damascena bifera see 'Quatre Saisons'
Rosa x damascena semperflorens see 'Quatre Saisons'
Rosa x damascena versicolor see 'York and Lancaster'
Rosa davidii 36, 217
Rosa x dupontii 33, 217, *217*
Rosa ecae 31, 217
Rosa eglanteria see Rosa rubiginosa
Rosa elegantula 'Persetosa' 30, 217
Rosa farreri persetosa see Rosa elegantula 'Persetosa'
Rosa fedtschenkoana 30, *30*, 218
Rosa filipes 'Kiftsgate' 41, *41*, 88, 218
Rosa foetida 27, 218
Rosa foetida 'Bicolor' 27, 218
Rosa foetida 'Persiana' 27, 218, *218*
Rosa forrestiana 36, 218
Rosa x francofurtana 'Empress Josephine' *see* 'Empress Josephine'
Rosa gallica 26, 29, 218
Rosa gallica officinalis 56, *56*, 224
Rosa gallica versicolor see 'Rosa Mundi'
Rosa gallica 'Violacea' *see* 'La Belle Sultane'
Rosa gentiliana 40, 41, 218, *218*
Rosa gigantea 28–9, 112, 218
Rosa glauca 34–5, *34*, 35, 218
Rosa gymnocarpa 28, 218
Rosa helenae 38, 40, 218, *218*
Rosa hemisphaerica 31, 218
Rosa hibernica 218, *218*
Rosa hugonis see Rosa xanthina hugonis
Rosa indica see Rosa chinensis spontanea
Rosa x kochiana 32, 218
Rosa laevigata 28–9, 194, 218

Rosa laevigata cooperi see 'Cooper's Burmese'
Rosa x l'heritierana 192, 193, 247
Rosa longicuspis 40–1, 218
Rosa lutea punicea see Rosa foetida 'Bicolor'
Rosa x macrantha 32, 219, 219
Rosa macrophylla 34, 36, 219
Rosa x micrugosa 30, 219
Rosa moschata 26, 38, 40, 219
Rosa moyesii 27, 28, 219
Rosa mulliganii 40, 219
Rosa multiflora 40, 184, 219
Rosa multiflora 'Carnea' 184, 189, 246
Rosa multiflora 'Grevillei see Rosa multiflora 'Platyphylla'
Rosa multiflora 'Platyphylla' 184, 199, 246
'Rosa Mundi' 11, 56, 57, 58, 224, 224
Rosa nankiniensis see Rosa chinensis spontanea
Rosa nitida 28, 29, 219
Rosa nutkana 219, 219
Rosa x odorata see 'Odorata'; Rosa chinensis spontanea
Rosa x odorata gigantea see Rosa gigantea
Rosa x odorata 'Ochroleuca' see 'Parks' Yellow'
Rosa omeiensis pteracantha 36, 37, 219
Rosa pendulina 193, 219, 219
Rosa phoenicea 27, 219, 219
Rosa pimpinellifolia 26, 29–30, 29, 62, 219
Rosa polyantha grandiflora see Rosa gentiliana
Rosa pomifera see Rosa villosa
Rosa primula 30, 219
Rosa x richardii 32–3, 32, 219
Rosa rouletii see 'Rouletii'
Rosa roxburghii normalis 33, 33, 219
Rosa roxburghii 'Plena' 33, 219
Rosa roxburghii roxburghii see Rosa roxburghii 'Plena'
Rosa rubiginosa 8, 9, 22, 26, 96, 220
Rosa rubra see Rosa gallica
Rosa rubrifolia see Rosa glauca
Rosa rugosa 27, 35, 100, 220
Rosa rugosa 'Alba' 100, 101
Rosa sancta see Rosa x richardii
Rosa sempervirens 220
Rosa sericea pteracantha see Rosa omeiensis pteracantha
Rosa setigera 199, 220, 220
Rosa setipoda 36, 220
Rosa simnica see Rosa chinensis spontanea
Rosa sinowilsonii 41, 220
Rosa soulieana 36, 36, 200, 220
Rosa spinosissima see Rosa pimpinellifolia
Rosa stellata mirifica 29, 33, 220, 220
Rosa sulphuria see Rosa hemisphaerica
Rosa turkestanica see 'Mutabilis'
Rosa villosa 33, 220, 220
Rosa virginiana 28, 30–1, 31, 220, 220
Rosa virginiana 'Plena' 220

Rosa viridiflora see 'Viridiflora'
Rosa webbiana 34, 220
Rosa wichuraiana see Rosa wichurana
Rosa wichurana 22, 41, 174, 220
Rosa willmottiae 33, 220
Rosa woodsii fendleri 28, 31, 220
Rosa xanthina 220
Rosa xanthina 'Canary Bird' see 'Canary Bird'
Rosa xanthina hugonis 34, 220
Rose d'Amour see Rosa virginiana 'Plena'
'Rose de Meaux' see 'De Meaux'
'Rose de Rescht' see 'De Rescht'
'Rose des Peintres' 54, 223
'Rose d'Isfahan' see 'Ispahan'
'Rose Édouard' 84, 230
'Rose Edward' see 'Rose Édouard'
'Rose-Marie Viaud' 190, 190, 246, 246
Rose of Provins see Rosa gallica; Rosa gallica officinalis
'Rosée du Matin' see 'Chloris'
'Roseraie de l'Haÿ' 100, 104, 104, 233
'Rosette Delizy' 115, 235
Rote Max Graf see Red Max Graf
'Rouletii' 212, 250, 250
Royal Pageant see Della Balfour
Royal William 123, 237
'Rubrotincta' see 'Hebe's Lip'

S
Sacramento rose see Rosa stellata mirifica
'Sadler's Wells' 139, 240
'Safrano' 115, 235
'Salet' 70, 227
'Sanders' White Rambler' 11, 15, 182, 245
'Sanguinea' 76, 228
Savoy Hotel 125, 237, 237
'Scabrosa' 105, 105, 233, 233
Scarlet Fire see 'Scharlachglut'
Scarlet sweet briar see 'La Belle Distinguée'
'Scharlachglut' 135, 240
Schneewittchen see Iceberg
'Schneezwerg' 105, 233
Scotch rose see Rosa pimpinellifolia
'Seagull' 19, 190, 246
'Semi-Plena' 44, 47, 221, 221
'Semperflorens' see 'Slater's Crimson'
Seven sisters rose see Rosa multiflora 'Platyphylla'
Sexy Rexy 126, 126, 128, 238
'Shot Silk' Climbing 169, 244
'Silver Jubilee' 123, 124, 125, 237
'Single Cherry' 65, 225, 225
'Sir Cedric Morris' 200, 247, 247
'Sir Frederick Ashton' 12–13
'Slater's Crimson' 72, 76, 228, 228
Smooth rose see Rosa blanda
'Snow Dwarf' see 'Schneezwerg'
'Snow Queen' see 'Frau Karl Druschki'
Snowball 212, 250
'Soleil d'Or' 116, 237
'Sombreuil' 157, 242
Sommerduft see Summer Fragrance
Sommermärchen see Berkshire

'Sophie's Perpetual' 76, 228
'Souvenir de la Malmaison' 86, 230, 230
'Souvenir de la Princesse de Lamballe' see 'Bourbon Queen'
'Souvenir de Mme Léonie Viennot' 14, 157, 242
'Souvenir de St Anne's' 86, 230
'Souvenir du Docteur Jamain' 95, 232
'Spanish Beauty' see 'Mme Grégoire Staechelin'
'Spong' 54, 223
'Spray Cécile Brünner' see 'Bloomfield Abundance'
St Ethelburga 142, 240, 240
St John's rose see Rosa x richardii
St Mark's rose see Rosa virginiana 'Plena'
'St Nicholas' 222
'Stanwell Perpetual' 65, 225, 225
Sulphur rose see Rosa hemisphaerica
Summer Damask see Rosa x damascena
Summer Fairytale see Berkshire
Summer Fragrance 123, 237
'Summer Sunrise' 208–9, 249
'Summer Sunset' 208–9, 249
Sunnyside see Avon
'Sunsprite' see 'Korresia'
Sussex 209, 249
Sweet briar see Rosa rubiginosa
Sweet Dream 213, 213, 250, 250
Sweet Magic 213, 250
Sweetheart rose see 'Cécile Brünner'

T
Tall Story 209, 249, 249
'Tanfudermos' see Summer Fragrance
'Tanlarpost' see Polar Star
Tapis Magique see Magic Carpet
Tea-scented China see 'Parks' Yellow'
'Thalia' 16
'The Fairy' 138, 202, 209, 249
'The Garland' 188, 190, 246
'The Queen Elizabeth' see Queen Elizabeth
'Tipo Ideale' see 'Mutabilis'
'Tipsy Imperial Concubine' 115, 115, 235
'Tom Thumb' 213, 250
'Tour de Malakoff' 6, 54–5, 54, 223
'Trigintipetala' see 'Kazanlik'
'Tuscany' 224
'Tuscany Superb' 8, 59, 225
Twenty-fifth 213, 250, 250

U
'Unique Blanche' 54, 223

V
'Vanity' 20, 111, 234, 234
'Variegata di Bologna' 86, 231
'Veilchenblau' 73, 190, 191, 246
'Velutinaeflora' 225
'Venusta Pendula' 38, 193, 247
'Vierge de Cléry' see 'Unique Blanche'
'Village Maid' 55, 223, 223

'Violacea' see 'La Belle Sultane'
'Violette' 190, 246
'Viridiflora' 77, 77, 228

W
'Wedding Day' 198, 199, 247
'Wekroalt' see Crazy For You
Westerland 138, 240
'White American Beauty' see 'Frau Karl Druschki'
White Bells 207, 249
'White Cockade' 160, 243
'White Flight' see 'Astra Desmond'
'White Grootendorst' 102
'White Pet' 197, 213, 250
White Provence see 'Unique Blanche'
White rose of York see 'Maxima'
'Wickwar' 200, 201, 247
'William III' 65, 225
William Baffin 143, 241
'William Lobb' 6, 70, 70, 71, 227
'Williams' Double Yellow' 64, 225
William Shakespeare 148, 148, 241
Wiltshire 209, 249

X
Xenia see Berkshire

Y
'Yellow Cécile Brünner' see 'Perle d'Or'
'Yellow Cochet' see 'Alexander Hill Gray'
'Yellow Maman Cochet' see 'Alexander Hill Gray'
Yellow rose of Texas see 'Harison's Yellow'
'York and Lancaster' 51, 222
Young Mistress see Regensberg

Z
'Zéphirine Drouhin' 84, 85, 230, 231
'Zigeunerknabe' see 'Gipsy Boy'

Author's Acknowledgments

At the time Mitchell Beazley invited me to write another book on roses I had already turned down invitations from other publishers and had no desire to write any more. When it was explained however that they wanted a book more about my lifetime's experience with roses, rather than a manual or encyclopaedia, I found it impossible to say no.

My first acknowledgement therefore is to roses themselves, for my lifetime is but a moment in their history; they will go on for ever. My passion for roses has given me the opportunity to meet lots of like-minded people all over the world: people I consider, not too presumptuously I hope, my friends. All of these have contributed to my love of roses and therefore, indirectly, to this book. Thank you.

I count my family among my closest friends and thank them for their invaluable input, especially my wife Joan, who translated my difficult-to-read handwriting into computerized text, never once complaining; also my daughter Amanda for her research for the Directory, and my son Richard for running the business in my absence. Special appreciation to Oscar, our Golden Retriever, who took me on many long, therapeutic walks when I had run out of inspiration. Another person who helped translate my difficult handwriting into printed text is Betty Gardener, my secretary and PA.

Thanks Betty for all those long hours at the keyboard. My thanks also to Helen Lee, our office manager, for never once noticing (or so she said) my absences. Thank you, too, to Ian Limmer for proving that the production side of the business runs just as well when I am not there; appreciation, also, to Tina Limmer for long hours sorting transparencies. My gratitide, too, to Peter Chinnery, for his help in the recognition of non-rosa genera in some of the photographs. In fact, I acknowledge the many little contributions made to the book from all my staff and thank them for their ongoing support.

Special thanks go to photographer Marianne Majerus for capturing so many lovely "roses in the landscape" pictures with her camera, and also to the owners of the gardens (detailed below) for allowing Marianne the freedom to take her photographs.

Thanks to all the Mitchell Beazley team, especially commissioning editor Michèle Byam for her support and guidance, Miranda Harvey and Sarah Rock, the designers, for between them making all the words and pictures fit together so well, and my editor, Lesley Riley, for her sensitivity, constructive suggestions, and for being a joy to work with. I hope everyone who has been in anyway instrumental in the making of this book will feel that a little part of it is just for them.

Photographic Acknowledgments

All photographs are by Marianne Majerus, with the exception of the following.

Peter Beales Roses: 13, 27, 31, 78, 83, 91, 94, 95, 98, 99, 110, 113, 114, 115, 117, 122, 125, 126, 128, 130, 140, 143, 156, 160, 163, 169, 173, 181, 186 below, 190, 192, 193 above and below, 198, 199, 200, 204, 211, 212, 213; Andrew Lawson Photography: 36, 41, 141; Garden Picture Library: photos by Mark Bolton 52, Howard Rice 53, Mayer/Le Scanff 175, Ellen Rooney 176, Eric Crichton 182; Mise Au Point/A Descat: 16; Octopus Publishing Group: 112; Photos Horticultural: 28, 104, 120, 129, 135, 149, 159, 165; S & O Mathews: 121.

All Directory photographs (pages 217–250) are courtesy of Peter Beales Roses, with the exception of 221 above and below centre, 222 below, 225 above and 236 below, which are by Marianne Majerus.

We would like to acknowledge the following photographic locations and designers:

Astley Abbots House, Shropshire: 56; Cerney House, Glos: 177; Clinton Lodge, Sussex: 9, 57; Coughton Court, Warwicks: 11, 127, 146, 147, 153, 178; Eastgrove Cottage, Hereford & Worcs: 15; Elsing Hall, Norfolk: 19, 54, 88, 97, 185, 194; Ephraim Gardens, Kent: 202; Helmingham Hall, Suffolk: 8, 48, 148; High Cleabarrow, Cumbria: 87; Killieser Avenue, London: 82; Lawn Farm, Norfolk: 179, 184; Lime Kiln House, Suffolk: 75; Malvern Terrace, London: 24; Mannington Hall, Norfolk: 17, 22, 108, 118, 170, 186a, 214; Mount Ephraim Gardens, Kent: 138; The Old Manor, Hemingford Grey: 40; Peter Beales Roses, Norfolk: 21, 29, 49, 61, 62, 64, 65, 137, 167, 197, 205, 206, 207; Pound House, Wilts: 92; RHS Hyde Hall: 103, 133; RHS Wisley: 20, 111, 188; Shepherds Lane Gardens, Surrey: 162; Sun House, Suffolk: 6; Wyken Hall, Suffolk: 71; Miranda Holland Cooper: 155, 172; Pedro Da Costa Felgueiras: 187; Lynette Hemmant: 191; Chris & Toby Marchant: 73; Mary McCarthy: 84; Helen Pitel: 157; Tom Stuart-Smith: 79.